PRAISE FOR

TELL THE STORY

A HOLLYWOOD ODYSSEY

"A touching and humorous true-life account of a storyteller's journey from a Georgia farm to a Hollywood mansion. Terrell Tannen's incidental journey is a clear and candid look at the joy, heartbreak, success, and failure that awaits all of us who arrive with ideas, desire, and a dream."

—Phillip Noyce, director of *Rabbit Proof Fence* and *Clear and Present Danger*

"A challenging account of one man trying to make a living in what seems to an outsider like a toxic and shallow world of inflated importance and radical uncertainty, driven by money, illusion, ego, and image. One comes away admiring the author's stamina, tenacity, and talent."

—Judson Mitcham, author of *The Sweet Everlasting*, Georgia Poet Laureate 2012-2019

"Want to hang out on a tropical island with the legendary director John Huston? Have a long liquid lunch with the iconic writer Jim Harrison? Get a flattering phone call from Oscar-winning director

Sydney Pollack? In *Tell the Story: A Hollywood Odyssey*, Terrell Tannen recounts, in lively prose, how he managed to do all those things and more as he rose in the Tinseltown ranks from an unknown documentary filmmaker to a sought-after screenwriter and director. Tannen's romp through 80s and 90s Hollywood is as fun and eye-opening as it is cautionary, for though it provided him nice cars, a mansion in the hills, and dates with starlets, quirks of fate deprived him of that ultimate Hollywood payoff—fame. Still, Tannen tells his story with wit and self-deprecating humor as he takes readers deep inside the star-making machinery as only a Hollywood insider can. Everyone who loves the movies will love this book."

—Ken Wells, author of *Swamped* and *Meely LaBauve*

"I'm generally a slow reader, but I devoured *Tell the Story* in one big gulp. When I was forced to put it aside for work, I found myself thinking about it. Terrell Tannen not only tells the story—many stories, expertly—but he sucks us into the very tapestry of life itself, from the frustrations and loneliness of youth to the nuts and bolts of working in Hollywood and the beguiling, funny, and sometimes heartbreaking trappings of near-fame. There were moments when I laughed, growled, and even gasped out loud. Tannen talks about the 'almosts' of Hollywood, but there's nothing 'almost' about this book—it's a full-on, full-tilt stunner."

—Joe Schreiber, *New York Times* bestselling author of *Chasing the Dead, Star Wars: Death Troopers*, and *Au Revoir, Crazy European Chick*

"Every writer comes to Hollywood with a unique story, and Terrell Tannen tells his with warmth, style, and a familiarity that every artist with a drive to perform can embrace. It's a personal yet universal tale about ambition and why we persist in the inscrutable faces of success and futility. Tannen reminds us how the drive to step off the porch can far exceed the need for a destination and how tantalizing yet elusive dreams can become when we have nearly made them a reality."

—Roger Birnbaum, owner of Spyglass Entertainment, cochairman, MGM Studios, and has overseen production of over 100 movies, including *The Sixth Sense, Seabiscuit, Angels in the Outfield, While You Were Sleeping, Unbreakable, Robocop,* and *Rush Hour 1, 2* and *3*.

"Tell the story he does. Terrell Tannen delivers an intimate account of what many of us have lived. We struggle, maybe succeed, struggle, maybe succeed, then do it all over again. And the ride is always worth the price of admission. Tannen's story is funny, frustrating, endearing, and inspirational. A truly inside view of a life seeking, finding, and climbing inside the movie-making machine, from canasta and crickets in the cotton fields to corruption in the halls of Congress to visions of Oscars from Hollywood's elite. A terrific read."

—Rosie Shuster, cocreator and original writer of *Saturday Night Live*

"If you think you heard it all when it comes to Hollywood memoirs, I urge you to read Terrell Tannen's refreshingly honest and hugely entertaining *Tell the Story*. Tannen's career has taken him to all corners of the globe, working with Tinseltown royalty (John Huston! Sydney Pollack!), but he doesn't shy away from detailing the far more common Hollywood experience: the agony of the near miss—to the point where his life story begins to feel like a thriller."

—Duane Swierczynski, *New York Times* bestselling author of *California Bear*

TELL THE STORY: *A Hollywood Odyssey*
by Terrell Tannen

© Copyright 2024 Terrell Tannen

979-8-88824-505-7

All rights reserved. No part of this publication may be reproduced, stored in a retrieval system, or transmitted in any form or by any means—electronic, mechanical, photocopy, recording, or any other—except for brief quotations in printed reviews, without the prior written permission of the author.

Design by Suzanne Bradshaw

Published by

köehlerbooks™

3705 Shore Drive
Virginia Beach, VA 23455
800-435-4811
www.koehlerbooks.com

TELL THE STORY

A HOLLYWOOD ODYSSEY

TERRELL TANNEN

VIRGINIA BEACH
CAPE CHARLES

Robert Landau / Alamy

PROLOGUE
THE ONCE, THE NOW, THE NEARLY, AND THE NEVER

I once worked with an actor who was a major movie star in the fifties and sixties. He starred in films helmed by the most respected directors in Hollywood, and in his prime, the actor's name and face were recognizable throughout the world.

The actor's career hit a wall in the seventies, probably because his afflictions and habits made him a liability on set. By the eighties, he was accepting small parts in low-budget exploitation films.

The actor was not alone in this position, and it was a sad and accepted state for many world-famous stars in their later years. Those who didn't need to work often chose not to rather than appear in lesser projects, but some just hated not working, had expensive needs that could not be ignored, or, in many, if not most, cases, just did not want to surrender what they had worked so hard to attain.

In the early eighties, I worked as a consultant on one of these films. The actor had agreed to work one week for $25,000, but he insisted on a contractual "rider" guaranteeing an additional $1,000 per day for "incidental" expenses, which, in this case, was cocaine. The production would be responsible for procuring the drug from the actor's designated dealer in Los Angeles and delivering it to the star on location an hour east of LA.

I wasn't aware of this rider when I first met the actor. I was relatively new to Hollywood, excited to meet one of the biggest stars of my youth—one who had appeared in landmark films by great directors.

When I met the star, he was anxious and aloof, with little time for anyone extraneous to his life, and I understood that. I also understood that he was a noticeably discouraged and frustrated man, unhappy with having sunken to making appearances in films like the one we were working on. The disillusion was written in the scowl lines and permanently narrowed eyes that had replaced his youthful, handsome innocence that once charmed millions around the world.

That was not the world we occupied that day in what is known in Southern California as the "Inland Empire." He made everyone aware without saying that he was a star, better than this, but he needed us like we needed him, and we were punished with verbal assaults filled with a life's sad and begrudged reckoning. Fame had been his, and he just couldn't give it up.

This star, now dead, had become known for famously losing his temper for frivolous reasons and yelling at whoever was in earshot, and when he yelled, everyone heard. It became clear to the crew why the star was yelling and how it was related to his "incidentals" rider. There is a level of anger, normally self-directed, distinguishable in a cocaine addict's rage. Most anyone working in Hollywood in the eighties heard it often.

The film was shot at a VA Hospital in a small suburban community not far from Palm Springs. Redlands is a quiet town mostly inhabited by retired couples and young, working families. One morning, just after sunrise, the production manager was hastily summoned to the hospital administrator's office to discuss a serious problem.

A victim of an auto accident had died in emergency surgery. His family had just been informed and apparently entered the hospital chapel to pray, where they walked in on our star, engaging in freebasing cocaine in the front row. Startled, he screamed at the family to get out, and they immediately sought refuge at a nursing station.

The administrator requested that the star not be allowed to bring drugs into the chapel. The star suggested locking the chapel door, so the production was faced with finding a solution.

The allure of Hollywood prevailed. For the remainder of the week, whenever the star made his frequent entrances to the chapel, an assistant director stood guard outside the door and prevented the grieving or distressed from disturbing the sacred bond between a man, his God, and his glass pipe.

When I heard of this and went to the producer, I learned everyone on the set knew the situation, and no one would do or say anything because they all had a job that week, and if anything interfered with the production, they would not have one.

According to Ibisworld, a respected market research firm, nearly 50,000 people work in the US film and television industry. Of those, fewer than 200 would be recognized on the street, and fewer were recognizable by name. But 80 percent of those 50,000 include low-, middle-, high- and super-high-income people who have enjoyed, endured, or suffered through the highs and lows of a career making movies or television. Almost all of them labor in relative anonymity, performing the tasks—creative, technical, mechanical, supervisory, and financial—that make it possible for the movie industry and movie stars to exist. I have been one of those people for nearly fifty years.

I did well for a while. You could justifiably say that I reached the ceiling and almost broke through it. You might even say I was nearly famous, for I certainly had my brushes with fame and the verifiably famous. I also realize my story could be the story of countless others.

CHAPTER 1
WHAT WE WANT

To warrant an obituary in the British Medical Journal, *The Lancet*, candidates must either belong to an exclusive group of pioneering scientists or physicians, most of them either Nobel Laureates or nominees for that prize, or be responsible for an impactful discovery creating worldwide attention. Occasionally, the subject is a previously anonymous person responsible for some obscure and often unrecognized feat that profoundly changed science. An obit in *The Lancet* can deliver fame to the obscure, a fact well known by the scientific unknown.

For a period of nearly a year, I wrote American assignments for the journal, including obituaries, which sounded solemn but, in actuality, became a tonic.

When writing an obit, I would call the subject's colleagues who were somehow involved in the discovery process, even if peripherally. This was a fun part of the job because there were very few notables I couldn't get on the phone, simply because they all wanted to be quoted in *The Lancet*, and they were all excited to talk about this milestone and their part in it. For some, it had been their life's work.

When I left messages explaining why I was calling, I would receive return calls from airport lounges, taxis, limousines, and conference and hotel rooms across the globe from the scientist's colleagues eager to say something quotable, and they often had it prepared.

These scientists were talking about something that had driven them most of their adult lives, and it became infectious to me that I could share in that excitement and almost relive it with them—that magic of a momentous discovery, the eureka moment—which gave me goosebumps.

Being affiliated with greatness, even talking about it in a respected publication, is another step closer to it. My interview subjects knew this, which is why sometimes I had trouble getting them off the phone. But it was good trouble.

The major question it left me with is this: Why do we care? Why does it matter to be close to that level of significance?

Of course, it becomes a rhetorical question, but that doesn't mean there is no answer. We all want to be great at something or at least in the running. Even if we never admit to wanting it nor feel the drive for it, it seems to exist in the human ego in some form, even if greatness is simply the ability to provide for others.

This is the drive that makes us do things and makes us feel dissatisfied when we don't. Sometimes, we fall into complacency and reduce our goals to what is more readily achievable, but only after a process of reevaluation that inevitably leads there.

I believe ambition is part of the human instinct, and everyone has their own interpretation of it. To me, instinct drives us to date, love, marry, work, produce, and contribute however we can. It changes shades as we age, but it remains for all our lives. We want recognition, we want support, and we want approval, not necessarily in that order.

Ambition is the instinct that drives us to avoid stasis at any cost. It is why we are curious and why we (if we can) leave home when we are young. We are driven to seek validation from any entity or anyone, including ourselves.

It is a drive that we are only able to consider with clarity as we approach the end of our lives, and we study the lives of others.

CHAPTER 2
THE WHALE

A couple in conflict sets across the Atlantic in a thirty-six-foot sailboat, clinging to a blind conviction that one month in the confines of open sea will incite negotiation, reignite cold passions, or mercifully dissolve the rancid remains of their once fiery marriage.

The voyage begins with valiant efforts to communicate, but failures mount with the days. After two weeks, civility is left in the boat's wake, and the only open question is who despises the other more. Nearly two thousand miles and three weeks of silent companionship lurk like a thunderhead.

One clear morning, with explosive force on a fatefully calm sea, the boat strikes an object heavy enough to move the keel, sending the couple crashing into the cabin wall, falling hard onto a deck covered by fiberglass shards.

Shocked and bleeding, the battle-fatigued pair slowly rise to their knees, now carefully eyeing each other not with suspicion or anger but with the gift of a forgotten mutual experience, that of a shared state, and it is fear.

This was the end of act one of three, the product of sequestering myself in an attic at least ten degrees warmer than the lower floors of a wood-framed country house built in 1935 on an excavated marsh in Northern Virginia, which, in August, was a sauna.

I had never written a film script and had no understanding of how to do so, but I desperately wanted to change my life. I appreciated the expansive imagery and emotional arcs available in an ocean voyage, had some personal experience on the open sea, and was drawn to stories set on water in childhood. With that, I embarked on developing what had been described to me as an extended "treatment," or a fairly detailed overview of a story, as told in three acts.

Researching the process, I learned that the first step is to establish essential plot points and commit them to outlined stages. The drama is initiated by establishing the conflict in act one, developing it in act two, and ideally providing a resolution in act three.

Once the story is set, the drama on the page pales in comparison to that in the head while awaiting judgment. Of course, you hope that friends, peers, and colleagues will like it, but what really matters is the opinion of a potential investor. A screenplay that doesn't become a movie is but a doorstop. Investors hold power, and we are slaves to it.

The first investor to read my treatment was Jay, a client who, among other politicos in Washington, had been paying me to make documentary films to promote causes. If Jay could be impressed, I was ready for the next step.

Jay wanted to read the treatment at my house so we could talk about another project afterward. I had the manuscript ready for him to take wherever he chose, but he insisted on sitting in my attic office, the sauna, while I awaited his appraisal.

Jay followed me up the narrow stairs, removed his jacket and loosened his tie, picked up the neatly stacked pages, and perched on an uncomfortable wooden chair procured from Goodwill.

He set the stack of pages on the seat of a second chair, slid his glasses over his ears, and leaned forward studiously, arms crossed, feet flat on the floor, focused exclusively on the open page in front of him. He remained like this for several minutes, eyes darting back and forth, turning each page quietly. When he finished, he sat back, thought a moment, and turned to me. His eyes hovered over the wire frames of his glasses; his eyebrows dramatically arched.

"Really? A whale?"

"It was a collision," I told him. "What's wrong with that? Something had to happen. It was kind of obvious, no? It's the perfect metaphor. It was what they needed."

His face remained sour with confusion. "Why not a boat?"

"Blind collisions are dramatic. They'd see a boat, and a boat doesn't mean anything."

"But a whale?"

"It's the biggest living thing in the ocean. Biggest on the planet. Again, isn't it the perfect result of their struggle?"

"I don't buy it."

Like me, Jay was in his mid-twenties. Unlike me, he owned a successful public relations firm in DC, drove a new Mercedes, lived in an expensive row house in Georgetown, was marrying a Broadway star, and could talk nearly anyone into whatever he chose because he had no pause and no filter. He didn't need them because he didn't need to think about what he said before he said it. It all came out like a press release.

Straight out of college and post-graduate internships, Jay had trained on Capitol Hill as the press secretary to John Rhodes, the Speaker of the House of Representatives. He could fluidly describe the speaker's political position, or lack thereof, or deftly avoid describing it at all. He'd developed this talent by standing in the spotlight for extended periods while describing someone else's belief system, which he didn't necessarily share, while often revealing nothing. It is a very refined skill. Now he was using this skill as a political strategist, a highly esoteric and highly paid position.

Jay knew that the secret to conquering self-doubt was confidence. I was successful, considering my youth, but Jay was far more so, and he knew something I didn't. At least, we both thought so at the time.

I thought about Jay not long ago while sitting in a screening room waiting for a film to start. We had worked together nearly forty years earlier, and I always liked and admired him. He displayed all the traits of a successful businessman, including confidence, but like so many of us, underneath, he was still a confused and insecure teenager. He hid it well, but that type of fear tends to rise to the surface. I liked that about him, for it elevated our friendship beyond business.

Sitting in the screening room, I searched Jay's name on my phone and was pained to discover he had recently died, apparently of a heart attack. His firm was still very successful, now in the hands of others but carrying Jay's name along with his partner's, who had also died young.

Jay remained in my head for weeks, and I remembered how he had dissuaded me from writing the story about the couple on the boat. At the time, I figured he must know better than I did because of his success.

I was unfulfilled and had retreated to the attic to find stories to hopefully change my life. Forty years later, I realized that as successful as he was with political consulting, Jay was wrong; the whale was right, and I should have followed my gut.

CHAPTER 3
IT STARTS WITH DESPAIR

I spent my freshman year at the University of South Carolina in Columbia, the heat-soaked capital. It was a miserable time because I didn't much like college and felt displaced among the freshman dorm students whose professional ambitions I didn't share, whose world seemed so removed from mine. I was lonely, but I was eighteen, where loneliness thrives.

I had fallen in love with music and embraced the idea of pursuing it professionally, but as I reached college age, I doubted my ability and possible success. Whenever I heard a spectacular drummer, it humbled me. I knew I was good, inventive, and steady, but I just wasn't that special.

I went to college instead of sticking with bands and immediately doubted my choice. As a result, I played when I could find a band needing a drummer, continuing through my first two years, and I found R & B groups to join and tour with locally, but my grades suffered. I later became a motivated student, but that was primarily because life was put on hold due to an accident, and I had to do some serious reconsidering.

The South will always be familiar to me, so I was comfortable with the meat-and-three meals, sweat-soaked clothes, and warm anticipation of an afternoon thunderstorm. But hanging over it all was an unwavering cloud of despair, a daily reminder that no matter how familiar it all was, I just didn't belong. Without question, a common malady among eighteen-year-olds throughout the world.

When my grandmother, Azalea, became seriously ill, Doris, my mother, cleared out her house in Virginia to either rent or sell. She put the furniture in storage and moved to the family farm in Monroe, Georgia, to look after her mother. Doris took a job at the local hospital as a nursing instructor and hired an aide to care for Azalea during the day, spending evenings and nights with her at home.

I would occasionally hitchhike from Columbia to Monroe, roughly a 200-mile trip on a two-lane blacktop with sparse traffic, save for occasional short-run trucks hauling textiles west from the Carolinas. Sometimes, single drivers would be traveling to Atlanta to shop or visit relatives and would be eager for company on a lonely road, even a teenager with a duffel, so I always held hope. There was no east-west interstate in Georgia north of I-10 in 1966, so travel was slow.

On a Saturday morning after my 8 a.m. class, I would load the duffel bag and walk up the hill to the Kollege Korner, where I could fortify myself on a teenage-sized load of sausage, eggs, grits, biscuits, and red-eye gravy. This was my way of readying myself for a long day as a hopeful hitchhiker, much of the time spent standing off a lonely road, waiting for the next ride.

West of town, the main drag, Gervais Street, becomes Route 1, and after several miles, intersects with US Route 378, a commercial road curling like a snake through the South Carolina pines. The highway eventually crosses the Savannah River into eastern Georgia, where, in the historic town of Washington, the Civil War officially ended in May of 1865, when Jefferson Davis dissolved the Confederacy. There, the road melds with US Route 78, or Charleston Highway, leading directly from what was once the largest slave port in the country, where 150,000 Africans were delivered onto the docks in chains, through Athens, Monroe, and ultimately downtown Atlanta.

Once on the commercial highway, I would again stand on the pullout, lift my arm, and let fate take its course. Sometimes, it would be minutes, other times hours before a car would stop. The drivers were generally of two types: loners looking for conversation or generous souls eager to help what could be an Army boot recruit from nearby Ft. Jackson headed home for a visit or a USC freshman looking for adventure.

Four to six hours later, I would most often be dropped alongside a Civil War monument memorializing the Walton County confederate dead, erected more than fifty years after the war and directly in front of the historic courthouse in downtown Monroe.

Since George Floyd's death in 2020, local activists have pushed to move the monument to a museum, but there is resistance within the county. I assume the same type of resistance followed the passage of the Civil Rights Act of 1964, which legislated the removal of segregation signs reading *WHITE* and *COLORED* from the Troy Theater entrances and the restrooms and drinking fountains at the Monroe bus station.

Two years after the Civil Rights Act, I noticed the signs were gone, but the separate facilities remained. And it was well known that if you drank from the "wrong" fountain, you still might well get a friendly yet threatening "reminder" not to do so. This was true in many places across the Southeast. The laws had changed, but only with a wink and a nod. People were still being murdered either for being the wrong race or helping the wrong race, often with no accountability for the murderer(s). I was a hapless teenager, but I recognized a systemic culture of brutality and fear permeating the air. It would reinforce my decision to leave, and years later, I was and still am astounded by how little Americans, in general, understand the lingering, pernicious impact of Jim Crow. It seemed too fantastical for people to believe—unless you were a Black Southerner.

Outside the courthouse on Broad Street, also known as Highway 11, I would catch a ride straight north to the farm, arriving in the mid to late afternoon. My mother Doris and grandmother Azalea (pronounced Asalee) would greet me with hugs and cheery Southern voices, feed me a sandwich and sweet tea while serenading me with local news and farm talk, then return to their Saturday routines while I walked the fields to soak in childhood summer memories.

Raised a God-fearing Southern Baptist, Azalea had a strict policy regarding alcohol—none was allowed in her house. Even when my grandparents would come to visit in Virginia, my parents would hide the booze. I once blew their cover when I was very young by innocently asking, "Why you got your drink bottles" stashed in the basement laundry hamper?

Azalea shook her head, for she understood as well as anyone the lure of a cocktail, good or bad. One reason she kept her policy was because my grandfather, Emory, would announce "important business to tend to" in town and bring me along as cover while he lounged on the loading dock at the local icehouse, drinking moonshine whiskey with other farmers while the kids threw a baseball out back. I discovered much later that the icehouse had been a notorious hub where the Ku Klux Klan planned its nefarious doings in the county. Emory was never a part of that crowd that I was aware of.

After dinner and an hour or two of three-handed-canasta on the porch, the ladies would retire to their bedrooms to read. I'd borrow Doris's Buick Riviera to put it on the highway in a fashion the car was built for but experienced only when I came to visit.

I would commandeer the car's 340hp V-8 to Barrow, the next county north where three-point-two beer was sold, buy a six-pack, and cruise the empty country roads for hours while sipping Pabst Blue Ribbon, windows rolled down just enough to let the evening breeze through, yet keeping out the night bugs riding its wave. The only light was starlight; the only sounds were a purring high-performance engine, the evocative hum of high-speed rubber on asphalt, and the nightly chorus of courting country crickets.

Inside the car, a tinny speaker would share local sermons, WLS in Chicago or WABC in New York, for some reason, all available on the AM dial after dark throughout the Southeast. After 8 p.m., I rarely saw another car, just bugs and bats fluttering in the headlights, roadside orchards with overhanging pines, wooden fenceposts, and barbed wire passing like a kaleidoscope of connected sentries.

If another car was on the road late at night, it would often have the out-of-state tags of motorists heading to Florida. Back then, such tags would almost guarantee being pulled over by the local sheriff or police—there was money to be made from fines for real or imaginary infractions. If the tags belonged to any place north of Tennessee, they might expect some bullying to go along with their speeding tickets. If the drivers happened to be Black, the bullying might turn into a beating.

My own father had been a victim of out-of-state harassment when he was jailed in China Grove, North Carolina, while driving from Washington, DC, to Georgia years earlier. He hadn't pulled to the side of the road when a funeral procession was passing in the other direction. The reason, of course, was that he had no idea that he was supposed to do so, which the officer fully understood because it was such an obscure infraction. But our car had Virginia plates and an Arlington County sticker on our windshield. Back in the fifties, that was northern enough for some Reconstruction payback.

Dad was jailed for hours while we waited outside the station. Eventually, Doris was allowed inside, and she demanded to know why her husband was being held. After paying a fine, Dad was freed and not to be toyed with for the remainder of that trip, including fielding a child's questions. I had never seen him that angry. It was a visceral lesson that helped me understand the outrage over police harassment—or far worse.

When the beer was gone, I'd head south on Winder Road and look for the landmark giant pecan trees flanking the circular dirt drive of our farm, Azalea's Acres. I'd pull behind the house and quietly park under the protective spread of the grandfather oak tree, which was at least as old as the antebellum house.

Careful not to slam the weighty door on the coupe, I would gently exit the car and make my way across the dirt and stone path up the concrete steps to the porch. There, I would take off my shoes, gingerly enter through the screen door, and cross the kitchen, lightly treading in stocking feet to quiet the inevitable creak of ancient linoleum.

On the far side of the kitchen, I would step up into the tiny attic doorway, which was, for some mysterious reason, barely two feet wide and nearly a foot off the kitchen floor. There, I faced the harrowing climb up the ominously steep service stairs leading to the narrow confines of a vaulted attic, where a welcome bed awaited.

In the morning, I would rise with the attic temperature, wash in the child's sink while stooped to avoid the roof's exposed shingle nails, take a morning walk in the fields with a cup of coffee to visit the animals, and walk back and share what we called Sunday dinner, even though it wasn't yet noon. I'd then pack up the duffel and a paper bag full of leftover fried chicken, slaw, peaches, and baked goods, and Doris would drop me downtown by the courthouse, where I would cross over to Highway 78 and stick out my thumb once more.

Sunday was the worst day to travel because traffic was so light. No one worked on Sunday. A few people went out to eat, and some got in the car to visit relatives or church. The trip back to school was often a long and lonely one.

The journey would take six to eight hours, depending on my luck that day. Sometimes, a trucker would pick me up, which was a godsend because that would often take me nearly the whole distance back to Columbia. Truckers were discouraged, if not forbidden, from picking up hitchhikers, but I encountered drivers, including older ones, so desperate for conversation that they wouldn't stop talking the entire trip.

Occasionally, a friend from school would come with me just for the home cooking and a day in the real country, and it still amuses me to realize that elderly couples would stop on a lonesome road to pick up two eighteen-year-old boys with duffel bags. That was the midcentury South.

One benefit of playing music while in school is that, unlike most of my student friends, there were times when I had expendable income. When the semester ended, I had saved enough to buy an old Corvette from a bored student of surplus means who had tired of the two-seater and was anxious to offload it for something plush.

I drove myself to Georgia for the first time, which, instead of hitchhiking, could be called leisurely. Only one ride, and straight on through, in a car that had never set rubber to, much less belonged on a dirt road and captured plenty of looks in the outer expanse of the Charleston Highway.

Life was far easier on the farm with my own car, but the heat and humidity remained the same, as did the torpor of life in the country. It wasn't long before I understood the powerful relationship between socialization and mental health. I helped the best I could on the farm, but the long days in the Georgia heat wore me down, and I realized how difficult life in the country was for a teenager looking for what Tom Waits called "the heart of Saturday night."

The only entertainment was driving around the dark countryside for hours or sitting at a college bar in Athens, which just accentuated my solitude. I spent long hours sitting on that porch, walking in those fields, and lying in that attic. Like most teenagers, I spent so much time alone, yearning for something or someone.

Ultimately, I succumbed to the loneliness and asked Doris and Azalea if they would mind if I left. I contributed very little to the farm and felt out of place. Our house in Virginia was empty, and Doris was willing to let me stay for the summer if it would rest easier on my psyche. I was three months shy of turning nineteen.

I loaded up what would fit into the two-seater and headed north. With a beautiful body and loud and powerful dual carburetor V-8 engine, the Corvette looked and sounded as advertised, but on the highway, the car handled like a misloaded cargo truck with risky suspension and an oversized steering wheel. This was a vehicle built to be admired, not driven. It was a punishing ride, but I was thrilled to take it, and when I hit the highway out of Monroe, life felt renewed.

Thanks to my mother's generous spirit and my grandmother's understanding nature, the opportunity for luck had once again presented itself, waiting to be recognized.

I never returned to the farm until it was sold to the adjacent farmer after Azalea died. I was in a distraught state when she passed, and Doris advised me to stay in Virginia, which I did, to my regret. It's possible Doris had enough grief on her hands, and the weight of concern for her depressed child would be overbearing, so she advised me to stay away. If true, I'll take it, and the regret can be struck from the list.

CHAPTER 4
THE LUCKY ONE

I knew the house in Virginia was vacant, but I had never seen it actually empty, as in nothing but a carpet. I had a sleeping bag with me, so I spread it on the living room floor, bought a radio, chair, lamp, pot, skillet, plate, drinking glass, knife, fork, and spoon at the local Goodwill, and then purchased toiletries, a towel, and laundry soap at the nearby drug store. I had my old home back, or at least a shell of it.

The radio had been my most insightful purchase, for it was my constant companion during waking hours. I had cooked for myself often enough while my mother was either working or in class, so I stocked up on basics at the grocery store and basically had everything but an income. Not much for an eighteen-year-old boy to spend money on in my limited world of that time, but that world was empty without steak and cheese subs, beer, and friends to consume them with.

A friend was working a summer job in the boiler room at George Washington University Hospital, and there was an opening, so he brought me on. The job was in the engineering department, which, given how little I had learned about how anything works in my youth, promised to be a rewarding experience. This became true, but certainly not in ways I would anticipate. The conditions of the job were so hapless, only a teenager would consider them normal.

Local folklore claims that Washington, DC, was built on a swamp. This isn't true, but the city is surrounded by rivers, which, in tune with the area's humidity index, provide excellent mosquito breeding grounds, making summer an endurance test for residents. In 1966, the GWU hospital was mostly heated by radiators, with air cooled by fans and a few window air conditioners. Central air-conditioning had yet to be installed in most older buildings other than movie theaters, which used the allure of cool, dry air as an enticement to come inside, so most patients and employees of the hospital just endured the heat.

The boiler room, which provided steam for radiators and kitchens throughout the complex, was a dark, warehouse-sized space with dim overhead lighting, the constant hiss of four fully fired tractor-trailer-sized boilers keeping the entire hospital basement at least one hundred degrees, and in the summer, it was often ten to twenty degrees warmer than that. The space had the appearance and personality of a set from a mid-twentieth-century era science fiction film, lacking only the theremin soundtrack of *Forbidden Planet*, which I began to use as a reference to our workspace.

The only access to the *Forbidden Planet* was through a service elevator that was for the exclusive use of two departments, Engineering and Pathology. The elevator, which I soon dubbed "the chute," had three stops: the Main Hospital level near the kitchen, the morgue, and the boiler room on the bottom level. Occasionally, workers from the boiler room would find themselves joined for the ride by a lab technician either bringing a corpse to the morgue for pathology or from the morgue to the crematorium on our level. It made for a discomfiting, often quiet trip to be sharing the chute with a dead body.

The "engineering crew," which my friend Don and I were a part of, wore dark green thick cotton uniforms, which could be easily identified throughout the hospital. We were normally carrying tools to or from the chute, performing a repair, or moving discarded items from one place to another.

Don and I were clearly summer employees because our names

weren't above the pockets of our uniforms, which we were responsible for washing ourselves. This was a sketchy requirement for an eighteen-year-old not accustomed to separating colors with multiple laundry loads, particularly after cleaning a boiler.

Every other week, one of the boilers would be shut down for a power wash. Lacking seniority, Don and I had the responsibility to perform this task. It sounded like an interesting assignment since both of us were intrigued by the thought of squeezing through a narrow metal gate designed like a mail slot into what is essentially a giant incinerator, struggling to haul the power equivalent of a fire hose on our shoulders. What could go wrong?

This intrigue can only be felt by very young men, and it didn't last beyond donning goggles and a jumpsuit, climbing into the cold boiler, lugging a heavy canvas tube on our shoulders with the potential to spread us onto our backs like human mops, and peering up at the ash-caked walls and soot-covered pipes hanging under layers of brick, dark as midnight and dirty beyond description. The intrigue was brief.

We would flash the okay through a slit of embedded glass similar to the opening in a welding helmet, dig our feet in, and wait for the blast, which came like a jet-propelled body slam. Feet planted wide while holding the hose with both hands, struggling to stay upright amid the force, we vaporized hardened ash and soot from the walls and pipes, east-west and north-south.

We did this while standing in the center of the boiler being pummeled mercilessly with blackened backwash and liquified dirt from all sides and above. It was like kneeling underneath a flooding sewer during a desert monsoon. But while there is something sublime about rainfall, this was hell.

The entire process took around thirty to forty-five minutes, and when completed, I would be covered with soot from head to toe, including so deep inside my uniform that even my white jockeys became permanently blackened, never to be used as a cleaning rag, much less worn again. To this day, I still don't understand how that much soot could find a way through all those layers. Eradicating all that filth in a tub, shower, or washing machine was impossible, which made me quickly understand why Don and I, young, dumb, and broke, were given the jobs.

There was a small, air-conditioned office in the center of the boiler room, possibly eight feet square, with an overhead fluorescent light over a small desk where a clerk was seated. His job was to communicate with the hospital administration and nursing stations needing maintenance assistance. The small size of the office was designed to discourage employees from gathering inside to cool off, which worked about as well as that idea can in three-digit temperatures.

The clerk, Mr. Kauch (pronounced like a sofa), welcomed the company of college boys because he enjoyed talking about his time in "university." Being college students made Don and me the subjects of scorn from the "engineers," who I soon learned had received no formal training in such but were referred to as either "maintenance engineers" or "steam engineers," depending on whether their specialty was fixing a squeaky door hinge or unblocking a balky steampipe. It was all some form of engineering, just not the kind that required several years in classrooms to master.

Mr. Kauch, prematurely bald and always dressed in a short-sleeve button-down shirt, clip-on tie, and one of two plaid nylon sports jackets he owned, had a sheet on the wall of his office where everyone would sign in at the beginning of a shift, and out when finished for the day or night. Normally, signing in would also include a visit with Kauch, a frustrated comic who loved to talk about the world he envisioned outside of his cube in the *Forbidden Planet*.

The "college boys" could relate to this world better than the permanent engineering crew, which created resentment among the engineers toward us beyond the normal reason of assumed entitlement, which, in this case, was far from deserved.

The foreman, whose name was Mr. Napier (always mister), was my toughest nut. Some foremen seem to always have it in for one goat in every crew, and I was Napier's. He was a sour-faced, scowling man with thick white hair and bushy brows guarding nervous eyes forever locked into a squint. A man who never displayed satisfaction, Mr. Napier's disposition was one of perpetual negative judgment, and he would openly sneer and mock me whenever I talked about school or what my goals were, which, as a college freshman, I clearly had none.

On my first day, Mr. Kauch asked what my plan was beyond college. I answered off the top of my head, "I don't know. Maybe go to law school?" From that day on, Napier would mockingly refer to me as "Mr. District Attorney," a moniker that he used indiscriminately to cast his jaundiced judgment on me, whether referring to my opinions, clothes, or job performance. The appraisals were never complimentary.

"So, the district attorney doesn't know how to cut a pipe?" "So, the district attorney needs an hour for lunch?" The DA became a target on the *Forbidden Planet*. In retrospect, I realized, at the very least, my incompetence provided some form of entertainment for Mr. Napier during his otherwise disagreeable day.

In the summer of 1966, the hospital was renovating one of the wings and was in the process of modernizing the facilities. Part of this renovation was to install new beds, sinks, and dividers in semiprivate rooms. My first failure in the engineering department came from being given the assignment to assist the person installing these dividers. His name was Wynkoop, and he was one of the friendlier engineers, a youngish, energetic man with dark hair and a bored expression. He rarely communicated, but he quietly did his job, which, on this day, was for us to attach a privacy curtain to railings already installed in a patient's room.

Wynkoop climbed a ladder and began threading the hooks onto the curtain, then sliding them onto the railing. My job was to gather the hooks from a box and hand them to Wynkoop, who attached them to the curtain and rail.

This was not an interesting job, and while passing the hooks, I scanned the room, seeking some source of entertainment. While doing so, I noticed the bed had operating controls. I had never seen an electric bed, which was a complete novelty in 1966. There were switches controlling the height of the bed and the angle of the head and foot, but when I turned them one way or the other, the bed remained still and silent. I tried every switch, back and forth, on and off, but the bed didn't seem to move or make a sound. After several tries, I gave up and sat with my boredom, handing Wynkoop hooks, which he intently threaded onto the rail.

First came the quiet vibration, growing into a shake, then a slow creak, quickly becoming a groan, followed by an ominous rumble from the adjacent wall. I jumped off the bed and flipped every switch I could find, but it was clear that the bed was indeed powered, had been silently elevating, and, being positioned directly under a wall sink, was now vying for space with the water pipe feeding the faucets. The pipe rattled, whined, and shook defiantly for several seconds until Wynkoop turned from the ladder and screamed, "Jesus Christ, man!"

The pipe burst, exploding from the wall, followed by a propulsion of water into the room, not as strong as the boiler hose but more powerful than anything I'd seen coming out of a pipe. Within seconds, there was almost a foot of water on the floor of the room, and Wynkoop was off the ladder, digging through his tool kit for a wrench. "What the fuck, man? Jesus Christ!" he kept yelling, not actually asking how I had managed to break the pipe off the wall and fill the room with water in a matter of seconds. I don't think I was ever asked that question, but my responsibility was never doubted.

Wynkoop quickly shut off the water and called for custodial help with a walkie-talkie. But as soon as he'd holstered his device, two nurses ran into the room, looked quizzically around at the newly formed wading pool, and told us we were directly above the doctors' dining room; it was the middle of lunch, and water was pouring from the ceiling onto the diners.

More chatter on the walkie-talkie. Within minutes, mops arrived, custodians went to work, and Wynkoop and I hurriedly threaded the hooks and slithered out of the room. I remained silent and barely visible the rest of the day.

But this didn't end my career as an engineer's assistant, which lived to crash another day in the rebuilt wing of GWU hospital.

Part of the renovations included installing forced-air heating throughout the hospital and replacing the aged radiator steam heat. As the heating ducts were installed throughout the wing, radiators were disconnected and scheduled to be recycled. My assignment was to remove radiators from the renovated rooms and take them, two at a time, to a storage yard behind the hospital, where they would be collected for scrap.

With no electric devices within reach, it was assumed I could do no damage, but this assumption failed to consider my persistent desire to seek a quicker, if not easier, method when faced with boring repetition.

My tools were heavy gloves and a high-capacity pushcart. I was never told what this cart's capacity was, but it was heavier than most pushcarts and had larger wheels, so I assumed, fairly, it could hold much more than a regular cart.

I took the cart to the first room and began loading up old radiators, which had been removed from the walls and were stacked on the floor. These were cast-iron radiators, which were easily 75 to 100 pounds each, minimum. It was a struggle to lift them onto the cart, and once loaded, a strain to push the cart with two radiators aboard.

To access the storage yard, I had to load the radiators onto the front service elevator, take them down three flights to the basement, around the entire hospital, and through the crowded hallways, careful to avoid dense foot traffic. At the other end of the hospital, I had to take the other service elevator up to the first floor and find a way through the service doors, meaning I had to secure the doors open while I pushed the cart through to unload in the yard. Each trip consumed over half an hour.

In my opinion, taking two at a time wasn't nearly efficient enough. If I could put four or more on board, it would cut the time in half or even better. It was, after all, a heavy-duty cart, so why not take advantage? Also, when I scouted outside the hospital, I realized another gate to the storage yard was easily accessed from outside the emergency entrance ramp.

If I took the radiators out the side entrance and around the hospital on the sidewalk along New Hampshire Avenue, cut across at Washington Circle, then back up at Twenty-third Street to the storage yard back entrance, it would be half the distance as going through the hallways and further cut the time spent on this dreadful task. Done.

Proud of the fruits of my ambition, I loaded five radiators onto the cart and tested it. Heavy, but manageable if I took it slow. I pushed the cart to the service elevator and brought it down to the first floor and out the side entrance. The cart seemed to be getting heavier as I pushed it from the hospital to the sidewalk, obviously an incline I hadn't noticed, but going slowly and carefully, I was able to keep it steady. Still better than going the long way with a lighter load.

When I scouted this option, I didn't realize the minute angle of the sidewalk leading from the hospital entrance along New Hampshire Avenue to Washington Circle. It was very subtle and never noticeable to a pedestrian, but it was slightly, ever so slightly, downhill.

As I began pushing the cart with at least 400 pounds of radiators on board, I noticed something very disturbing. The cart was soon moving faster than I was and quickly picking up speed. Within seconds, I couldn't hold it any longer and had to let go.

I yelled and waved my hands at the people on the sidewalk, and all managed to jump out of the way as the rogue, industrial-sized super-wagon rattled and banged its way down the path. As it gained momentum, each crack in the sidewalk created a cringe-inducing gong of hundreds of pounds of hollow cast-iron pipes crashing into each other, sending terrified workers scattering in all directions. The cast-iron death cart that I had unleashed eventually ran out of sidewalk, crashing over the curb and into Washington Circle, where it hit the pavement, overturned onto its side, and scattered radiators into every lane of midday traffic.

Miraculously, no cars were damaged, but traffic in the circle was halted. I ran down the sidewalk, apologizing to shaken pedestrians for the runaway hand truck and asking if anyone was hurt—thankfully, no one was. I carefully entered the circle with waving hands amidst blaring horns and the shouts of furious drivers. I righted the pushcart and began to slowly lift the radiators and replace them on the bed.

The yelling and honking were drawing a lot of attention around the circle, and it became a keen topic of amusement for everyone watching, except for me and one other person.

As I was crouching among the cars loading the radiators, I glanced at the storage yard entrance on Twenty-third Street, where, peering at the circle from outside the yard, scowl in full bloom, with fists on his hips, stood Mr. Napier. I sure could have used the help collecting the radiators, but Napier had something else in mind. He met my eyes, shook his head, turned around, and walked into the storage yard.

I did get help from some sympathetic pedestrians who took pity on the kid in the heavy green uniform picking up one-hundred-pound radiators in the August heat and humidity of downtown Washington, and within a few minutes, I had collected the radiators and deposited them into the storage yard. There was no sign of Napier.

I finished transporting the scrap, two at a time, along the interior route, which took the remainder of the day. I didn't have the courage to take lunch because that would require signing out and confronting Napier, who would clearly be anxious to berate me. But when I was finished, I skulked down to the Planet to sign out for the day.

Kauch was alone in his office when I walked in. He looked at me and half-smiled, half-smirked. "So, I hear you had an interesting day!" I agreed that I had and turned to the chart.

At first, I couldn't find my name, but when I looked closely, I saw that it had been blacked out with Magic Marker. Not just lined through but blackened with enough willfulness that no part of my name was legible, just thick, black Magic Marker, which alone would have required some effort to find in Kauch's office. It must have taken some time for Napier to create such a prejudicial disbarment for the district attorney, but I know he relished it.

The next day, Don and Mr. Napier were riding the chute down to the Planet when a lab technician wheeled a cadaver onto the elevator. When the technician pushed the gurney out the doors to the morgue, Napier watched them go and snickered.

"There goes the lucky one."

CHAPTER 5
THE SEEDS OF A STORYTELLER

The remainder of the summer showed little improvement. The Corvette died, or at least that is what the mechanic told me when he realized I knew nothing about engines. He did offer to "take it off my hands" for $250, which I sadly accepted before heading back to school for my sophomore year, which fared better musically but not so grade-wise. With my mother's subtle encouragement, I decided to avoid the expense of returning to college in South Carolina the following year and instead came back to suburban Washington, DC, where life took another turn.

My time there ultimately led to a move west to pursue a career in filmmaking, but only indirectly. I decided to give up music and apply myself academically. I would have to essentially restart my studies, with only basic credits on my transcript, but I was prepared to do that with borrowed money to start, then aim for scholarships. I knew grades wouldn't be an issue if I just did the work and went to class rather than on the road with a band or my friends.

I would make it my goal to become a stellar student. I only had to decide on the field of study, and since I grew up in a family that traveled for the US government, that was what I would pursue. I would have to start back at a community college and make straight

As, then move a step up from there and keep doing so until I was where I wanted to be. My interest at the time was diplomacy and international relations, with a career goal of foreign service, which only deepened during the time I spent incapacitated by an accident.

In the spring of 1968, I was riding a motorcycle past a road construction site, and, trying to avoid a dog that ran in front of me, I crashed into a road grader. I flew off the bike, hit the grader, and landed on the street. My injuries required a long period of bedridden rehabilitation, wearing a lower body plaster cast. This lasted throughout the summer and continued through the fall.

I spent most of those months in bed reading or watching television. My mother worked during the day and was in class many evenings, pursuing an advanced degree for her teaching. Our neighbors took turns volunteering to bring meals, and friends would stop by with sandwiches and beer. By the end of the summer, I was able to position myself in a wheelchair, and friends would prop me lengthwise into the back seat and take me for rides.

We would drive for hours, drinking beer, talking, and listening to the radio. It became a ritual I looked forward to, which ended late one night when several of us stopped at an overlook on the George Washington Parkway to relieve ourselves in the woods. Needing two hands to perform the task in this setting, I had to prop my crutches into the unstable and uneven ground covered with soft earth, leaves, and sticks on a hilltop overlooking the Potomac River.

The crutches failed to hold in the wet mulch, and I tumbled down the hill. I stopped short of the river but caught a number of branches, dirt, rocks, and leaves along the way. It was a struggle for all of us to get me back up the hill and into the car, now with a broken cast, stuffed with dirt, twigs, leaves, and pebbles rubbing against my atrophied leg.

My mother, who was hosting me during this rehab, was not pleased, so the visits continued, but the joyrides were discouraged.

I read newspapers, magazines, editorials, nonfiction, and novels regarding world politics, which had always interested me. I followed every conflict over the globe, Vietnam at the forefront, which, in 1968, was the theater for nearly 550,000 troops, the greatest concentration of American forces since WWII. It was an interesting year to be bedridden, for the world was changing at a pace unlike anything in my lifetime. And it was all playing out on television.

Walter Cronkite and David Brinkley guided me daily through the Vietnam war, the grief, and the riots across the nation in response to the assassinations of Martin Luther King, Jr. and Robert Kennedy, the police riot in Chicago during the Democratic convention to nominate Hubert Humphrey, and the violent reactions to protests in Miami when the Republicans met to nominate Richard Nixon.

I saw newspapers change as their cities did, shedding light on the social and racial inequities that were becoming national news for the first time in my life. I watched the music on television develop from sweet, soulful ballads and dance numbers to frenetic psychedelic pop and incisive political protest songs. My physical condition left me a captive audience for the news of the world.

I was incapacitated for nearly six months and in rehab for another six. Exactly fourteen months after the accident, I began walking without the aid of a cane or crutches. But all this time spent mostly by myself in a hospital or bedroom enabled me to focus on my core interests. It was an epiphany. I'd fallen in love with stories.

Everything was a story: history, politics, current events, civilizations, and unquestionably music. I had been an avid reader since childhood, but somehow, that time spent in front of the television made me start looking at stories in a new light. I began to see film as a form I could be a part of. Movies were not just entertainment but an instrument for a voice. I was captivated and moved by them and curious about how they were made.

If I was captured by a film, I began noticing who the director and screenwriter were and remembered to look for them again. I was still more interested in reading the news of the world and how governments and people interacted, but I was beginning to understand that the potential films had to influence and affect those same people. I wasn't thinking, *I'm going to make movies*, but the pot was simmering.

When I recovered, I returned to school with the intention of earning scholarships, graduating with honors, working a year to save money, and proceeding to graduate school in international relations to look for a job in the State Department working overseas. That was the plan.

CHAPTER 6
THE ADULT WORLD

After graduation from college, I began driving a taxi to earn money while looking for a more permanent job, which would, of course, turn out not to be permanent.

One morning, I picked up a professionally dressed, serious woman who asked me to take her to the Longworth House Office Building on Capitol Hill. We began to talk, and I learned she ran the office of the Joint Committee on Congressional Operations, a relatively new committee formed to monitor congressional oversight, which was about to hold hearings on a reporter's right to remain silent when questioned by the executive branch.

After the publication of the Pentagon Papers by the *New York Times* in 1971, President Nixon ordered the formation of the "plumbers unit" to stop leaks to the press from the White House. This unit was responsible for the Watergate break-in in June of 1972 and had targeted the *New York Times* and *Washington Post* to pressure journalists to reveal their sources of information inside the White House. The Watergate break-in had occurred the previous June, and investigations were in full swing.

President Nixon had threatened to incarcerate journalists who refused to reveal their sources, and this had become one of the historical stories I was interested in learning more about, so this committee intrigued me.

I told the office manager about myself, and she asked for a résumé. Like all young graduates driving taxis, I carried mine in a pouch on the front seat of my cab, so I handed her one; she paid and disappeared into the Longworth HOB.

Several days later, she called me to come in for an interview. It turned out to be the first of three, the third being with the chair of the committee, Rep. Jack Brooks of Beaumont, Texas.

Mr. Brooks, a slender, bald man wearing a starched white shirt with rolled-up sleeves held tight by red suspenders over his shoulders, sat behind an oversized mahogany desk with his feet propped on the blotter. He sat at such an angle that my field of vision was limited to the soles of his shoes on my left, his frowning face in the center, and a framed Marine Corps logo on the right.

Mr. Brooks never smiled, and the crease in his forehead never lifted during the interview. With his hands clasped together on his stomach, he was simultaneously chewing on an unlit cigar and sucking tobacco under his lip. Once every minute or so, he would remove the cigar, lean over a large brass spittoon stationed to the right of his desk, let out the discharge, and resume his pose.

It was clear to me that my position would be one of relative unimportance, and this was simply a formality, but the goal he had in this interview was to make one thing perfectly clear. Like all employees, I had to understand the scope of his power. The last thing Mr. Brooks said to me in the interview was, and he removed his cigar to be heard clearly, "If you ever fuck with me, I will personally see to it that you never work within one hundred miles of this city. Understood?"

I wondered if it was possible to hide my combined shock and amusement. Why in the world would he threaten a new kid before he even had any responsibility? "Yes, sir."

"Okay, that's it."

He took his feet off the desk and hit the intercom to his secretary.

"What else we got?"

As I was leaving, he called out to me. "One other thing. Get a haircut."

That came as a surprise, considering this was my third interview. I had been advised to get a haircut at each, which I had done. By now, I felt like my hair was close to boot camp length. But apparently, it was not boot camp enough for the ex-Marine, so I complied and was hired.

My job was twofold: to conduct legislative or legal research when assigned to do so (though most of this was given to committee clerks who seemed incapable of boredom) and to interview candidates for job openings in congressional offices. This became the interesting part of the job, simply because when an office had an opening, they had to follow the protocol of filling out an interview request form and submitting it to the Congressional Placement Office, where I had a desk.

On the interview form, the submitting office was required to list any and all job qualifications, the lack of which would exclude someone from being considered. For example, you might need a certain degree or have so many years of experience to qualify for a particular post.

What shocked me when I went through the job requests from different offices were specific requirements that seemed patently illegal. "White only" was the most glaring example, but others specified "a Southern accent," "preferably blond, but must be attractive," "needs to be pleasant looking," or "have an unquestionably good figure." Clearly, these were expressly forbidden by, or violated the spirit of, the Civil Rights Act of 1964, which had passed less than ten years earlier.

Most of the racist and misogynist demands were for receptionists, but not all. Even an occasional request for the highest paid jobs in an office, those of administrative assistant and legislative assistant, would occasionally ask for White candidates, and in some minority offices, Black or Hispanic.

I was a young liberal, always supporting Democratic candidates. When meeting a member of Congress, I would immediately look up their ratings in the ADA and ACU booklets. These publications rated members' voting records to express a measure of their liberal or conservative views.

ADA, or the Americans for Democratic Action, was founded in the 1940s by Eleanor Roosevelt and promoted progressive policies. The ACU, or American Conservative Union, was relatively new, since 1971, and rated members according to their support of individual liberties and opposition to what they considered overregulation.

Being young and naïve, I was content to judge members' character and trustworthiness according to how their ratings matched my biases. A high ADA rating meant someone I would like; a high ACU meant someone I should avoid. This was how I navigated the halls in 1972. At the time, my youth led me to evaluate character according to political leanings.

The blatant disregard for the legalities of the Civil Rights Act among offices in the US Congress was the first disturbing discovery in my job. The second was that I noticed the Congressional Record published monthly disbursements to each committee, which was public record. Something about the amount our committee was receiving didn't seem quite right to me, but all employees had access to a listing of committee salaries and pay scales, which was also a matter of public record. Adding up the salaries and comparing them against total appropriations showed a vast amount of money disappearing into the ether—sums that couldn't simply be explained by overhead and office supplies.

The committee had just formed in the 1971 Congress, so all the employees were relatively new. Most of the staffers were close to my age, recent college graduates eager to make a statement in their first position on the Hill. All the major publications were chasing Watergate figures like cats after crickets, and Nixon had ratcheted up his nefarious plan to plug White House leaks to the press, doubling down on his threat to jail journalists who wouldn't reveal their sources. The hearings were being held to determine the constitutionality of this threat.

Researching these stories was a juicy assignment for new staffers and provided riveting conversation when we met after work for drinks and meals. The committee's work was the hottest item in all of Washington, and we were thrilled to be at the center of it. Less thrilling was that everyone knew the racist and sexist games being played by the Placement Office, and everyone knew that committee money was going down some kind of dark hole. But to dwell on those things would've required some hard choices, and so they were rarely discussed.

I'd made some good friends, particularly with three staffers close to my age and background, as we lunched, drank, and bonded over our mutual experiences. But one thing would soon become clear: as much as the committee money trail intrigued me and the Placement Office postings bugged me for their blatant discrimination, my pals weren't so interested in that. To go there seemed too risky for Hill careerists. But I was not that, and I didn't see it as a risk—I saw it more as a duty to slip the engine into gear and was convinced that it would gain momentum once engaged. Of the two issues, the Placement Office seemed the best target.

Starting with the new Congress in January 1973, the chair of a Joint Committee would switch to the senate side. The senator in line to assume the chair was a Democrat named Lee Metcalf of Montana. Senator Metcalf was known on the Hill as affable, fair, and extremely sensitive to environmental and social justice issues. His ADA rating was over ninety-five, so he was someone I could feel comfortable trusting.

I knew I was on my own, so without mentioning it to my colleagues, I photocopied job orders excluding applicants for reasons other than education or experience. That editing still left me with a considerable number to copy. And, since I was already at it, I also copied Congressional Record issues with the committee disbursements listed.

I called Senator Metcalfe's office and made an appointment. I told the office manager that I was a committee staffer and needed to talk to the senator about urgent committee business that I felt was private but he should know about before he assumed the chair.

In retrospect, I gave too much away about the seriousness of what I wanted to discuss with him, inviting a preliminary interrogation that I should have avoided. Regardless, the manager was friendly and welcoming and made an appointment for me that coming Friday at 5 p.m.

I showed up at Senator Metcalf's reception area on time, and the office manager immediately led me into his office, which was a Montana travelogue with photos of wilderness, presidents among wildlife, mountainous scenery, and Native American chiefs with Montana lawmakers and lawmen. I struggled to keep my eyes away from the walls and on the desk in front of me.

I had copies of all the questionable job orders, Congressional Record pages, and salary tallies in my briefcase.

The senator, a ruggedly handsome man with a friendly manner and Western style to match the office décor, welcomed me and invited me to sit across the desk from him. As I did, he sat down and began in a fashion that alerted me as to where this would be headed.

"So, what's on your mind?"

Considering the reason for the meeting, the more germane question should have been what was on his mind, but I was too inexperienced to turn the conversation in that direction. I stammered my way through my concerns, telling him my history, how long I had worked there, how I discovered the illegal job requests, and then the payment discrepancy. I told him what high regard I had for him as a senate member, which I immediately realized was a mistake because it was so irrelevant. I said I had not felt comfortable approaching the previous leadership but that he was a man I thought I could trust.

While I spoke, I laid the materials onto his desk, and he silently looked them over, occasionally looking up at me as I described my personal interaction with offices to emphasize how open they were with the discrimination. He never said a word.

When I was finished, he looked up as though waiting for me to continue. When I didn't, he asked, "Anything else?"

My heart dropped. "No, sir."

He stood up and put out his hand.

"You were a good citizen to come in here today."

I took his hand, unable to formulate a viable response, aware that I had made a major mistake. "Thank you, sir."

He rang his office manager, and she came in to escort me out. I have no memory of the small talk she offered along the way, simply white noise following me into the marble hallway.

I carried the hollow feeling all weekend. *A good citizen.* That's what I was? That's what it meant to him? I knew I had done the wrong thing, but I didn't know what the right thing would have been. It became a weekend of functioning in a haze until I showed up for work at 9 a.m. Monday morning.

Several minutes after I was seated at my desk, I was summoned to the executive director's office. I had only been in his office once before. He had been my second interview for the job and the source of my second haircut. He got right to the point.

"We're going to do some restructuring of the committee staff and won't be needing your services any longer."

"Starting when?" I asked.

"Starting now. Go home. We'll offer you two months' severance."

Congressional offices are above the laws they create, as is evidenced by what happened in the Placement Office in 1972. Even though, by federal law, employees were guaranteed two weeks' severance pay when terminated, this did not apply to the US Congress. When you were fired from a congressional office, you were paid nothing beyond the day you were terminated. In my case, however, I had been offered two months' severance, which, from my understanding, was unprecedented among lowly staffers.

I was incredulous. "Two months?" Then trying to add some levity. "That almost sounds like a bribe!"

He went ice-cold. "Are you making an accusation?"

I realized the possibility of a recording device in the office. Since

President Nixon's usage of them, it was assumed congressional offices were also bugged. I weighed where to go with this exchange and swallowed the rest of it.

"No, sir. I'll take the severance. Thank you."

I left the office and went home.

I paced the rooms, trying to figure out what I should have done differently until it became the obvious rabbit hole, so I gave it up, or at least I tried to. Later that afternoon, I got a phone call from Rachel, one of my colleagues from the committee with whom I would socialize after work.

"Where are you? What happened?" She had seen me that morning at my desk; then, suddenly, I was gone, and the desk had been cleared.

"I was fired."

"What? Why? What did you do?"

"I don't think I should tell you that. For your sake, not mine."

"Well, will you come meet us for lunch, then?" I agreed to do that, and we planned to meet on Wednesday in the senate cafeteria.

Rachel and I met for lunch, along with two other colleagues we hung out with after work. It was a somewhat sad but enjoyable goodbye lunch, and we promised to keep in touch and continue to visit the same watering holes on the Hill. I think we silently knew that would never happen.

I had mentioned up front that I wouldn't talk about work, that we should forget it and just have a good time, which we did.

That afternoon, Rachel called at the end of the day.

"You have to tell me what happened with you."

"It's best I don't. It would just put pressure on you to make a choice that I don't think you want to make."

"After lunch, all three of us were called into the executive director's office and fired. Wasn't an hour after we got back."

"What? What reason did he give you?"

"He didn't, but clearly, someone saw us having lunch with you today. You have to tell me what happened."

So, I did. She listened intently, then sighed in resignation. None of the information was news to her, but she didn't know that I had collected the evidence, much less gone to see the incoming chairman. "So, what can we do?"

"If I go to the press, will you all come with me?"

"I'll have to ask them, but I sure will."

The next morning, I called the office of Jack Anderson, a storied investigative journalist who had inherited Drew Pearson's column in the *Washington Post*. Anderson had a reputation as someone who would fearlessly call out people in power. He was writing columns about illegal behavior in the executive branch but would listen to anyone from inside the government who had information regarding government misconduct.

I told the assistant why I was calling without too much detail, that four members of a congressional committee staff had been terminated for trying to expose illegalities in congressional offices, and we wanted to come see him as a group. That would get his attention.

The assistant called me back with an appointment to see Mr. Anderson at 10 a.m. Friday morning. I called Rachel, who contacted the others, and everyone joined in their enthusiasm about what this could mean.

We prepped each other and listed certain instances in the Placement Office where each of us had to exclude candidates from positions because of their age, appearance, gender, or ethnicity. With four of us now going in to see Mr. Anderson, we felt a certain power in numbers.

Thursday evening, Rachel called me. I had prepared the documents for the meeting and was going over who should speak and what they should say. The last time we spoke, which was Tuesday, her tone, like mine, was that of a soldier preparing for combat. Not this time. I remember most of the conversation like I just got off the phone.

"We're not going with you tomorrow."

"Why not?" I already felt two steps ahead of her. Somehow, I knew this would happen.

"Senator Metcalf called us into his office this afternoon."

"Wait, he asked all three of you to meet with him the day before we were going in to see Anderson? Didn't that stink to you?"

"It doesn't matter. We went to his office, and he hired us."

"Back on the committee? To do what?"

"Not the committee. His personal staff."

I wasn't expecting that. "And all of you accepted."

Silence to that. There was one point I had to make; then, I knew we were finished. "You realize what this makes you, right?"

"See it however you choose. We want a career here. All of us."

"I just want to be certain that you are aware of what this means. This is an important decision in your life. Seems you made it without even thinking."

"Listen, you never cared about a career on the Hill. You never even thought about that. This is what we all chose and what we want. Sorry."

"This isn't insignificant. It's going to stay with you. That's the only point I want to make."

That was the end of it. I don't know what became of any of them.

The next morning, at 10 a.m., I went to Jack Anderson's office. He couldn't be there, but he had me sit with his investigative associate Brit Hume, now a well-known broadcast journalist, but at the time, he had been recently celebrated for securing confirmation of the infamous Dita Beard memo. Beard was the ITT lobbyist who admitted to Hume that the memo detailed a $400,000 offer by ITT to fund the 1972 Republican National Convention in San Diego in return for the Nixon administration DOJ dropping an antitrust suit against ITT protesting the company's merger with Hartford Fire Insurance.

Anderson and Hume's reporting on this scandal ultimately resulted in legislation mandating public funding of political nominating conventions, an act sadly overturned by a bipartisan Congress in 2014. Conventions are parties, and politicians like lavish parties.

Sitting in Anderson's office with Hume, I laid out the job requests from the individual offices, the Congressional Record issues, and the salary totals for the committee. He looked them over, said he would take them to Mr. Anderson and call me, which he did that afternoon.

"I spoke with Mr. Anderson, and his feeling is that it would be a big mistake to go public with this right now."

"Why is that?" I asked.

"These are Democrats running this committee. We're after the president, and chances are very good that Watergate could bring down the administration. If we go after any Democrats right now, it can only hurt our current goal. Mr. Anderson really appreciates you bringing this to him, but he thinks the timing is bad. Best to sit on it."

Not likely. I threw everything away, booked a flight to Jamaica, escaped to the Caribbean, and never wanted to set foot in any US government office again, including the Capitol, House or senate office buildings, and the US Department of State.

CHAPTER 7
THE DARKNESS

I returned from Jamaica with a new blend of disappointment, disgust, and despair, trying to accept those feelings as liberating, for I was now free to find a new direction.

I had no identifiable goal and no income to help me look for one. I did have youth in my favor, and certain jobs are easily attained for even slightly skilled young people. I soon found a job writing for an information clearinghouse for The National Institute on Alcoholism and Alcohol Abuse. Not an obvious destination for one looking to escape gloom and malaise, but sometimes what is available is what looks best.

Our offices were in a bland, boxy converted warehouse in the middle of what was then farmland in Gaithersburg, Maryland, now part of the suburban sprawl of Washington, but in the early 1970s, it was mostly dairy, dirt, and horse farms. The sign above the door to the warehouse read NATIONAL CLEARINGHOUSE ON ALCOHOL INFORMATION above the NIAAA logo. It was surprising to find this sign amongst all the farms, where the most common traffic was either trucks or tractors.

The warehouse directly south of ours was being leased by Robert Redford's production company to create the *Washington Post* newsroom in which to shoot the film version of *All the President's Men*. This film set was often the topic of office gossip among staffers, who would find a way to drive by the set looking for stars. Passing the set daily was a sour reminder of my last job on the committee.

To eradicate the stigma of alcoholism, the clearinghouse mantra was "Alcoholism is an illness." We were not allowed to refer to alcoholism as a "disease" in publications because there was no infection, and it was not contagious; therefore, it was an "illness." This was decided at great expense by consulting physicians, attorneys, and PR firms, and I'm sure this conclusion was reached after legal and financial discussions concerning health insurance and employee rights.

Many of the employees were sober alcoholics active in AA, which statistics proved to be the most successful treatment. NIAAA was testing Antabuse and other chemical treatments with mixed results, but AA was proven to work on a reasonable percentage of those able to stick with it.

My area of specialty was skid row, simply because I took an interest in how so many people ended up there, including many with successful jobs. Was it strictly alcohol or more than that? Did the personality create the alcoholism, or vice versa?

While working at the clearinghouse, I visited many areas around the country considered "skid row." This was a sad assignment but interesting due to the personalities I found in these communities. Everyone had a story, each unique, yet with the same conclusion. In his 1985 *Playboy* interview, John Huston, the iconic, Academy Award–winning director of classics like *The Maltese Falcon*, *Treasure of the Sierra Madre*, and *The African Queen*, was asked why most of his films were about losers. His response was "Because they are more interesting than winners."

During these travels, I learned the origin of the term "skid row," which referred to the hills above the loading docks in Seattle. During the depression era of the 1930s, lumber trucks would unload timber at the top of the incline, and the logs would "skid" down the slope onto a waiting barge where they would be stacked by loggers. The area near the docks was known as "the skid," and the road at the bottom was "skid road." This is where jobless and homeless people—referred to as hobos and bums back then—would hang out, looking for work on the barges or just a place where they weren't bothered and could sleep, drink, and cook in relative safety. A common warning among those in Seattle who were concerned about someone's excessive drinking would be "You better watch yourself or you'll end up on skid road." That designation was later shortened to "skid row." This is the story I was told, which I was happy to accept.

I also spent three weeks inside the Manhattan Bowery Project, a former men's shelter founded by the Vera Institute of Justice in 1967 as a detox center for alcoholics on the Bowery and an alternative to jail for those arrested for public intoxication. The Project still exists under the name Project Renewal and, according to the Vera Institute, treats over 20,000 homeless alcoholic men and women every year.

I was looking for these people's stories and trying to find common threads among them, originally thinking the men would be eager to share their tales. I anticipated talking to characters damaged by alcohol and failure, seeking empathy from one another and compassion from those more fortunate. But when I tried to elicit their stories, most were reluctant to share with me; some would be downright hostile.

My time at the Project became a harrowing experience, like GW hospital without the humor, with genuine hardship. In the view of many of the men at the shelter, I represented the privileged, one who would soon return to the comfort of my home and cash my paycheck earned by documenting the despair of the skid-row alcoholic, thus adding to my fortune by exposing their damaged lives. A number resented me, some strongly.

I couldn't argue with this perception, though I tried to present myself as sympathetic. Most of these men (it was only men on my side of the Project) were extremely angry about their lives, and many lacked hope or pride. Those who willingly shared with me told stories of emotional, physical, and economic tumbles that were heartbreaking and extremely dispiriting.

The one common element in most of the stories I heard was that these men seemed incapable of avoiding their downfall, even when given opportunities. As I heard their tales, I couldn't help but feel that there appeared to be some way of avoiding this fate if they had only made a different choice at some point. It felt like an obvious choice, but for some reason, they were incapable of making that decision, inclined to go another direction, or simply unable to act due to a psychological block.

I remember that my opinion at the time, though I couldn't document it with any statistical support, was that some people, for reasons perhaps only a psychiatrist could determine, are just incapable of doing what is best for them both physically and emotionally. It was almost as if—perhaps because of sadness, hopelessness, or anger—self-destruction becomes a choice. The upside of this insight was a peculiar inspiration. I knew, based on my experience with these men, that I wanted to tell stories. Such as my limitations allowed me, I wanted to try to capture the human condition, as best I could, and that became my story.

This period became my most difficult. Though I didn't seem to share the addiction affinity with these lost men, I suffered from many of their maladies. I was somehow incapable of making the best choices, without the reasoning to support them.

I was losing hope for myself, feeling depressed to the point that I couldn't find motivation to live beyond the banal. I felt lost and pathless. To where, I didn't know, but just as I felt that summer in Georgia, I had to find a road leading somewhere different.

One night, I went to a jazz club in Georgetown to have drinks.

One of my friends, also a musician, mentioned how good the pianist was and that I should hear him.

I was impressed and went up to the stage to tell him so during a break.

He told me he didn't tour because he had a full-time job practicing psychiatry during the day and played at night to maintain his sanity. This interested me, and I asked if I could come for a therapy session. He gave me his card, and I called the next day.

We met in the late afternoon, when traffic was starting to clog the avenues out of the city. His office was in the lower floor of a brick Georgetown townhouse off M Street, most likely where he lived. It was cramped and dark, with posters of jazz greats on the walls. He asked me why I needed help, so I told him that I felt I had to change my life, or I feared for my emotional stability. I just kept spiraling in a free fall, and I had to find a way to stop it. Something must happen, but I really didn't know what or how to make it. Unlike my summer on the farm, I couldn't just get in a car and drive.

He asked me several questions about what I did with my time, my interests, and my family background, and I told him the truth as I saw it. He listened, made a few notes, asked about my history, and I answered while looking out the window. He paused and said it was very clear to him what my situation was.

I have a very distinct memory of staring at the metal garbage cans in the dank alleyway outside his window, thinking about how noisy the collection-day mornings must be, when he spoke up to tell me that it was very important that I listen carefully to what he was going to say next; he was going to tell me what I had to do.

I faced him, eager for a light on the path.

"You have a creative reservoir inside you, and you must draw from it." He was very serious. "If you don't, you are going to die. Prematurely by natural causes, or your own hand even sooner. Don't think about it. Just do it. Reach into yourself, or you will never find your way, and that will be fatal."

He shook my hand, accepted my check, and ushered me out with a serious, unfriendly goodbye. I didn't quite know what to make of him, much less his forecast. But I never forgot him, nor his insight.

CHAPTER 8
THE LIGHT ON THE PATH

I was assigned a limited amount of work each day at the clearinghouse, which I normally finished by lunch. I was required to stay until 5 p.m., though I had nothing to do, with no supervision. We were corporate employees under a government contract, so although salaried, we punched time cards each day and were required to arrive before 8 a.m. and leave after 5 p.m., entering and exiting through the back of the building to an employee parking lot. Executives parked in the front and were mostly invisible the entire day. No one knew when they arrived or left, and they pretty much worked behind closed doors, with little employee engagement.

This described my workday as well, though I did enjoy a discrete frolic with the executive director's secretary, but that was more about two bored people escaping an existentialist prison than anything else. The affair gave the two of us something to look forward to beyond the soul-crushing days of staring at lost, defeated faces among the beige industrial walls. Though we both knew the risk of being exposed, discovering inventive methods to disguise our trysts became a game worth playing.

The clearinghouse was run by the General Electric Co. An odd choice, one would assume, but I soon learned that when the US government cut NASA funding by two-thirds in 1973, NASA had existing contracts with companies like GE and was obligated to honor them. With no rockets being built, the feds needed to give scientists something to do to earn the obligated money, thus the decision to have weapons and space exploration companies run information clearinghouses on alcohol and drug abuse.

Because of this, all my bosses at the clearinghouse were aeronautical engineers, or engineers of some kind that had nothing to do with steam or pipe repairs, rendering my DA experience at the hospital useless. Most were trained to put rockets into space and were responsible for publishing materials designed to aid people suffering from alcoholism. Several of the executives had mobile airplanes or rockets hanging from their ceilings, and ironically, many kept bottles of booze in their offices.

This was a concern to several employees at the clearinghouse, many who happened to be AA members and didn't want to be anywhere near alcohol. But these engineers were clearly depressed and discouraged by the work they were doing, in a field they had absolutely no training or interest in, serving out GE's contract with NASA, hoping something would come along to give them the opportunity to do what they were driven to. Just like me.

One afternoon, a young man who looked much older than his years walked into my office. He was about my age, perhaps a little older, with long, scraggly hair, a pocked face, a tie-dyed shirt, and stained bell-bottom jeans. He had clearly not bathed in some time, with breath to match, and had a folksy, Tommy Lee Jones manner about him. His name was also Tommy, and, unwittingly, he was about to change my life.

Tommy explained that he was a part-time film student at American University and had secured a contract with an alcoholic treatment center in the Catskills to produce a short film to raise money to help fund the center. The center planned to focus on skid row in Manhattan and, with government assistance, bus their patients to the facility from the Manhattan Bowery Project. Tommy wanted to know more about the Bowery Project, and he had been told I was the man to see. Not just about the Project, but I had in my office the most extensive file on skid row anywhere in the nation, with a government database to access whatever else I needed.

After I told Tommy about the Project itself, we talked about his film. He explained that he was being paid very little by the center, was using the university's equipment to shoot 16 mm film, and planned to do everything himself, including camera, sound, and editing.

Having no experience with filmmaking, this intrigued me. I did have a lot of experience with tape recorders during my band days, so I offered to work sound for him.

Thankful for another body to help carry equipment, Tommy welcomed me, and we loaded up his borrowed vintage Chevy station wagon and drove (slowly and noisily) to the Catskills that following weekend.

When we arrived at the location, I felt like I was at home. As if discovering an instrument I inherently knew how to play, I gave Tommy ideas on where to set up, what kind of questions to ask, when to move the camera, and when he had what he needed. As any filmmaker will acknowledge, so much of the process is intuitive, and I clearly felt it. I had found what I wanted, and I wasn't about to waste any more time.

I helped Tommy with the Catskills film and another about psychic phenomena. I learned whatever technical details I could regarding camera, lighting, and editing. When I felt as though I'd learned enough, I quit my job at the clearinghouse. I'd found my career.

CHAPTER 9
POTOMAC VOICES

I discovered the newly formed Environmental Protection Agency was planning to make a thirty-minute film about the Potomac River to celebrate the nation's bicentennial on July 4, 1976. This was spring of 1975, and the agency wanted the film completed by early the following year.

A friend who worked in public relations for the Potomac River Basin Commission confided in me that the EPA wanted to focus on the history of the river, and he understood that the Agency planned to accept the lowest bid, an aberration from the standard government policy of choosing bids in the middle range.

I had no idea how much to bid, so I figured I would find a way to make the film as cheaply as possible and submit a ridiculously low number, figuring necessity would birth invention. I would just plug the holes as they appeared. If it didn't turn out as well as I hoped, I was certainly no worse off than before.

For content, I proposed a film not about the history of the Potomac but a contemporary portrait of the towns and communities along the river from the headwaters in West Virginia all the way to the mouth of the Chesapeake Bay.

I was a fan of Frederick Wiseman's documentaries. Devoid of

narration, his point of view was exposed subtly through the voices of the participants with no interviewer, no voiceover, and no subtitles to guide or inform the audience. Wiseman made feature-length documentaries that felt like stories, not just packaged information. They were also unpredictable, which, as any filmmaker will confirm, is any storyteller's primary goal.

My plan was to begin in October, when the leaves were turning, and shoot for one month. The crew and I would follow the Potomac from its origin, interviewing the residents of the towns and villages along the banks of the river from its headwaters to the Atlantic Ocean and let them talk about how the river has affected their lives and the lives of their ancestors. I would find interesting, unusual people who felt and sounded authentic and indigenous to the area, and I would call it *Potomac Voices*.

This is the concept I pitched to the EPA along with my proposal. After three months of classic bureaucratic stalling and red tape, they accepted my bid of $6,500 and gave me a deadline for delivery.

Even in 1975, this budget was easily $93,500 less than any close-to-successful film company would have bid, and I had no idea how, but I was determined to make it happen. I figured I had everything in the world to gain—and nothing to lose.

I started by interviewing every local filmmaker I could find in Washington, DC, picking brains one at a time. Filmmaking was such a specialized field in that era, with so few competing companies, that much of the film community was collegial and familial. I told them what I intended to do, and most were enthusiastically supportive and offered bountiful advice. Others were snarky and dismissive to the newbie amateur who was trying something impossible. I was surprised by the extreme generosity, as well as the petty competitiveness. I also had one other thing going for me. Pretty much every local filmmaker possessed a healthy ego and was anxious to impress upon me how much more knowledgeable each was than the others.

What I understood very clearly was that nearly all of them had found their niche, which was making sponsored films for either the US government, candidates for office, or an organization whose purpose was to somehow affect governmental policy.

No one was really that interested in creating fiction, and certainly not in making feature films in Hollywood, which, if things worked out like I planned, was exactly where I saw myself eventually. People in Washington were mostly dismissive of Hollywood, seeing it as superficial, flakey, and not to be taken seriously. Any concepts of feature films would be colloquial stories conceived to be shot in 16 mm with a local cast and crew, destined for a regional film festival (or New York, in a best-case scenario). When I asked about any Hollywood plans, local filmmakers derisively referred to LA, like many who have only lived it from a distance, as "la la land."

Happily, I found an exception. A local enthusiast who held a graduate film degree from NYU and had produced a feature-length black-and-white picture on a minuscule budget as his MFA dissertation. His name was Michael, and when I met him, he was recovering at home from knee surgery. While this had temporarily sidelined his film career, it didn't keep him from going to see classic films at the Kennedy Center virtually every night. He was a film buff who loved movies. When I pitched him to join my project, he jumped at the chance and pledged to teach me whatever he could.

I also found Chris, a camera assistant who was struggling to obtain his first director of photography credit. Chris had been stymied because no one making a sponsored film was willing to risk offering an assistant the job of DP. Then again, no one had a budget as low as mine.

I offered Chris the job in return for meals and the credit, and he accepted. He owned a van, which could ferry the crew to the locations, and he was willing to provide transportation for the price of gas, acting as our driver as well. I was upfront with Chris. I confessed I knew little about the technicalities and terms, but I promised one thing—that I knew what I wanted on film. It would be a powerful point since I would later learn that indecisive directors are the bane of film crews everywhere. Now I needed equipment and a crew.

Having learned from Tommy's experience, I approached the American University Film Department and met with the head, whose name was Glenn. He had never been approached with an unusual proposal like mine. Our conversation went something like this, with Glenn starting.

"So you are making a sponsored film about the Potomac River for the bicentennial?"

"I am, and it will be unlike any film the US government has made before. There will be no narrator, and the only talking heads will be people who live and work on the river. The audience will experience their lives firsthand."

"That sounds interesting. Different."

"Different from anything you've seen before . . . in a government film, that is."

"And you want to use our equipment?"

"In exchange for that, I will teach your students how to shoot a film firsthand."

"Wait, you want my students to go on the shoot?"

"As my crew. They will learn the process hands-on. We will camp along the Potomac for a month!"

"Wow. Have you done this before?"

"No, sir."

"What is your experience?"

"Well, most recently, it's been exclusively with Tommy."

He brightened at this. "Oh, really? That's interesting."

I didn't think it was that interesting, but what I didn't know at the time was that he thought I was referring to the Ken Russell film of the Who rock opera *TOMMY*. I only learned this later from the students. I don't think anyone ever corrected his misunderstanding, but I was sure curious as to what he thought my job was on that film.

Satisfied, he shook my hand and smiled. "Okay. Let me know what you need and when."

I now had a DP, editor, equipment, and crew. We were ready to begin production—and I had yet to spend a cent of my tiny budget.

I convened the crew the last week of September to sketch out my plan. Our October would begin in the high Appalachians in the Potomac's headwaters. We would wind our way among the coal mines and paper mills and drive through horse country in Maryland and Virginia, stopping in DC to film the sights on the river. Our last leg would be traveling on the Chesapeake in oyster boats with the watermen, past Smith Island, Delmarva Peninsula, and the Eastern Shore, ending south of the Chesapeake Bay Bridge, where the estuary empties into the Atlantic Ocean.

I also explained that living conditions would be lean—camping, cheap motels, and sleeping in the van when nothing else was available.

We set out for the Appalachians, unsure of what we would find but anxious to capture it. I was the sole producer. Two members of the crew helped me make phone calls for shooting arrangements, but those efforts were fitful. Basically, we just drove until we found something that looked good to film, whether it was a coal mine, paper mill, trailer, raft, boat, riverside hut, ghost town, or water so polluted by acid runoff from the mines that no organism could live in it.

I would ask Chris to stop; then I would hop out and talk to whoever would agree to an interview. We'd unload the gear and shoot that person on the spot. The reaction was mixed: some subjects were wary, some downright hostile, some coldly friendly, some curious. What they shared was confusion as to why we were there in the first place. Cameras were rare in these mountains. *National Geographic* had sent a photographer a year earlier to capture the disappearing culture of the Upper Potomac, but that was the extent of it.

We found dying towns and actual ghost towns. We saw shuttered mines and paper mills and those on the brink of closing. We found a river that had become too polluted by these mines and mills for boaters or fishermen to use. There were no children and few men and women of childbearing age. They had all gone to seek a better life.

What was left were broken-down grandparents and the downtrodden former workers of the now defunct mines and close-to-dead paper mills and logging camps. They told their stories and showed us their homes, vacant docks, and porches. It was a landscape littered with old cars and a handful of decrepit restaurants serving ham and eggs to people with little hope.

One good example of a cold interview took place at a neglected mobile home situated off the banks of the river not far from an abandoned mine. I knocked, and an older man's gravelly voice barked through the closed door. "What do you want?"

When I explained that I wanted to talk about the Potomac, he barked again, "What the hell you want to talk about the damn river for, and who wants to know anyway?"

I told him why I was there, and he opened the door. He was an older, unshaven man in faded plaids, jeans, and a trucker's cap. He scrutinized me and shook his head. "Whatta *you* wanna know about it?"

"Well, sir. I'd just like to hear how the river has changed since you first moved here."

"Moved here! Hell, I didn't move here."

"Well, since you can remember."

"I've always been here. Can't say that for these others."

"Well, can you tell me how the river has changed?"

"Of course, it's changed. Damn Army Corps of Engineers. It's what they do!"

"What exactly did they do, and why?"

"Pork barrel. That's what and why. All I'm gonna say."

"What?"

"Pork barrel." He closed the door.

Not all interviews went like that, but until we reached cleaner water, more than a few did. I never discovered what he was referring to, but for a government sponsored film, it would certainly be irrelevant.

October in the Appalachians. Under a bright sun, autumn leaves painted a stunning palette of red and yellow, but the lively colors cloaked a dying community. A hundred years ago, tens of thousands of young workers had flocked to this region to work the mines and factories. Now no one knew what was next for this part of the world.

This all changed when we descended into the Eastern Seaboard. The river, now fed by fresh streams, regained its health. The farms were productive and the inhabitants optimistic. The fishermen along the banks were cheerful and welcoming.

This made for a nice lead-in to Washington, where we were pleased to sleep in our own beds and enjoy the comfort of a boat to ferry the crew and equipment, shooting the monuments from the river. After the claustrophobic, dreary slog through Appalachia, this was a welcome change for all of us.

Below the city, the river opened in every respect. We traveled aboard the oyster boats, which, in the lower part of the Potomac and across the Chesapeake, were only allowed to harvest oysters with "tongs" to preserve the beds.

These "tongers" would operate a ten- to twenty-five-foot-long device, like two extended garden rakes, cut from hardwood and joined at the center to convert into what looked like a giant pair of scissors except with conjoining metal teeth at the bottom. Holding the tongs over the stern, the watermen would lower the closed rakes to the oyster bed, vigorously opening and closing the scissors back and forth to collect the mollusks in the teeth. Then, they would haul them up hand over hand, like descending a rope while pulling deadweight.

These were among the strongest people I had ever seen. The power in their shoulders necessary to lower the tongs that distance, open and close the heavy devices multiple times to dig deep in the bed, then haul up a load of oysters against the force of a strong current, was extraordinary.

I was a young man, but when I tried to copy their process, I found it painfully difficult to extend my arms away from the boat, scissor the tongs back and forth hard enough to collect a load from the bed, then lift the tongs up and out of the water and swing the load to the culling board in the center of the boat. I was beat after a single try, but these men repeated the process possibly a hundred times a day. And this was a family affair, where waiting wives and children would hand scrape the teeth of the tongs to pry off the clinging mollusks and sort them into tanks.

But the tongers were cheerful and friendly. Many had heavy mid-Atlantic Chesapeake accents, which is a vernacular both unique to that area and unmistakable. They loved to laugh and sing and always had a bottle of Tabasco within reach. Over the course of the day, we snacked on freshly shucked raw oysters straight out of the water. I had never tried them before and became hooked; they were one of the most singularly satisfying delicacies I had ever tasted.

It was a grueling month, with long days of driving and shooting followed by uncomfortable nights with bad food and fitful sleep, but when the month ended, everyone agreed the experience had been unique, rich, and a fond memory. Well, almost everyone. One or two crew members, young men close to my age, were understandably embittered by the fact that I was a complete novice posing as an instructor. And two of them didn't stick it out for the entire month.

But most of them completely bought into my charade and were rooting for my success. It was a learning process for all of us, and young as we all were, it was tiring but unforgettable. We each offered the skills we carried; we worked well and hard; we were young, flexible, and keen for the adventure we found.

When the shooting was finished, I rented an editing room in the basement of a high-rise apartment building in Rosslyn, VA. The room belonged to a man named Bob Velasco, who owned a company that licensed stock music and sound effects. It was a one-stop shop for me.

Michael came in and taught me the basics of editing: how to use a Steenbeck editing machine, mark the work print and splice it, and overlap sound—everything I would need to know except the craft—and he taught me a lot about that as well.

Like Frederick Wiseman, I had intended to use no music in the film, but I found that the Chesapeake section had so much life that I wanted something joyful to accompany it. I was a fan of Keith Jarrett's solo improvised albums, but when I listened to his composed record, *Belonging*, with Jan Garbarek, Palle Daniellson, and Jon Christenson, I heard music that I felt fit perfectly into the segment.

One thing I could not afford with my limited budget was a composer, or music licensing, so I decided to use the same approach that had worked for me in securing a crew to find the right score. Keith Jarrett's publisher was Cavelight Music, with an address in New Jersey. Through 411 information, which hasn't existed now in decades, I was able to secure a phone number.

When I called, a woman answered with a solitary "Hello."

Surprised, I began the pitch I'd prepared for a music company executive. "Hello, I'd like to speak with someone about obtaining music rights for a film."

"Is it Keith Jarrett music?"

"Yes, it is. How did you guess?"

"This is his house. I'm his wife."

So, I discarded the prepared pitch. She put Keith on the phone, and I told him all about the film, how I had put it together, my complete lack of experience, and the minuscule budget. He listened carefully, laughing at the amusing hardships I described while shooting the film. I told him what a fan I was of his work, and I originally had no plans to put music in the film. When I heard sections from *Belonging*, however, I knew how these pieces would fit perfectly with the Chesapeake section. Would he consider letting me use them for free since I had no budget for music and there would be no price of admission for anyone seeing it?

Keith asked if he could see the film, which was a hurdle I had to think about, so I told him I would try to arrange something and call him back.

In 1976, the only way someone could watch a film that wasn't broadcast on television or projected in a theater was in a private screening room, and the only people I could think of with access to those were film distributors. I looked up the American distributors of small art house films in New York and found fledgling New Line Cinema. This was before the company was producing films, and they had yet to score big in distribution. At the time, they were handling mostly small foreign films for art house release.

I contacted Stanley Dudelson, New Line's distribution head at the time, and asked if he would screen a film of mine for Keith Jarrett if he came into the city from New Jersey.

Dudelson was skeptical at first but intrigued by the way I presented the film, as perhaps a bit more *avant garde* than it was, and he agreed to screen the synchronized work print with a special projector. I didn't mention the EPA to him, or that I didn't own the film, but he didn't ask, so, in truth, I never lied.

I took the work print and dialogue tracks to New York, where Dudelson screened it for Keith on a synchronized projector in New Line's tiny Midtown screening room. Keith liked what he saw, and over post-screening coffee, he gave me his blessing to use whatever music I chose. He wrote a release on a restaurant napkin and signed it. A memento I wish I had kept.

I brought the elements and the napkin back to Washington, completed the film, and submitted it, where the reception was as good as I could have reasonably hoped.

The film was shown at National Park facilities along the Potomac, including the Harpers Ferry National Historic Park, for ten years, and I used it to audition for a job as a resident director at a local film company. I started my own company a year later.

CHAPTER 10
TRICKS WIN FIGHTS

While my company was producing sponsored political films, I was able to fund my own feature-length documentary, which taught me the rigors of putting together a feature-length project.

Tricks Win Fights is the story of a year-long relationship between a twenty-nine-year-old African American heavyweight boxer and his manager and trainer, a married White couple who took him on as a reclamation project after ten years of alcoholic inactivity. The three had a strong and loving bond and barely a dollar between them, yet whatever one had, they all had.

Matt Robinson won the Golden Gloves of America amateur tournament when he was eighteen and never lost a fight his first year after turning pro. He became a promising young heavyweight in the mid-Atlantic region.

As his success grew, Matt started drinking heavily, which progressively became so bad that he was forced to quit the ring. He remained an alcoholic for nearly ten years, losing everything he had, including his apartment and car. Matt, who lived with relatives until they couldn't support him any longer, finally accepted that he had hit bottom. He was heading toward suicide either by will or neglect and had to turn his life around while he was still young enough to enjoy one. He decided he would stop drinking, get back in shape, and resume his fighting career at age thirty.

This was when Matt walked into a storefront gym in New Carrolton, a Maryland suburb south of Baltimore. The business was owned by Rocky and Pat Coleman, new residents of the area, who had recently opened and were looking for clients to train.

When Matt and I met, he had lost most of his teeth, making him difficult to understand when he spoke. He was also overweight from what had clearly been a diet of fast food and alcohol. He was sober and trying to maintain a healthy diet, but drinking and his lack of conditioning had clearly caused his body to falter, and Rocky was helping him build it back and turn him into a successful fighter. As Matt's manager and trainer, Pat and Rocky were planning to share the benefits.

Rocky, in his early fifties, had been a small-time thug and street hustler in New York City. His proud claim to fame was emceeing the Christmas show at Sing Sing prison for five years straight. Less than a week after he was paroled, Rocky met Pat in a Bronx dental office, where she was working as a receptionist.

After getting his tooth pulled, Rocky stopped by the reception desk and tried to convince Pat to walk off the job, promising her the world if she would get up and leave with him. They had first met when he arrived with his infected tooth, but for Rocky, it was love at first sight, and he was a man with big plans.

Pat, fifteen years his junior, was flattered and intrigued by Rocky's brash approach, but she was reluctant to quit her job. However, when the dentist came out to reception and tried to throw Rocky out of his office, Rocky floored him with a right cross.

Pat was charmed. As she recalled the courtship in her heavy Bronx accent, "Nobody nevah done knocked nobody out ovah me befoah. Nevah!"

They got in Rocky's car and drove until they ran out of money and gas, which was about 200 miles, stopping in Baltimore. Rocky had learned how to plaster in Sing Sing, so he used his skills to start a mobile business, got Pat licensed as the first female professional boxing manager, rented a suburban storefront, and put in some mirrors and bags, then began his quest to, as Rocky liked to put it, "crash out."

Rocky was a colorful, loquacious, energetic hustler who claimed he could talk his way into anything, and if that didn't work, he had other methods. He wasn't tall, but he was solid, tough, and threatening to anyone who disrespected him.

His motto was "tricks win fights," which meant exactly that in his world. Like Pat, Rocky also spoke with a heavy Bronx accent, hard on the consonants, rarely ending a word with a soft letter (always youse rather than you, doze over those). He wore a white jockey T-shirt, often a tank top, tan trousers, sneakers, and a golf cap every day. I never saw him without a white gym towel hanging around his neck, including at his home.

Rocky's goal was to "crash out," which became his motto when cheering on Matt during a training session. "Come on, Matt. Lessee watcha got. Gib'm dat kidney shot we been workin' on. Datzit. Datzit. Gonna crash out, Mattie. Crash out!"

Since he worked most mornings as a plasterer, Rocky's arms, shirt, hat, and often hair, face, and glasses would normally carry some residue of dried gypsum by the time he showed at the gym. The clothes were freshly clean each morning, but the glasses and hair kept collecting bits and specks of white, which became one of Rocky's endearing fashion statements.

When he was sober, which was normally during daylight hours, Rocky was welcoming and friendly. He often bragged about their two small children, Rocco and Roxanne. "Dat Rocco's gunna make some kinda money. Kid ain't even in foist grade annie awreddy knows how to fight!" This would be a typical Rocky pronouncement. Preschool tough kid makes a dad proud.

Rocky's wife, Pat, a thin, laconic platinum blond, wore bright, color-coordinated outfits with what were then known as white go-go boots and an angled knit cap to match. She was always heavily made-up, with deep red lipstick and enough pancake to mask facial scars. She sported a bent nose to match Rocky's that we assumed was the result of their drinking. Everyone knew that the drinking began when the crew left early. You could feel the barometric pressure dropping when Rocky was drunk—and no one wanted to be around.

I came to know of Rocky, Pat, and Matt through my photographer friend Michael, who happened to see them training Matt through the window of the storefront gym and was captured by the colorful scene. He went inside, took photos, showed them to me, and I knew there was a story waiting to be told.

When I met the trio in person, I was convinced. Michael and I filmed the three through eight months of training in the gym. We'd follow them to local restaurants and on Matt's training runs around Haines Point in Southeast Washington every morning at 7 a.m. It was quite the scene: Matt, trying to keep up with Rocky, and Pat, who would drive alongside in their red Cadillac convertible, blasting Fats Domino's classic "I'm Gonna be a Wheel Someday." It was a natural soundtrack.

Occasionally, they would be joined by Sugar Ray Leonard, at the time an up-and-coming DC welterweight who had just turned professional and would drop by the gym to work out. Ray was friendly, as were most all boxers I met through Matt. It seemed the fighters got their aggressions out in the ring and stayed casual outside of it.

When time for the big fight arrived, we all traveled to Newark, NJ, and checked into the Lincoln Motel off Interstate 95. There, we prepared for the event, which would take place at the local Newark arena, a reputed mob-owned venue designed for boxing, Roller Derby, and pro wrestling. Matt's share of the purse was $200 for the fight, win or lose—a reasonable sum for an unknown.

But Rocky was determined to spend less than half of the purse on the trip. He was careful to monitor what Matt ate for dinner, delivering it personally and making sure Matt stayed in his room the hours before the fight. Female companionship was available for rent right outside the motel, but Rocky was a strict trainer. He would yell through Matt's door, in earshot of everyone staying on the floor, "Matt! No pussy before a fight. Y'got me? Pussy and fightin' don't mix! Eat your steak!"

Rocky would leave his door open until fight time so he could hear if Matt left his room or someone wanted to enter.

The fight was a good one and ended in a draw. Matt fought well against a tough opponent, and the three celebrated in the dressing room. After Matt, Rocky, and Pat left to return to the hotel, the skeleton film crew and I began packing up—when we were surprised by a determined knock on the dressing room door.

Chris, the DP who shot *Potomac Voices*, opened the door to reveal two surly characters who looked like generically cast thugs on a daytime soap. They told Chris they wanted to see "the boss" of the crew, and when asked why, they explained that nobody had asked for permission to film the fight, and the owner of the arena wanted to "make arrangements."

Hearing this from the back of the dressing room, I asked for some time to unload the cameras and can the film. The men at the door agreed, but they requested I bring the film with me when I joined them.

While the visitors waited outside the door, I asked Chris to put all exposed film into a changing bag and, just as soon as I joined the goons in the hall, pack it surreptitiously into a duffel and lock it in the van parked on the street, where I would meet him when (if) I returned. I figured if things didn't go well, at least the footage would be secure.

While the arena guys waited outside, I taped several unexposed film cans, marking them as exposed, and labeled them as to which rounds of the fight were inside each can. Raw film stock was expensive, but certainly not as expensive as what these guys could threaten.

I put all the cans into a carrying bag, walked out of the dressing room, and accompanied my escorts to an office that, if it were created by a production designer, would have been quickly rejected as too obvious a choice for a wise-guy clubhouse. Before we entered, my companions checked the bag, and, once satisfied the contents were the film of the fight, led me inside.

It was a darkly lit office, filled with loosely sorted boxing and celebrity magazines strewn about clumsily carved tables and chairs, multiple oversized ashtrays perched on metal stands, enclosed by painted cinder block walls covered with garish event posters, and carnival-quality art pieces. The man in charge sat behind a peeling varnished wooden desk in the shadow of a spot lamp, posing like Edward G. Robinson while my two escorts stood behind me blocking the exit.

I sat in a chair across from Mr. Robinson, the taped and labeled cans of unexposed film in the carrying bag at my feet.

Edward wanted to know who I was, who was paying for the movie, and who would be paying him 50 percent of the budget, which he considered a fair percentage. Plus, of course, 50 percent of all profits. If I wanted to take the film with me, I had to sign over his share. No negotiating.

I initially tried telling him the truth, that I was paying for the film myself, there was no budget and no money and no signs in the arena about cameras, and no one had said anything about filming not being allowed.

His expression never changed with this explanation. He said he knew movies were expensive to produce and made a lot of money, and I'm the guy sitting in front of him, so I'm the guy he's getting the money from. If I had none with me, I had to sign over his share.

I told Edward that I was just the director, not the ultimate boss, and would have to consult with any distributors and financiers if the film were to be shown theatrically. I had no money, they would be the ones paying him, and I would have to get back to him about his offer.

As I anticipated, he told me if I wanted to leave, the bag stayed with him until he had his signed agreement from whomever would be responsible for 50 percent of the income.

So, it did.

I don't know what became of him, my carrying bag, or its contents.

I cut *Tricks* between shooting my sponsored films, so it took nearly a year for me to finish. I was proud of the completed film, seeing that the story worked as an introduction to the three and their unique relationship. It showed all the hard work preparing for Matt's comeback and the tension leading up to the fight, culminating in the fight itself and Matt's deserved sense of accomplishment. After ten years of incapacitating alcoholism and near homelessness, he had a boxing career once more—and a renewed life.

I was excited to show the film to Rocky, Pat, and Matt, so I set out to contact them and set up a meeting. I discovered Rocky's number had changed, but I found him in another Maryland suburb closer to Washington.

Over the phone, Rocky told me they no longer had the gym but were training out of a newly rented home in this suburb. I excitedly told him the film was complete, and I wanted them all to see it. I rented a projector and planned a screening party at their home.

Finding an address was far more difficult in 1978 than it is today, for all you had was a folding map without house numbers. I drove around the suburban neighborhood, looking for the address Rocky had given me, but none of the numbers were easily visible in an area filled with nearly identical 1940's-era red brick ramblers.

Turning a corner, I noticed a van with a ladder attached to the top and a crude logo on the side advertising a plastering company. I laughed when I saw it was parked in front of an aging brick rambler with a chain-link fence surrounding the backyard, boxing bags and mirrors hanging from the trees behind it.

When I went around back, I found Rocky, Pat, and Matt training a fighter in front of the mirrors. Matt was in street clothes, wearing an eye patch, supervising a young man in a tank top punching a heavy bag hanging from a limb, in front of a mirror propped against a tree. When I approached them, they enthusiastically welcomed me as an old friend, and I asked Matt about his eye patch. Without breaking the celebratory mood, the three told me the story of the past year since the fight.

Matt had successfully reestablished his career. He turned pro once more and was moving up in the rankings, with a respectable won-lost record since returning to the ring. His purse had built to a minimum of $500 per fight, which was, at the time, very respectable. He had moved into his own one-bedroom apartment, sparsely furnished, sleeping on a box spring and mattress on the bedroom floor.

Matt kept a television on the floor by his bed, which he would watch before falling asleep every night. One morning, Matt woke up and leaned over the side of the bed to put on his shoes. In doing so, he bowed directly into the television rabbit ears, where one of the antennae poked into his right eye, puncturing the cornea and permanently blinding it.

Matt could no longer fight, so Rocky and Pat decided to accept him as a partner in training young fighters. They had helped cover the medical bills for Matt's eye and paid to have his lost teeth replaced, perhaps with plastering money and whatever they had earned from Matt's fights. Matt was now easily understandable for the first time.

Matt helped Rocky with his plastering when he could, or if they had a new fighter, he would come over to the house and train him while Rocky worked a plastering job. Rocky, Pat, and Matt would have strategy sessions at the end of the day, for they were now equal partners in a new boxing management venture.

I quickly decided that I had to shoot an epilogue, which I did, in their backyard, with the management trio and their new fighter, and sure enough, Rocky chose his own ending by again reiterating how they were going to "crash out" with this new plan and what became Rocky's signature line: "Tricks. Datz whutitakes. Tricks win fights!"

The finished film received notable acclaim at the Telluride and

Venice Film Festivals, with legendary Serb director Aleksandar Petrovic personally writing me to say he considered the film to be "the most accurately profound and critical examination of American society that I have seen in a documentary film, capturing both the American dream and the American myth."

Praise I took to heart, because that was precisely how the film was conceived, as an insight into both. In 1979, documentaries were rarely seen, receiving very little fanfare at festivals. Any notice was considerable. But I felt like the film had accomplished what I hoped it would. Petrovic's analysis went right to the heart of the spirit and milieu I was after. I'd found a receptive audience, no matter how limited, and for the first time, I began to feel realized.

CHAPTER 11
THE INTRODUCTION

Building on the positive reception to *TRICKS*, I expanded my film company, purchased cameras and editing equipment, and started to work consistently all over the United States and beyond, traveling to every continental state, Mexico, and the West Indies, producing sponsored political and issue-oriented films for lobbying purposes.

During this time, I wrote the treatment about the couple colliding with an unmovable force, that being the whale, and was discouraged enough by my client Jay to put it aside. A lesson I didn't forget.

In making my documentaries, I often hired a cinematographer named David who lived and worked primarily out of New York. David called one evening and recommended I come meet a German director who was looking for an editor to work on a low-budget horror film to be shot on the Eastern Shore of Maryland.

I had no experience as a feature editor, but I had saved enough to cover my mortgage for an extended time, and I had also learned that in filmmaking, a few natural skills combined with a willingness to work for nothing was far more valuable to potential employers than experience.

I met Max, the director, at his loft in Soho. I say his loft, but it obviously belonged to his new wife Sylvie, a strikingly attractive and talented young actress who seemed somewhat connected in New York art circles.

The year was 1979, and punk rock was finding its way into American culture. In line with this, Max dressed in black leather boots, pants, a jacket, and a motorcycle hat. The costume was a strange hybrid of SS officer, Hells Angel, and Village Person.

As an actor, Max had enjoyed considerable success as a teen heartthrob in his native Germany, supported by garish images of his younger, pouting face on the cover of German fan magazines placed about the loft. At the time, European cinema, particularly German, was in fashion in New York, and Max found it easy to promote himself with the right phone calls to arts and culture publications in Manhattan. He had starred in several of the "German new-wave" films, now known as New German Cinema, which, incomprehensible as many were, had become fashionable in New York's art scene. He carried just enough cachet to gain entry to Andy Warhol's Factory and convince Warhol to get involved in two of his films. Warhol figured these films would not enhance either his career or his reputation, so he soon dropped out.

Max had mischievous, almost menacing eyes, thin lips, and an extremely slight, almost hairless body. He barely weighed more than his wife, but he carried himself with an officious air of self-importance, using his acting skills to impress upon his audience (meaning anyone in hearing distance) that he was focused only on the subject at hand. Any interruption of the profound flow from Max's musings would draw a sardonic rebuke, Max noting that any "genuine artist" would react this way.

"Ach" preceded most of Max's negative opinions, and a giggle for most positive ones, and there was little room in between. Max had just recently moved to the US, and though he had learned excellent English in Germany, he added certain American words or phrases to exclamations because he thought he was using the appropriate phrase, even if it didn't make sense. He was most fond of the words "so great," "the greatest," and "the worst," and he concluded his descriptions, and most sentences, with "here." Anything unpleasant was described as "depressing."

"Ha, this is the greatest sausage here," or "Ach, this is the worst food here. It is so depressing."

Max saw himself as an anarchist, whose black leather outfits represented an antithesis to what he described as "the bourgeois mediocre," which he pronounced "mediocker." Ultimately, though, Max lived a completely comfortable, bourgeois life in an expensive house, driving a Cadillac and eating at nice restaurants.

Journalists, however, could be reluctant to call out artists for political hypocrisy for two reasons: an interviewer did not want to alienate other potential interviewees, much less the current one, and in the social and political climate of the time, considering the fresh interest in German cinema, the audience was looking for someone to believe in, not judge.

After our meeting in Soho, Max invited me to dinner to discuss his project, where we had a lengthy talk about movies past and present. Reflecting on that night, I recall how much fun it was to talk about films when I had so much to learn. All I knew was how much I loved them, and I could find a kernel of joy in most any movie. (Unfortunately, there seems to be an inverse "fun" factor in discussing films, related to one's experience in filmmaking. Perhaps unsurprisingly, the more seasoned one becomes, the more tiresome the subject.) But in New York in 1979, I was fresh and eager, so I couldn't get enough. Whatever Max could tell me about German cinema, the New York art scene, or low-budget filmmaking in general, I was anxious to hear.

After dinner, we made plans to meet three days later to look over locations on the Maryland Eastern Shore. In the meantime, Max would watch *TRICKS*, and they would overnight a script for me to read.

It never arrived, which would not be surprising to any experienced film worker since promised deadlines and deliveries are often unmet. But for me, at the time, it became the first of many lessons learned in the feature-film business, and perhaps a lesson as valuable to a novice as William Goldman's wisdom in *Adventures in the Screen Trade*, when he referred to his most important maxim: "In the film business, nobody knows anything."

I would add the suggestion that in the film business, it is wise to take absolutely nothing at face value—be it the promise of a script to be delivered overnight, a job, a gift, or a favor or request for such, admiration, defamation, praise, disrespect, success, failure, love, hate, or unconditional, uninhibited sex. My incognizant introduction into how the film business really works is that it doesn't really, but it sustains itself through the powers of love, ego, and greed.

If the job to edit the movie was offered to me, I was prepared to work for nothing just to learn how feature films were made. I had earned enough through my company to manage at least a year without income, if necessary. I knew the first skill any aspiring filmmaker should learn is editing, and this was the perfect opportunity. I had embarked on a career as a documentary filmmaker and had quickly become successful enough to earn a more-than-sufficient income. But that wasn't my goal, ever. I wanted to make feature films, and I saw this as a golden opportunity to learn how to do it without going blindly all-in like I did with *Potomac Voices*. The investment would be far greater for everyone, including me, in the world of feature filmmaking, and with this opportunity, I would be going to school tuition-free, gaining hands-on experience in the process. If it didn't work out, I could always go back to the documentaries, but if it did, my life had changed. I talked it over with my partner, Pam, who I shared a house with, and she was fully supportive. She knew what I wanted to do, and she believed I should be doing it.

Just from my experience with docs, I knew that a firm belief in yourself is more than half the battle, and there are no regrets for effort, only the lack of it. Regardless of how good or bad the film turned out to be, and even if it ended up costing me money, it would be a life-changing experience, and I would come out ahead. I would never forget the torpid emptiness and despair that overwhelmed me when I was eighteen, sitting on the porch at the farm in Georgia, listening to the crickets in the fields and trucks on the highway. Just looking for a path, any path that felt right. I would also never forget the afternoon in the jazz-playing psychiatrist's office and what he told me I needed to do, though, at the time, I didn't know where or how. I was lucky enough to have found the path and felt destined to follow it, no matter what the result.

Max called the next day, and if I was willing to work for expenses and a small profit participation, I had the job. I accepted, ready to move on.

CHAPTER 12
PIGLETS, POLICY, AND A KARO-SOAKED WIFEBEATER

Following numerous funding delays, seemingly synonymous with low-budget filmmaking, I met Max three weeks later at a Maryland farm owned by Sylvie's aunt and uncle, located two hours from Washington on the Eastern Shore of the Chesapeake Bay.

Sylvie's uncle was a major policy advisor under several US presidents, from Truman to Carter, and an active figure in Washington intelligence think tanks. He and his wife had agreed to let Max and Sylvie film on the farm, clearly without having read the script, believing they were lending a location to an art film.

While we were there to look over locations, a town car would arrive each morning, dispatched from Washington, to pick up Sylvie's uncle and take him to Washington. In another month, the car would be passing equipment trucks descending upon this genteel property to shoot a $300,000 horror film about the ghost of a murdered psychopath seeking bloody revenge. Sylvie's uncle would soon be advising negotiations on a nuclear treaty on Friday, posing as an extra in a slasher pic over the weekend, and returning to world disarmament on Monday.

Max, Sylvie, David (the director of photography), and I toured the farm for several days. It was an idyllic location, over a mile of waterfront property with acres of corn, tobacco, and green pastures reminiscent of the Southern landscapes of my youth. After deciding upon the locations, we adjourned home to wait for the crew.

When the crew arrived, we all returned to the farm, bunking in cabins built decades earlier to accommodate farmworkers. It soon became apparent that a feature-film shoot is much like summer camp, where lives are suspended, libidos blossom, and everyone adopts an interim personality (much like working on a cruise ship, but with sixteen-hour days).

Married people have affairs, the serious become frivolous, and those who generally tire at dusk will close out the local bar. The attachments become firm and passions overwhelming, whether love or hate. Actors, in particular, will take advantage of this fantasy world, partly because for a few weeks or possibly months, they will be living another person's life on screen. So, a committed actor will sometimes live the character's life off camera as well.

This can lead to the intense blooming of a relationship or painfully exposed and embarrassing behavior. Hollywood is full of stories about uncontrolled choices of actors on sets, particularly stars who are allowed to have a far greater margin for shame than lesser-known actors. The major difference between an actor and a star, aside from salary, is leverage.

The director, assistant directors (ADs), and production assistants (PAs) are normally far too occupied with job requirements to participate. But actors and crew spend so much time with one another while waiting for the next shot, and there is so much creative energy being expended on the set; physical chemistries seem to naturally detonate. It is hard to make a marriage last in Hollywood, and most that do last manage because both partners understand the threat and find a way to either avoid it, placate it, or accept the danger. Marriage in Hollywood is often a business merger, particularly among the most successful.

A sad story about shameful behavior played for leverage was

relayed to me years later by John Huston. The story was about Marilyn Monroe and Arthur Miller on the set of *The Misfits*, which Huston directed. Their marriage was dissolving, and Miller was infatuated with a photo archivist, whom he had met on set and would soon marry after his divorce from Marilyn. Marilyn had developed a barbiturate and alcohol dependency, which shredded her emotional filters, and she was hurt, angry, and unhinged.

Whenever the opportunity arose, Monroe would humiliate Miller in the company of the crew or cast. One night after the set wrapped, she drove off, leaving him abandoned in the desert to find his way home. She didn't want her husband to accept this behavior, which was so extreme that it became embarrassing to everyone in sight. But somewhere in their labyrinthine chemistry at the time, abuse was Marilyn's only form of communication with her husband, and he chose not to reciprocate. So, she punished him, beating him emotionally until he finally left and returned to New York.

The shoot closed down while Marilyn went to a hospital to recover. Huston told me that a lot of people misbehaved on that set, including himself. Part of it was because he and the producers seemed to know that the Miller/Monroe marriage was in trouble before they began. Marilyn had confessed to Huston that she had read Miller's diary, and it revealed his feelings of disappointment in her that struck Marilyn's most vulnerable nerve. She would never measure up to what he thought she was, and that would kill her. So, she did the only thing she could to seek power against that which rendered her powerless. She sought whatever leverage she could find, even her own vulnerability, and used it the best way she knew how.

Nothing so dramatic happened on the set of our film. Actors and crew members dallied with one another, and the group in general treated the property and its inhabitants without proper respect, but to many on the crew, it was an opportunity to live on a farm for the very first time, see piglets being born and cattle being fed and milked, and walk to the water's edge, cast out a line, sit in the grass, and absorb the transcendence of watching water move while waiting on a fish. In a time before cell phones, lives were pleasantly suspended in the country.

As for the crew and actors, it was a diverse collection of New York stereotypes of the 1970s, and considering it was work, we had fun. There was an anarchic atmosphere around the film, and not much went according to plan, which only made it more memorable.

The actors were assembled from several ensembles with varying levels of talent and temperament, as well as actor/investors who were seeking exposure on screen. The crew was composed of mostly young assistants or struggling filmmakers looking for an experience that could lead to an upgrade on the next job, or, like me, figuring it wouldn't take long to put it all together and make something happen. For a few of us, it didn't. Others weren't as fortunate.

Dinners were prepared and served in the main guesthouse, with various actors and crew taking turns preparing. There was help in the kitchen and in housekeeping, but it never seemed professional. We ate meals together, and that is how most of us got to know one another. The farm became a party site where one would never know what to expect driving from one house to another.

We would spend hours working on a take where an actress would scream and cower while holding barber scissors to her own throat, pretending she had no control over this harmless-looking tool. Or perhaps shooting close-ups of a knife thrusting into what is supposed to be the back of a man wearing a white cotton tank top—a "wifebeater." It is actually the same white tank top the actor wears, pulled over a Styrofoam-packed box filled with Karo syrup blended with red food coloring. The syrup would bubble out each time the knife plunged in.

Between takes, we could wander outside and play with calves, watch the piglets, or gaze at the field hands working the October harvest. When the next setup was ready, we would return to the simulated killing. Being so close to the simplest reality while creating such a dark and disturbing fantasy was so surreal that it became haunting.

CHAPTER 13
A MIROAR BREEZES

Our film in Maryland became amusing for how bad parts of it were. In my opinion, notoriously so. Most of the actors had never been in a film before, and they didn't quite grasp the not-so-subtle difference between film and stage acting, where performers are projecting to an audience, not blown up onto a seventy-foot screen. The director's job is to recognize when subtleties are at their most potent on-screen, and this can be a grueling but extremely important distinction in maintaining a character's credibility with the audience.

Making a good movie is extremely difficult, even for experienced filmmakers, and our film clearly showed we were not that. The characters rarely moved in frame, and their dialogue of "country" niceties became a parody of itself. The violence in the film, which was to be its selling point, was often comical both in conception and execution, but in the end, these factors worked in its favor.

The plot of the film is that an abused brother and sister murder their tormentor, their mother's lover, in front of a mirror, which captures the image of the dying man. Twenty years later, the mirror is shattered, and the victim is freed to seek revenge against—everyone. When the spirit leaves the mirror, the shattered pieces glow with a pulsing red light, and whenever the action is presented from the killer's point of view, we hear the sound of breathing through a stocking mask, which the man was wearing when he was killed.

Once freed from the glass, the invisible spirit controls objects and people's movements to the point where they appear to murder themselves and those around them in inventive, cringe-worthy fashion—with knives, scissors, ice picks, pitchforks, corkscrews, and assorted household items and farm implements.

The finished product actually received a few glowing reviews from critics who loved the fact that a German "art house" director was making an American horror film. Some found the mirror idea to be clever and original and managed to excuse the clumsy and flat staging; in some cases, they even applauded it. Many were kind and, to our own confusion, forgiving and even complimentary of some of the film's worst moments. Certain critics seemed determined to praise the film, regardless of its demerits. Of course, not all saw it this way, but enough to give the movie its own notoriety among a limited group, even today.

Max would direct the murders with manic intensity. His thick German accent, coupled with the absurdity of what we were doing, often made it difficult for the crew to ignore the comedy while shining a pulsing red light onto a mirror piece while Max yelled.

"Miroar breezing! Miroar breezing!" he would scream while the gaffer (lighting technician) and best boy (gaffer's assistant) would pulsate a red light on the mirror, keeping pace with Max's commands. Max's English was not yet to the point where he pronounced every word as intended. The letters "th" still came out as "z," and no vowels were silent. Breathe became "breeze" and mirror was "miroar!"

"Breeze! Breeze! Miroar breezes! Miroar breezes!"

In the sound mix, one of us would breathe through a stocking while the loop of a heartbeat would play along. This would synchronize with the red light pulsing on the mirror piece.

"Stab! Stab! Miroar breezing! Miroar breezing!" If everything was going according to plan, Max would offer an excited cheer. "Ha, ha! This breezing is so great here!"

If an error was made, Max would throw up his hands and slap his forehead. "Ach! This is so depressing." And we would start again. This expression fit a German stereotype every crewmember had seen numerous times, unfortunately, in comedies.

One actress cuts off her top to expose her breasts before inserting the scissors into her own neck. Another character dies of head trauma when hit by an opening door on a wall medicine cabinet over the sink. Another victim is killed when a wooden window sash closes on his head. They all are assaulted by the invisible ghost, using whatever objects are easily available and inexpensive.

We were generous with the syrup and food coloring. There are many sound effects filmmakers use to heighten tension, particularly in a "slasher" movie like this one. They give the scene added authenticity, like footsteps, doors and drawers opening and closing, punches, stabs, gunshot wounds, etc.

A stab, for example, depending on the weapon, is far more effective when paired with the sound of a screwdriver or larger blade entering a watermelon or potato, accounting for the victim's size and the wound's location. The chest will sound far different than the neck. These are known as "foleys," named after Jack Foley, who introduced the concept of providing sound effects in the first days of "talking" pictures. He was so skilled that the profession was named after him.

When editing the sound, I performed foleys on a recording stage myself. For larger budget films, professional "foley walkers" worked on a stage in a recording studio while the film was projected on a screen; their experience in learning how to synchronize footsteps and sound effects to the film's action resulted in a shorter rental time for the studio. This made the best "walkers" valuable to the producers.

This is rarely done today, with even low-budget films contracting out to "sound houses" for a package price to create all the sound effects, background voices, and crowd noises known as "walla" effects and atmospheric sounds of the city or country. These houses employ full-time walkers and voice-over actors to create all the sounds and voices needed in a television show or film. In 1979, however, editors on low-budget pictures produced and recorded most of these sounds and voices themselves or with their friends and then manually synchronized the sounds and action on 35 mm film and tape. Now fully digitalized, it is a far different, and far more efficient, business.

After weeks working on a film like this, one easily becomes depressed and lonely, and I couldn't wait for the company of friends and family who represented my previous life. This level of independent, ultra-low-budget horror filmmaking had a gloom attached to it, which is why I tried to make as much light of it as possible.

There's also a letdown when the film wraps. When it's over, it's over, and most members of the crew vanish into their old lives, usually to meet again only on another job or at a party. Exceptions come with the department heads who do the hiring. Crew members stay in touch with them to keep up with what jobs are on the horizon, normally done over coffee or drinks. It's important to not let those who can hire you forget you.

When the shoot wrapped, most of the actors and crew returned to New York. I returned to Virginia, planning to edit the film in my house with rented 35 mm equipment and, if necessary, taking a quick documentary job while doing so. Max would contact me with the postproduction schedule and plans.

Unlike most of the films I have worked on, our experiences on the farm were so extreme and spontaneous that I established several close friendships, some to become lifelong. Over forty years later, the vernacular we coined to lighten our long days and nights still has the power to entertain.

CHAPTER 14
PARADISE AT TWENTY-TWO DOLLARS A NIGHT

Max and Sylvie decided to move to California for postproduction. Since New York was the only major American city Max had visited, they planned an extended drive across the country to see the sights and promised to call when settled in Los Angeles. I figured I had two to three weeks to decompress before post began.

The long drive across the country turned out to be four days, which is about as quick as anyone can drive the distance with sleep included. Less than a week after I arrived home, I received a call from Max.

"We are in the middle of Hollywood. It is so great here."

I was growing accustomed to Max's use of excitement as a form of manipulation, so I rarely matched his enthusiasm. "Where exactly are you?"

"In the greatest hotel. It is like a paradise with all the palm trees and swimming pool. When can you be here?"

That was the call. They wanted me to join them. I tried to avoid commitment as long as I could. "Where are you cutting the film?"

"We will do everything at the hotel. You must come right away. It is so great!"

"I'll see what I can do." I did have a business at home, as well as a life, and responsibilities I couldn't abandon at will.

Max never wavered from his intensity level. "I can't believe how beautiful and warm it is in LA. Just the greatest! You will love it. When can you be here?"

"I'll let you know."

Max hadn't mentioned how long he wanted me there. I had agreed to work for credit and profit participation. I could afford to do so, but it must have some limits. Moving into a Hollywood motel for an undetermined amount of time? I talked it over with Pam. She was supportive of me going west and scoping out a potential move for us to Hollywood. It was in the plan, so might as well hit the accelerator.

Three weeks later, Max and Sylvie picked me up at LAX in their new black Cadillac El Dorado and brought me back to the "greatest hotel here!"

Max had purchased the car in New York and driven it across the country. To Max, a black Cadillac was the perfect vehicle for a new-wave German anarchist filmmaker, freshly arrived in America. Expensive but not elitist, big, somehow threatening to the norm, and definitely not bourgeois. It was a statement, and more imposing than functional.

The Tropicana Motel in West Hollywood, now defunct, was at the time a famous haven for hipsters, druggies, and rock 'n' rollers of all ages, as well as the site of Duke's Coffee Shop, a gathering spot for the same, with lines of waiting customers stretching down Santa Monica Boulevard.

Oddly enough, the Tropicana was owned by Dodger legend Sandy Koufax, a curious choice for the Hall of Fame pitcher to purchase what punk poet Iris Berry called the "Chelsea Hotel with poolside astroturf."

The Tropicana pool, facing two stories of simply furnished rooms on all four sides, was surrounded by plastic: palm trees, umbrellas, tables, or grass. The clientele were mostly young men and women in search of a party, favors, or a spot to recover from such. Alternating waves of stoned rockers, gawkers, sex workers, promoters, and hangers-on mostly arrived as a package and spread out over white nylon lounge chairs, before leaving empty cases of Pacifico or Corona, still an American novelty in 1979.

I would pass by, appreciate the scenery, dive in and splash about, appreciate a few minutes more, dry off, and return to work. I spent very little time at the pool because of my work schedule, but the experience, much more than work, would ultimately grow to become a fruitful part of my education.

Los Angeles, west of downtown, had the feel of a small town in those days, and it certainly was and remains to be a company town. Most everyone in this part of Hollywood knew each other's faces at that time, if not their résumés. Young people wanted an alternative to the crowds of Sunset Strip, known as the weekend playground for Valley teens and cruising low riders, and the starched pretense of Beverly Hills. They wanted a place where comfort and music were offered and welcome. There weren't many hip places around, and Duke's was the chosen spot.

The Tropicana was also the hottest scene in music at the time. Aside from American rockers like the Doors, Janis Joplin, the Ramones, Blondie, Ricki Lee Jones, Sly Stone, Warren Zevon, Tom Petty and the Heartbreakers, the New York Dolls, the Runaways, Joan Jett, Iggy Pop, and more, all the British, Australian, and West Indian pop and ska bands stayed at the Tropicana when they came to town, including the Clash, Bob Marley and the Wailers, the Specials, Madness, the Bad Seeds, Nick Lowe and Rockpile, the Pretenders—UK groups just hitting the charts in America.

We first lived in a corner suite by the parking lot at the corner of Santa Monica and Westmount, but when Tom Waits, a motel veteran, vacated the bungalow in the center of the lot, I moved in to cut the film. It felt like a genuine venture into the artistic experience, living like a true bohemian, among bohemians, in a setting where no one spent money on much other than minimal nourishment and maximal drugs. The cheapest rooms were twenty-two dollars nightly, and we paid $800 by the month for a suite with a kitchen and an entrance directly into the private lot.

Santa Monica Boulevard was not a desirable location in 1979, before West Hollywood became a city and gentrified the neighborhood. Drug dealers and prostitutes of both sexes used the area to ply their trades, and assaults and robberies were fairly common in front of the motel. One night, I heard a noise outside the door and opened it to find a young man leaning against the wall, moaning in pain and holding his side. His shirt had been ripped from a knife assault and was soaked in blood. When I told him I was calling 911, his eyes popped open, and he shuffled away, leaving a bloody trail, which the housekeepers hosed away the next morning as if it were a daily chore.

We leased a Kem flatbed film editing table from Gary, a fellow who lived in Malibu and rented equipment from his house. He personally delivered gear to the site to size up his clients in case repossession became necessary, which it often did. We rented several tables from Gary, at times needing more than one. The machines broke down often, and Gary would return to make the repairs. There were very few moving parts in these machines, and in the best tradition of German engineering, each was easily replaced. It was ten years later that editing software became commonplace and these cumbersome tables became obsolete, and nearly ten years earlier, these flashy, quick, accessible machines had replaced the upright, noisy, and slow film shredding Moviola.

Like many of us, Gary was a transplanted easterner but had immediately bought into the California dream. He was short and overweight but always wore what could be called "cabana gear," with a flowered shirt hanging too high, beach shorts too low, and a crusty pair of sandals that he never changed. What remained of his scraggly hair would bush out from under a different baseball cap each visit.

These caps were normally promotional gear for various technical facilities for what is referred to in Hollywood as "the business," or "the industry." Technicolor, Movielab, Panavision, Deluxe Labs, Birns and Sawyer, Sunset Sound—all the gear and service houses in town provided free merchandise for mutual promotion, usually T-shirts or baseball caps, which were the favored fashion accessory for balding men in Southern California, particularly those who drove convertibles.

Gary's convertible was a Porsche, and he found ways to fit the sizeable Kem into the car so he could enjoy "the drive from the beach," a sentence he always delivered to remind us he lived in Malibu.

When he arrived, Gary would show us the disassembled table crammed into the seat, boot, and trunk of his car and wait while Max wrote a check for the full rental plus security deposit. Gary would call the bank to verify the account, open his toolbox, and scurry back and forth between the parking lot and motel room, hoisting pieces like an industrious ant, running them through the door, and bolting them together on the floor of the room, leaving no time for thieves to help themselves to his parts, or his Porsche.

While on the floor assembling the table, Gary would proudly gossip about the numerous low-budget films he was currently renting equipment to, nearly all horror or comedies, being cut in the three- to four-mile corridor of Hollywood between Highland and Doheny, mostly on or just off Santa Monica Boulevard. It was a time when "Hollywood" was still in Hollywood because most of the support businesses were still within the confines. Today, some have moved to the Valley or Santa Monica; filmmakers now live everywhere, and many work from home.

Once the equipment was installed, Max would wake me at seven each morning, and we would discuss the scene to be cut that day. He and Sylvie would often disappear for the afternoon while I cut the scene. We would have dinner together, prepared in the small kitchen, and they would watch television while I went back to work.

On a restricted budget, we rarely went out to dinner, though

I realized the lack of spending was simply a statement about our production budget. Whatever they wanted to spend, they could afford, but that wouldn't be in keeping with our "mission." In the meantime, I would splurge on an occasional beer or hamburger.

My workday normally ended at one in the morning, leaving an hour before the bars closed—just enough time to walk east on Santa Monica Boulevard past the gumbo and Louisiana chicken carryout, liquor store, and Tropicana's competing Alta Cienega Motel, crossing La Cienega Boulevard to Flipper's Roller Boogie Palace, where I would usually peer inside to see if a band was playing.

Flipper's was a former bowling alley owned by Art Linkletter, converted just months earlier to a roller rink/bar/disco, with live acts often performing in the center of the rink while gaudily dressed skaters circled them under dazzling disco balls suspended from a domed ceiling. It wasn't a visual you could find just anywhere, and the striking combination of color, movement, and sound was fondly memorable.

The whole scene screamed *this is LA*. Filmmakers tried to capture the culture in the Linda Blair movie *Roller Boogie*, whose dismal box office performance accurately envisioned the brief life of the craze.

Cher, Berlin, the Go-Go's, Black Flag, Patti Smith, the Plimsouls, Talking Heads, and even Prince performed at Flipper's before it closed in 1981. The energy of performing while skaters circled the bandstand excited the musicians, who were like a spindle on a turntable. Though the sensory experience was impressive, I rarely stayed longer than a few minutes. Time is precious in the countdown to closing time, and I was more interested in a beer and pinball at Barney's Beanery.

My generation will recognize Barney's from R. Crumb's illustrations on the cover of Janis Joplin and Big Brother and the Holding Company's *Cheap Thrills* album. Barney's served good chili and hamburgers but wasn't a particularly friendly place, evidenced by a prominently placed sign over the bar: "FAGOTS STAY OUT." The misspelled sentiment was restated on the matchbook covers.

I would order a beer and occasionally a sandwich or bowl of chili and wait for a free pinball machine. Barney's was crowded, regardless of the time or day. Pool tables and pinball machines in the back were the centerpiece, with booths in the front for diners and screenwriters who liked to camp out for hours with papers spread across the table. One had to select a machine, claim a place in line, then find a way to play, eat, and order beer simultaneously. It was a unique skill, requiring several attempts before mastering.

Barney's was also where many nightcrawlers would go to score drugs, a priority made obvious by the surly, desperate nature of many of the patrons. Drugs were popular at the time, and I used my share, so I understood the friction they could cause.

Cocaine was the drug of choice, and cocaine does not promote submissive or even agreeable behavior. I saw many fights over the months I spent in that corridor, most of them in Barney's bar. I met a number of people there, some multiple times, but nothing took root, and Barney's doesn't rest calmly in my memory. We left the Tropicana in early 1980. Today, I live about three miles away and have never returned to Barney's Beanery.

When it was closing time at Barney's, I would walk back to the Tropicana and get a few hours rest. I knew Max would be at the Kem by 7 a.m., reviewing what I had done the previous day, with the volume turned up so he could clearly hear the actors. For an editor, it takes very little time to know every line, every delivery, every pause, every breath, every shout, and every scream in a film from beginning to end, and I heard most of them every morning, at high volume, after four hours of sleep, if I was lucky.

When Max had offered me the job to edit his film, I fully intended to be a greater part of the production team, learning every creative step from start to finish, simply because I had so much to learn about the process. To do so, I had to abandon my business to work for essentially nothing, which was not a difficult decision because I had money saved and was determined to switch to feature films. I knew how to make documentaries, and I could always go back to it if this didn't work out. But in my mind, that wasn't about to happen. The indisputable advantage ignorance provides.

Pam was fully supportive and fancied the idea of a move to LA, if that's the direction this venture took us. I let my clients know I was shutting down until further notice, recommended other filmmakers to replace me, and went west to scope out the territory, weigh the possibilities, and determine the future—which became reality.

CHAPTER 15
THE NEW WORLD

My first few weeks in LA, I found the transition lonely and difficult. The only people I knew were Max, Sylvie, and whatever friends from the Maryland shoot who occasionally came to visit or look for work. Max was overly proprietary and monopolized my time to the point where it felt worse than indentured servitude.

I had come to Hollywood to learn how to make movies, and I was learning by doing, but it was a friendless time in an unfriendly town, and I was desperate to find someone in a similar situation. What most aspiring filmmakers, actors, musicians, writers, and artists discover in time is that "the business" is an opportunist's game, not for the easily disappointed or discouraged.

None of us had much knowledge of LA, and each day was a discovery. The sky, hazy blue and cloudless, layered with a noxious haze so thick it had flavor, made Easterners instantly aware of why locals wear sunglasses. It wasn't to hide red eyes like we thought. It was shelter in a desert.

Baseball caps were a fashion statement, like sunglasses. Nobody but ball players and truck drivers wore baseball caps on the East Coast at the time, but of course, Birkenstocks and long hair were out of style in the east as well. In California, however, the sun can be oppressively strong, and "casual" rules the day, then and now.

Instead of submarines, or "grinders" or "hoagies," the favored quick lunches in LA were hamburgers and club sandwiches. The hamburgers were bigger and better than what we were accustomed to, but we missed the bread, oil and vinegar, and cured meats with peppers in a spicy Italian sub. Hamburger popularity has spread since then, even on the East Coast, but hoagies have yet to really hit in LA.

Rather than a week between rains, LA could go over 200 days. There would be little need for a jacket, or even a sweater; the penalty for wearing one to be fashionable was to suffer in the heat. The daily sameness created an intellectual lethargy, which I think is why so many writers leave town to work.

I came to realize that a lot of this was merely adjusting to this assiduously sunny reality. Once I became accustomed to the city and its weather, I developed a love for it. The transition from the East Coast probably took about four years, which I'd say is average for those moving here to work. I realized I could live much more cheaply in LA than in New York, and spending so much time outside seemed far healthier than in New York's crowded confines and cold winters. To this day, I enjoy writing here, simply because it's possible to sit outside on a terrace, under an umbrella, almost any day of the year with the most pressing consideration being the weight of the shirt you're wearing.

I admired Max's commitment to his work, which I shared. He loved every part of the process and enjoyed my enthusiasm for it as well. We sacrificed the lively LA social scene for time spent in front of the editing table. I had committed to this life so I could learn how to make feature films. Max, for all his ego and eccentricities, had worked as an actor with notable directors in the German New Wave and received lauding reviews from prestigious film critics internationally. He had won praise as a director to be taken seriously. Max had an unusual pedigree, one I wanted to benefit from. I did, but in a far different fashion than I imagined.

As soon as we began cutting the film, Max and I familiarized ourselves with all the necessary supportive industries that keep Hollywood functioning. The editing table was just the beginning. We needed what are known as "expendable" supplies like tape, gloves, splicers, benches, reels, notebooks, and markers—and that was just for the editing room.

Later, we would come to know the talent agents, casting directors and audition facilities, storyboard artists, prop and costume houses, labs, sound houses, postproduction facilities, mixing studios, screening rooms, supply houses, copy shops, and even research libraries. The industry employed thousands of people, and for everyone employed, there were hundreds more looking for jobs.

Max and Sylvie loved living in the core of the film center, and like children absorbing the culture of a new world, we visited the landmarks mentioned in grocery checkout line magazines. We never actually ordered food at Musso's, L'Orangerie, the Polo Lounge, Chasen's, or the Brown Derby, but we knew them through the front glass. We would eat at Schwab's drugstore occasionally, but most of the known restaurants catered to patrons who either carried their own expense accounts or hoped to benefit from another's.

Newly arrived ingénues or young leading men would hang out at the bar or counter, nursing a coffee or iced tea while trying to make eye contact with the most successful looking person who moved with a satisfied swagger. It had been known to work before, so why not?

Rather than meeting at restaurants like most do in New York, we would gather at someone's house or apartment; even the smaller units often had outdoor areas, and it was always nice in the evening when the sun went down. The air would cool off, and most Easterners were not accustomed to sitting outside without being bothered by bugs. Except in the heaviest rain seasons, there were very few bugs, including mosquitos, in Southern California. Screens were unnecessary. For reasons unknown to me, that seems to have changed in the new millennium. Mosquitos are now a pest in the best neighborhoods of Hollywood and beyond.

Most of those we met in our first few months in Hollywood were connections Max had made while working in Europe—producers who had success making films overseas but who now lived in Los Angeles.

Max and Sylvie would be invited as a couple, but they occasionally brought me along to these meetings, exposing me to a decadence I had not yet been initiated to.

Some of the European producers were spending money made by an ascendant several generations prior, whose descendants had grown accustomed to the lifestyle. Later in my time in Hollywood, I would become exposed to a much more nouveau riche group of the self-made, who, in reality, were much wealthier than the Europeans I met with Max and Sylvie. Although these parvenus lived even more lavishly than the Europeans, they didn't play the roles as well.

One of our first meetings after moving into the Tropicana was at the home of a producer Max had worked with in Germany. This producer had made a number of successful low-budget movies that were shot in Europe but distributed worldwide. He had recently been featured in a book about low-budget classic movies, and Max was interested in getting his advice and perhaps investment in our film.

The producer lived above the Sunset Strip in a hillside 1960's era house, with a pool and hot tub behind it. He was clearly in his seventies, but very vital, with a welcoming and cheerful manner. He introduced us to his Danish wife, who probably wasn't his wife, an aspiring actress probably forty years his junior.

Our hosts offered us margaritas and suggested we take them into the hot tub. I had never been in a hot tub, and it sounded like the proper way to begin a Hollywood dinner party, so we took off our clothes and settled into the tub. This was the California living I had heard about. Five people sitting naked in a hot tub, with at least a forty-year swing in their ages, the oldest being married to the youngest.

We spent at least two hours in the tub, and fresh margaritas kept appearing. They tasted like lemonade, and I quickly downed several, until the heat from the water and the ice in the drinks hit an impasse in my head. I needed a reset, so I asked to use the restroom.

The young wife offered to show me the way to the guest cabana, so we both climbed out, and on the way, I dove into the swimming pool to cool off. The water was at least thirty degrees cooler than the tub, and it hit me like an invigorating ice bath—until I climbed out. My head started to flutter as I entered the cabana, and as I was about to ask why she was dimming the lights, everything went black.

I came to with the wife lying next to me on a platform guest bed. I was more embarrassed than excited, but she was a considerate person, who seemed genuinely concerned for the health of her guest, even though we were nestled together in a sleeping bag—still naked.

"Are you all right?" she asked playfully.

"I don't know what happened." But I did.

"You went out. Right on the floor."

"Ouch."

She smiled. "No problem. It's why we have bags out here."

I noticed she was smiling more than she should, and it belatedly dawned on me that this must be part of their living arrangement. If they entertained guests, she was free to seduce them. She put up with being married to an old guy. So, when young men showed up, they were fair game if she was up for it.

"Well, thank you."

"Of course."

She didn't move, lying against me and waiting for results that weren't going to come. My head was still spinning.

"I don't feel so good." A reliable conversation stopper.

"Really?"

"I'd like to sleep, if that's okay." She wasn't expecting this and probably hadn't heard it before. I closed my eyes to emphasize the point. "Do they know what's going on?"

An exhale of resignation. "I'll tell them."

"I would appreciate it."

She got up and left. I was so dizzy that I couldn't think, though the irony of where I was after what I had been doing wasn't wasted, even in my fog. My first hot tub party in Hollywood, low-budget as it was, and a dip in the pool renders me unconscious. I awoke only long enough to appear confused, and she was kind enough to tuck me away and return to the party.

Sometime later, when I reappeared from the cabana, dinner was finished, and everyone was dressed and ready to leave. Max, Sylvie, and I drove home talking about the producer's career and what he could potentially do for the film. I felt like I had nearly suffered a heart attack, which could have been true, but I also considered what he could do for the film, which was why we were there.

Max called the producer several times after that, but it soon became clear that the hot tub party was what most gatherings in Hollywood were: dogs sniffing other dogs. Who can do what for whom . . . how soon . . . for how much? Deals always involve a seller and a buyer, but sometimes everyone is a seller, and sometimes those roles don't become clear until several phone calls, or lack thereof, after the meeting. In this case, everyone was looking for money, and no one was spending it, so we continued on, as one does in Hollywood.

CHAPTER 16
THE STARS ALIGN

After several months in the Tropicana, Sylvie wanted a home. We leased a house on Curson Avenue north of Hollywood Boulevard, across the street from Wattles Park. It's a community garden fronting the Wattles Mansion, built by Omaha banker Gurdin Wattles in 1907. This was before the movie industry arrived, when mostly agricultural Hollywood was a winter escape for wealthy Midwesterners.

The plots at Wattles were shared by several local residents who traded homegrown vegetables over the course of the summer, reminiscent of country living but still in the hub of the wheel. There were many jewels like Wattles Park throughout Hollywood: hiking trails, spectacular mansions from the early twentieth century, small, uniquely Western museums like the Hollywood Heritage and Gene Autry Western Heritage, and better-known landmarks such as the Hollywood Bowl and Greek Theater. Hollywood had not yet been overrun by development. You could reliably spot coyotes or even a mountain lion in the center of a residential and even commercial community.

The house was Japanese designed, sleek and open, located downhill adjacent to the estate of Carroll Righter, the "Astrologer to the Stars." Righter had appeared on the cover of *TIME* Magazine in 1969 and was reputed to be consulted regularly by Ronald and Nancy Reagan during the Reagan presidency.

While we lived on Curson, a stream of celebrities visited next door for "consultations." Righter also hosted garden parties to celebrate various signs of the zodiac. I remember the Leo parties, simply because I am a Leo. The guests would be nattily dressed, arriving mostly in town cars and limousines, and as each climbed out of the car, a young man would approach, wearing a tuxedo and pointing a video camera, shouting a welcome followed by personal interrogations. After awkward self-introductions and at times excruciating efforts at humor, the tuxedoed greeter would hustle to the next arriving limo and thrust the lens into the face of whoever stepped out of the back.

"Welcome to the party. And you are?"

It was amusing to watch this ritual from our own garden, comparing the awkward responses by befuddled guests with a lens in their faces, some known, some not. Not one, however, asked, "Why the interview?"

The guests would disappear into the house, and we could hear them being greeted by other guests, room to room, finally joining the bubbling crowd on the back lawn where more excited greetings would shriek. From the number and volume of shrieks, I was always curious for a glimpse of the back lawn, to see how so many party guests could fit.

The only time I was invited into the marble-columned mansion was when Sylvie was babysitting her brother's two Panamanian Amazon parrots and the birds escaped the cage and flew into a palm tree behind Mr. Righter's house.

Parrots are noisy birds, and the two were screeching the joys of freedom from next door. I rang the bell to the Righter mansion and was escorted into the back garden, where the merriment took place. Tall palms, ficuses, and bamboos enclosed a spreading park that extended nearly to the next block, with marble statuary and fountains connected by stone walks winding through a perfectly manicured lawn and solidly sculpted shrubbery. The entire back garden felt like a cemetery location from Tony Richardson's film adaptation of Evelyn Waugh's book *The Loved One*.

We located the tree sheltering the parrots, but they were out of reach. We tried to coax the birds onto a rake or stick, but they flew to a higher spot. Max and I suggested Sylvie call a bird wrangler since we were in a company town where such a skill is in demand and not that difficult to locate.

Sylvie, however, had other ideas. She knew a small camp of homeless people slept in Wattles Park at night, so she crossed the street looking for someone adept at climbing trees. Max and I were skeptical of this, but in Hollywood, any skill useful on film is in demand and easily found, particularly when the seeker is a beautiful woman.

A volunteer quickly appeared. Over our protests, Sylvie engaged the man and brought him back to the house, sending us off to the editing room to work. Later in the morning, while synching the image of an ice pick being plunged into a throat with the sound of a screwdriver thrusting into a potato, we got a phone call summoning Max home.

Figuring Sylvie would both help the homeless man and save herself some money, she had escorted the man up to the Righter house. She handed him two bird cuffs, similar to handcuffs but suitable for parrots, and instructed the man on how to bring the parrots down, careful not to harm them. For this, she would pay him $100. As would be expected, the birds were unhappy about being cuffed and let the man know it with beaks capable of crushing walnut shells.

After a trip to the emergency room, the episode ended up costing Sylvie far more than paying a bird wrangler.

CHAPTER 17
TACOS, SCREAMS, AND SIGHS— HOW IT *REALLY* WORKS

After leaving the Tropicana, our editing room was housed in a sound stage/editing facility in a part of Hollywood even seedier than where we came from. This particular stretch of Santa Monica Boulevard, at the corner of Highland Avenue, was known for drug deals and prostitute pickups, and several celebrities had been the victims of police stings on the block.

Of the four corners adjacent to the facility, one housed the film processing laboratory Movielab, which operated all night behind locked gates. Another corner contained a Chinese-owned porn-and-donut shop, later used as the primary location for *Tangerine*, Sean Baker's film about transsexual prostitutes. The third corner housed a gas station popular with drug dealers and prostitutes because of four available pay phones to conduct business, and on the fourth corner was a Taco Bell, our only accessible food option other than the Chinese donuts. If we got hungry at night, it often became an interesting adventure.

My assistant, Carrie, was a young woman recently graduated from CalArts, whose even younger friend, Lola, was the apprentice editor. Both aspiring filmmakers, they had little experience but worked very hard for little money (when they were paid) and were eager to learn.

The first floor of the facility contained sound stages for Foley and ADR recording. ADR (automated dialogue replacement), or dubbing, is when actors come into the studio and stand in a recording booth while scenes are projected on a screen in front of them. This system was used if the lines were not clearly understandable in the original recording or if ambient noise or crew mistakes made the line unrecognizable. A third reason was professional displeasure. If the producer or director wasn't happy with the performance, the actor would rerecord the line, synching the delivery and cadence to that on-screen. It is the same principle as Foley walking but for dialogue. Dubbing dialogue is a cultivated skill, and experienced actors can be astonishingly good at it.

The sound mixing rooms were on the first floor, editing suites on the second, and a shooting stage on the third. Most of the rooms and stages were used for porno films, which, in those days, were actual feature-length movies shown in specialty theaters around the country. Horror and low-budget genre films found a home here as well.

Though I used a flatbed Kem editing table, which old-fashioned producers considered a luxury because of its ease of operation and sizeable screen (making it more expensive), many of the editors in this facility still used the traditional (and far cheaper) upright Moviola editing machine.

Invented in Hollywood by Iwan Serrurier and originally intended for home viewing, the Moviola was quickly determined in 1924 to be the perfect editing tool. Douglas Fairbanks bought the first machine himself, and the framed receipt still hangs on the wall of the Moviola Co. in Hollywood, which remains today.

A Moviola is operated with a foot pedal, controlling the speed and direction of the reels. Nearly all the films being cut in this facility were shot in 35 mm and intended for theatrical distribution (as opposed to television, which could be shot and broadcast in 16 mm or on videotape). So, the editing rooms and work areas were spacious enough to handle big Moviolas, flatbed Kems or Steenbecks, and large 1,000-foot reels of 35 mm film. This was specialty merchandise, found only in a company town.

Before the age of digital filmmaking, a Moviola could be far more precise than a flatbed for manual editing. When a Moviola editor was trying to slowly move the images forward or backward to determine the perfect spot to place an edit, it would be done with taps of the foot or manually hand-guided frame by frame, which is one twenty-fourth of a second—bit by bit, forward, and back, until the perfect spot was determined. It could go as slowly as the editor chose, manually moving the film through the viewer inch by inch.

The flatbed tables were not geared like the uprights and were limited to several preset speeds, so this extreme slow-motion scanning, fully at the will of the editor, was not possible on the Kem or Steenbeck. The flatbeds, however, were much easier on the film stock, and editors spent far less time repairing broken sprockets with thick, clear editing tape, which often caused jams while passing through "the gate."

When a decision had been made for a particular edit, either alone or in concert with the director or producer, the editor would mark the work print with a dull washable grease pencil on the designated frame. This process would be repeated at will until the end of the 1,000-foot reel, which contained approximately ten minutes of screen time.

Before the digital age, every booth in any size theater held two projectors, each with a shuttering window between the projector lens and the screen. In the final positive print of a movie, each reel would be marked with one or two blue dots appearing in the upper right-hand corner of the screen between eight and eleven seconds from the end of the reel and again at about one second, both acting as cues for the projectionist.

The first cue was for the projectionist to start the second projector, and the last cue was to switch the projection gate so the open projection window would close, the second open, and the next reel be projected onto the screen. This normally came at a scene change so the audience would be less likely to notice any lapse, in case the projectionist was late with the switch.

Projectionists were skilled union employees and well paid to hit their cues. Start at the first dots, switch at the second, and the next reel will sync perfectly with the end of the previous. This procedure would be repeated back and forth for each projector until the final reel, until digital projection rendered the whole process obsolete.

Back in the editing room, working on what was called a "bench," a long table with hand-operated reels on either side, or "rewinds," the assistant would run the coordinated reels of picture and sound through a synchronizer, identified by matching code numbers on the edges of the film and tape, until arriving at each frame the editor had marked, either to begin an edit or end it. It was necessary for the editor to mark the picture because the soundtrack would be matched to the work print in the synchronizer.

Following the editor's marks, the assistant would know precisely where to insert the film and sound into the splicer, synchronized by common sprocket holes, identified by matching code numbers on the edges of the film and tape, and make the cut of sound and picture with a small guillotine. The assistant would then wipe it clean and seal the splice with clear adhesive tape. When each reel was completed, the editor would screen it on the Moviola or flatbed.

While screening, as the tape slowly moved across the sound head, the editor would crank up the track and watch and listen very carefully to be certain no sound cuts were made in the middle of a noise, which would be too jarring; the volume would have to be loud enough for the editor to hear the slightest sound, whether it be a word, gasp, shriek, laugh, or movement. This meant maximum volume at all times.

As the editor moved the film across the Moviola sound heads in slow motion, it created a particular noise, one heard exclusively in the hallways of a building that housed movie-cutting rooms.

Since this particular facility hosted mostly porn or horror pictures being cut across the hall from one another on the same floor, imagine the symphony of amplified sounds reverberating throughout the corridors. Shouts of fear . . . and pleasure, at maximum volume, first at regular speed, then slow motion, then regular speed again. Back and forth—again, and again, and again.

Editors hated wearing headphones because of their size and weight, so it was full volume, all day and much of the night, resounding through closed doors, covering the entire floor. Screaming in horror. Screaming in ecstasy . . . forward and reverse. "PHAAAAA—EEERRRRRRRG!" Back and forth. Back and forth. Slower. Faster. Constantly. "GRRRRREEEE—AAAAAAHP!"

Orgasms on one side and murders on the other. All speeds, both directions, blending together. All day. The smell of tacos. The crunch of their shells.

"PHAERG! GREAHP! PHAERG! GREAHP!"

But in 1980, headphones were just too damn bulky.

As the process of putting a film together became routine and I learned how it worked, I became exposed to the underbelly of filmmaking. An unfortunate component of every profession where considerable money—power—is involved.

As he grew comfortable living in America, Max pondered a series of fashion choices, determined by what he felt would best represent the image of the "German auteur in Hollywood." In New York, it was the full black leather costume, which, when not perceived as a sexual joke or musical irony, was not so appealing in LA, particularly when the SS gear is worn by an actual German.

Successful directors receive attention, and attention can help make directors successful. Some are indifferent, but in the early 1980s, most emerging directors hungered for it, including Max. The Cadillac was the first step, an impressive way for a New Wave German director to arrive in Hollywood.

Max had also realized Gary was on to something with the baseball caps. These were designed to actually shade the sun, a popular look in Hollywood twenty-five years before the bill was flipped to the back or side of the head to proclaim "cool slacker," or more succinctly, "doofus."

Max's original choice of hats was the LA Dodgers, although he had never seen a baseball game. Later, when he discovered Francis Coppola and George Lucas were from the San Francisco Bay Area, he switched to Giants caps but ultimately opted for whatever supply house was offering free gear to advertise their services.

The hair springing from under the sides of the hat could also be important. Never be uniform or flat, which would be far too conforming, but look naturally unkempt. This required training the hair. A partially unbuttoned shirt with jeans and running shoes would complete the preferred Hollywood director look of the time, accentuated by a serious stare when the head is lowered and framed by a lifted back collar, which implied the necessary gravitas.

If possible, a sweater would be draped around the shoulders and loosely tied below the open shirt, bordering the lifted collar. For Max, it was a look requiring time with a mirror until the hair direction, collar, and sweater placement was perfected.

Having been a child actor, Max had the patience and background to prepare him for this. Occasionally, he would wear makeup, mostly pancake and eyeliner, but he eventually decided that if this preference were discovered, fans could question his sexuality, which, at the time, could hurt his potential career.

Like many actors, Max was aware of his projected image. Over the years, I learned how important this is to everyone who wants to become successful in Hollywood. A successful talent agent once told me that in Hollywood, perception mattered far more than reality. An actor may adhere to any belief system or display any pattern of behavior he or she chooses, no matter how unsavory, but it's inconsequential if public perception can be controlled, which is why publicists are so valuable. Though skeptical at the time, I would later learn the unfortunate truth of what the agent said.

In the Hollywood studio system, a star's image was carefully cultivated and controlled by the studio, which monitored the flow of information through news outlets. It was a mutually beneficial arrangement between the studios and the press, so the stars' private lives remained that way. Marriages were faithful, no one was homosexual, and stars never had a drinking or drug problem. They loved children, animals, and the underprivileged, and when not vacationing in Ibiza, they spent all their time off the set with their family, feeding the poor, or volunteering at the shelter.

One morning, the editor of a German magazine called the cutting room, and after a telephone conversation in German, Max said that a writer and photographer would arrive from Germany. We had to find a location to take impressive pictures.

Max had avoided telling the editor what his new film was about, preferring to keep the content mysteriously vague and "alluring." He did tell the editor that the film was an application of "German thoughts contemplating American deeds." He did not dissuade the editor from understanding this was a political film. Max told all interviewers his film was "a political look at American society," careful to then avoid the interviewer until the next production, which would always be "far more political than the last."

When the German magazine editor had asked Max if he was working in a studio or on location, Max explained that he shot the film on location but was editing in the "heart of Hollywood." The editor was hoping to send a writer and photographer to capture Max at work, apparently on a studio lot, the heartthrob German actor now cutting out a career for himself as an acclaimed director of American films. The editor couldn't disguise his excitement over the vision that a new voice of German cinema was now entrenched in Hollywood's heart, unaware that this organ beat from a warehouse sandwiched between Movielab, the gas station serving as drug dealer and pimp headquarters, the Chinese donut/porn shop, and Taco Bell.

Max explained to the editor that his current film was a thoughtful, allegory-ridden political statement about America, and he had moved from NY to LA, where he was living in a Hollywood Hills mansion while shooting on location in the California desert.

To prepare for the journalists' arrival, Max bought a large cowboy hat, a Western shirt, and jeweled snakeskin boots, deciding this was the best look to present as a former European exploring the American West. Living the dream and wearing the trimmings.

When the writer and photographer arrived at the airport, Max and Sylvie picked them up in the Cadillac and provided a quick tour of Beverly Hills, followed by a drive past Paramount and MGM studios (years before the lot was sold to Sony). Since it was the journalists' first visit to LA, they were genuinely intrigued.

After the tour, Max parked in front of a drive leading through deep foliage to the front door of a large house above Sunset Strip in the Hollywood Hills.

Max got out of the car and posed by the front gate, telling the journalists it was his house and they were free to photograph him, but he wished to remain out front because he had important houseguests from Europe, and he didn't want to disturb them.

The photographer snapped several photos, with the house barely visible in the background. I have no idea what Max would have done if someone had walked out of the house, arrived, or even spoken through the intercom. But no one did. The photographer got his pictures, and they got back in the Cadillac and continued on.

There were several rental locations in the desert outside of LA offering what could be sold as nineteenth-century Western towns and ranches, good for staging gunfights and cattle scenes. Max found a spot on a hill far enough away from the set where he could take the reporter and photographer and pose for photos, with a Western set in the background, appearing as if he was on the set, with no location rental to pay.

Max leaned against a wooden fence and put one heel on the railing, an instant cowboy in his snakeskin boots and oversized Stetson hat, calmly and earnestly describing in German how he had discovered a vehicle to express his anarchist political views through an established, revered American tradition: the horror film. A new approach.

The interview continued in the editing room, where the photographer would take pictures of me and my assistants working while Max sat in the foreground expressing his views on American film and culture. We were instructed only to show dramatic scenes on the Kem, mostly featuring Sylvie in crisis. From there, Max escorted the two to Musso and Frank's for dinner and the Polo Lounge for drinks before dropping them at their budget hotel in the Valley. He gave them a souvenir Western belt buckle from Nudie's, the Western store made famous by providing performance costumes for Elvis Presley.

After another day of sightseeing, posing, and interviews, the journalists returned to Germany, and Max returned to his baseball cap and running shoes. I spent my days at the editing room, and Max spent more and more time away from work—and Sylvie.

As Max met more and more Europeans in the film trade in Hollywood, he took advantage of what the lifestyle could offer, and how easy it was to accept. Because of his celebrity as a teen actor, the perks of fame were something he enjoyed in Germany. Here, he was unknown, but he had a cachet among certain film cognoscenti, which he could exploit effortlessly.

Some critics would look for political imagery wherever it could be found, and as any filmgoer understands, it is all in the interpretation, like listening to a song.

Max found that many American critics were far more gracious with him than with American directors. As an example, we were preparing to shoot a dinner scene taking place in the country home of a Southern country cop and his family, when Max noticed the wineglasses were empty. He was furious. "Ach! Where is the wine? Get the wine! Who has dinner without wine?"

"A Southern cop and his family," I mentioned to Max. This was supposed to be a low-income family in the rural South in the 1970s, living in a small house on a farm where a cop, his wife, and her aunt and uncle all live together for some unknown and, in Max's mind, irrelevant reason.

The idea that this family would be drinking wine at all was a considerable stretch, but an expensive bottle of Chateauneuf du-Pape in what would very likely be a dry county in the Bible Belt? The only wines available within an hour's drive would be, other than Boone's Farm or scuppernong wine, perhaps one Louis Martini and one Gallo red option, and possibly the sweetest rosé, all of the lowest grade.

"Ach." He dismissed my plea for credibility and insisted the glasses be filled.

The props people poured the wine, but clearly someone had already taken notice, and advantage, of the expensive vintage sitting on the kitchen counter, and there wasn't enough left to fill all the glasses, so two were unfortunately left empty. These glasses were unconsciously placed in front of the characters next to be murdered in the story.

When the film was released, one critic, while gushing over Max's European pedigree, commented on his sensitivity to the characters' plight in life, using empty wineglasses to reflect on the prospective victims' impending doom, a sensitive insight rarely displayed in American films.

It is found gold for a director to be anointed with imagined genius by a major publication, and Max was thrilled. He proceeded to concoct his own validation for the critic's perception and responded to the European press that he was surprised and delighted that an American newspaper was able to spot such subtlety in the complex work of a German auteur.

This was a clear demonstration of Max's ability to improvise on cue, on or off a stage. It was impressive but strongly disturbing.

The risk is what carried the excitement for him. Once he saw an opportunity, he not only exploited it but carried it further than most of us would be capable of—like pretending an occupied house belonged to him and risking being exposed. He would do the same in almost any situation, like his interviews with critics, and almost welcome the challenge of having to spontaneously extricate himself from an impossible situation he created with a lie. He would never squirm, instead constantly doubling down, pushing it to an extreme the interviewer would have to challenge, accept, or move on from.

Max would later laugh about the absurdity of what he had created, referring to duplicity as a skill he had learned from his mentors in German cinema. Keep the conversation going by creating a political context for it, particularly when caught in a lie. Conjoin fantasy and reality; then play the role which serves you best. Max did this with a cold indifference, believing that, in his words, "The truth is whatever you make it to be."

CHAPTER 18
THE UNDERBELLY

Max engaged a foreign sales representative, also a German, to sell the film to markets around the world. Otto lived in Malibu with his young American wife and would often visit the editing room, watching the murder sequences as they were cut, making certain the scenes were graphic, but not too graphic for European audiences.

Occasionally, Otto would bring foreign buyers to the suite to watch a scene. While I rolled the film on the flatbed Kem, Otto would stand behind me with the buyer, narrating and embellishing the action on screen like the master of ceremonies at a burlesque show, orchestrating a reaction from his client.

During one of these visits, I was showing Otto and a French Canadian buyer a scene where a pitchfork is floating through a barn by itself, waiting to skewer the next person to walk inside. Otto put his hands on the buyer's shoulders and spoke into his ear like a boxing coach, preparing his victim for the onslaught.

"Oh, Serge . . . do you see what is happening here? Look, Serge, look! What is the pitchfork going to do? Oh, my God! Look! Oh, God. Look out! Look out!"

Then, he grabbed Serge's shoulders in a jolt as the pitchfork plunged into a victim's chest.

"*Hoooly mooooly*, Serge!" He extended the exclamation for dramatic emphasis, giving Serge's shoulders a friendly squeeze. Serge didn't know whether to shout, laugh, or shudder.

"Isn't that exciting, Serg? Very scary, isn't it? I can't take it. Come on, let's go. I need a blow job." And they walked out.

Otto would bring a different buyer around every two weeks or so, then huddle with Max to discuss strategy. Max felt that Otto could educate him on the business side of filmmaking and was constantly asking questions.

At times, I felt like a carnival handyman fidgeting away on the nuts and bolts of the Ferris wheel while eavesdropping on conversations between the barker and ride operator.

Max and Otto mostly spoke in German, but when crass American expressions seemed suitable, they would switch to English. Otto enjoyed using crude English denigrations like "crooks," "sons of bitches," and "assholes," but he was particularly fond of "bullshit." He would often interject these terms into the middle of a sentence in German, but mostly he would revert to English to savor the context and be clear to anyone who overheard him.

Whatever Otto didn't approve of was "bullshit." He was in the business to make money, and dramatic films rarely made money, so they were "bullshit." German art films were "European bullshit!" He would, of course, only use this reference when talking to Americans, like me.

Since I was not dependent upon a salary, and had none anyway, Max and Otto's conversations regarding how to save money were more a source of amusement than an issue for me. My assistant Carrie and her apprentice Lola were both recent CalArts film graduates with high aspirations for working in the business. They had learned editorial responsibilities and responded to Max's ad in a daily trade mag, anxious to work a paying job on a real movie. Max's policy, however, was to always keep them at least two weeks behind in salary. Since they were scheduled to be paid every two weeks, each paycheck was for work performed a month earlier. When Carrie mentioned this to me, I told Max it had to be corrected.

He scoffed. "They are spoiled. In Europe, it is always done like this."

"Not here." I assured him. "They don't want to be stiffed a month's pay at the end, in case you're running short."

"Ach. This is so bourgeois mediocker. There are thousands who want her job. Americans are so ungrateful." He never said they would be paid.

"We don't see everything the way you do, that is true. Unless they volunteer, people expect to be paid for the work."

Max decided to adopt a devious strategy he had learned while working in Europe. Always stay two weeks behind on pay periods owed and withhold the final two weeks' pay indefinitely. If Max continued to owe technicians money, they were bound to work on his next project to collect what was due, and Max could always remain two weeks ahead. To Max, it was a major victory to collect two weeks of uncompensated labor—a position of strength. When I asked how this strategy meshed with his leftist ideology, I was, of course, dismissed as "bourgeois mediocker."

Max refused to pay Carrie and Lola, feeling he had scored a victory. In response, Carrie quit and took the film home with her, immediately filing a mechanic's lien on Max and the film itself for what was due both to her and Lola.

Furious when he opened an official letter from the county recorder's office, Max's face glowed with a fury I didn't think he was capable of. He never thought these two novices would dare such a bold move.

"This slut will never get her money!" he screamed, ripping up the lien. I asked why he felt she didn't deserve to be paid for the work she had already performed, and he dismissed me like a housefly.

"How am I supposed to finish my film with this bitch? How?"

"Pay her."

"Ach."

He disappeared into the bedroom and consulted with Sylvie. I went for a walk since, without film, there was no work I could do. I figured each day he paid for an editing room without film to cut was costing him more than an assistant, so within a day or two, I would have the film back, with a new assistant, and I did.

CHAPTER 19
THE DAYS OF LIVING CRAZILY

Days at the editing room were long and laborious. The suites were windowless and, in retrospect, grim. Carrie, Lola, and I had bonded and filled the dead zones with exchanges of stories and ideas. I missed them when they left, to be replaced by Susan, somewhat unenthused, inexpensive, and emotionally afloat.

Susan was educated, opinionated, critical, and subversive. She loved conversation, but it often turned negative, Susan being determined to repeatedly emphasize, regarding movies and much more, "Don't listen to me. I don't like anything." Not a popular sentiment with filmmakers.

While I waited to screen each reel, Susan would prepare the assembly at the assistant's table, perched on a nicked gray metal barstool, arms cranking the rewinds at both ends of the bench like a contortionist owl, tediously spinning through 35 mm spools as she eyed the fleeting frames for white grease pencil marks, stopping every few seconds to cut, splice, and resume as if tending an assembly line. As Susan worked, she emanated a touching sadness to me, at times becoming a painful allegory for what we all were in that building: dispensable cogs in the wheel, toiling away in drab, colorless boxed rooms surrounded by walls never touched by the sun, unconscious of its rising and setting as we dutifully labored in cold fluorescence, determined to create meaning beyond our everyday lives, even in the most insignificant terms. Despite her capability, Susan's dry, disengaged persona cemented my dispirited but growing conviction that, as in nearly every company town in America, including Washington, DC, a sizeable portion of LA's entertainment workforce left home every day to perform a job that simply combined the most availability, least resistance, and highest return. Ambitions were left in a bedroom diary, and life became just what the day provided.

A running joke in the film business is the dismissive line, "Don't worry, it's only a movie." The only reason it's considered a joke is because although it is self-mocking, no one subscribes to that belief. As has been shockingly demonstrated by financiers, principals, and even technicians, making movies has at times superseded self-preservation. But movies are still an industry, and we are all cogs in the wheel.

Susan had grown up in Hollywood, and exposure to her jaded view of the world wore quickly. But although she acted like she had been everywhere and done everything, she did know where to find whatever we were looking for, and she introduced me to multiple ethnic eateries I would have taken years to find on my own. I learned much about the city from Susan, including its history.

Susan seemed to carry unfiltered judgments of people as well as movies, which probably included me, but she did kindly invite me to her parents' house one night for dinner. They lived in a privileged, older neighborhood in the flats below the Hollywood Hills, where I was warmly welcomed. While eating, the family explained to me how auto and tire manufacturers had sabotaged rail transit in Los Angeles. I was skeptical at the time, but like my optimism, my skepticism was ultimately defeated by experience.

Apparently, auto and tire lobbies had killed the proposition for streetcars in the 1950s, and there were many suspicions that the battle was ugly—and illegal. Susan's family was emotional and passionate about this and suspicious of my initial skepticism. When I told my hosts that I was the son of a military intelligence officer, my welcome noticeably cooled.

Susan worked hard, if not effectively, and was happy to contribute whatever she could to the effort. She didn't seem to mind not getting paid as much as Carrie and Lola, but she was paid more often, and she smiled when Max explained why she was being shorted.

In retrospect, I believe Susan was one of the first I knew to take antidepressants. She always smiled, even when talking about the most dreaded subjects. She never avoided a subject, but she rarely showed enthusiasm. She seemed hardwired with an automatic disconnect when facing emotional subjects, and indifference came easily to her. She was generous with her knowledge but rarely zealous and appeared to live without compulsion. I often wondered what was inside her heart, for she never gave any indication that it had ever soared or been broken.

Susan introduced me to The Farmer's Market and its village of shops and restaurants, the Watts Towers, San Pedro, Long Beach, and all the neighborhoods that make Los Angeles a metropolis. She quit the job about a month after starting, a pattern that I assume she continued indefinitely. I was skeptical that she would ever identify, much less find, what she was looking for. I hope I was wrong.

Another eager aide, Barry, replaced her. The most ebullient of all my editing assistants, he was young and motivated. Susan called for about a month, asking for her final check, then stopped. I don't know whether she got paid. Barry, as I had been, was more eager to learn than get paid, at least until the price seemed to exceed the quality of education.

Max's interview with the film magazine had been a success back in Germany, so various celebrity mags and television networks contacted Max for an interview. Knowing the value this could have with European investors, Max invited them at various points to come visit, scouted out appropriate private locations for each shoot, then went to Nudie's Western Wear to secure a few costumes.

For an interview, Max would pack a director's chair in the trunk of the El Dorado and drive the visiting crew to a carefully selected, quiet location in the Hills above Lake Hollywood. There, he would unpack the chair and place it in a preselected spot in front of a Mediterranean-style mansion, check the drive behind the gates to be certain no one was approaching, and sit like a despot on a throne. He would then assume a calmly reflective pose while the photographer snapped advertising stills, the Hollywood sign in clear view over Max's shoulder. The audience would, of course, assume the mansion was his own.

While squinting and looking into the distance with impassioned eyes, Max would soulfully express the trying struggle of a German auteur with the pained and heartfelt voice of the misunderstood, fighting to realize his art in the belly of the soul-gorging commercial beast. He would then curl his lips into a smile and turn to the camera, a playful twinkle in his eyes, as if sharing an inside joke.

Max was a very good actor, and he needed no preparation, for he was a true professional. I never saw him give a bad performance when he was selling a product, particularly if the product was him. When the interview was over, Max would fold up the chair, return it to the trunk of the Cadillac, drive the crew to the hotel, then return to our rental house to snack on wurst and cheese.

Between the interviews, Max was becoming more absent from the editing room. Sylvie would occasionally call looking for him, but I assumed he was off with Otto taking meetings to sell the film. I rarely put the pieces of their relationship puzzle together and was caught by surprise one morning when Max suggested that we had been working too hard, and we both needed a day off just to relax and talk. He called Sylvie into the living room and suggested a break for us.

"Sylvie, I think Terry and I should get away for a day and go to the beach."

"You don't want me to come along?"

"No, we need to clear our heads and talk about the film."

"Okay. What time will you be back?"

"This afternoon. You will be okay until then."

She nodded, unsure if that was true. A male director meets a lot of women, particularly through the job, and is in a position to help most of them. Women sometimes take advantage of that with a position of their own, to the point they are able.

Everyone involved in the film business who has any influence, be it a casting director, director, producer, financier, studio executive, or even the multiple assistants to the aforementioned, is in a position to help an actor, even if it's only providing access.

Actors are aware of this, and the most skilled and intelligent of them are able to capitalize on their qualities without giving away too much of themselves. It's about creating the illusion of promise, without the delivery, and sometimes delivery sweetens the deal. This is where the term "casting couch" originated, and far more performers than will admit to it—men, women, and transgender—have taken advantage of the opportunity.

Max would often brag about how many women he had slept with and how easy it was for him as a star in Germany. He said it required no effort at all, and he was bored with most sex he had with the German women. Conventional sex had become "bourgeois mediocker." This is why he had arranged a day at the beach, and I was the foil.

When we started out for Malibu, I noticed Max was heading east on Franklin, and the Pacific coastline is certainly west of Hollywood.

I asked him where we were going, and he said he wanted to pick up someone.

"Who?"

"Oh, the greatest. You will see."

He pulled the Cadillac to the curb. Within moments, an attractive young woman exited a building, climbed into the back of the car, and smiled.

"Hello."

"Wendy, this is Terrell."

"Hello, Wendy."

"Where are we going?" she asked, putting her hand on my arm.

"We're going to the beach. Wouldn't you like that?" Max smiled, looking at her through the rearview mirror.

"Of course, I would like that."

She smiled back at Max in the mirror, exchanging coded messages with winks and grins.

I wished I could look at Max as well because he wasn't responding to my questioning stare at the side of his face. He hadn't implied anything about this, and it would put me in an extremely awkward position with Sylvie.

I looked back at Wendy, who was dark-haired, slender, around thirty, and dressed in a pale-blue suit, cut extremely low at the neckline, revealing a black lace bra. She put her legs up on the seat, revealing stiletto heels. She was staring at me with a smile, but the silence was deafening. I tried to start something, anything.

"Do you work at the school?"

She laughed. "No."

"Are you in the film business?"

"Max, am I in the film business?"

They both laughed. Max was keeping his eyes on the road, hands on the wheel. "Wendy would be the greatest publicist here."

Wendy reached over the seat and gave Max's arm a familiar squeeze. He beamed at her through the rearview mirror and turned on the radio.

I took advantage of the music to keep quiet, as did Wendy, for the drive to Malibu. When we arrived, I opened the back door for Wendy, who scurried into the front seat and closed the door while I unloaded beach chairs and towels from the trunk. Max had not moved.

I stuck my head in the window. "You're not getting out?"

"We're going to be alone. Enjoy yourself. It's a beautiful day, no?"

"When are you coming back?"

"We'll meet you here at two o'clock. Have fun. Better than an editing room!" And they were off. It was shortly after ten a.m.

I walked the beach and jumped in and out of the ocean a few

times, which reminded me how long it had been since I had enjoyed invigorating pleasures as simple as warm sand, fresh air, and salt water. I spent the hours hiking the beach, diving in the waves, sitting on a bench eating a hot dog. I had not enjoyed a day to myself without working in quite a long time. But I would still rather be at the editing room. This just meant another day's delay before the film was completed.

At two o'clock, I walked back to the parking area where Max and Wendy were waiting. The car smelled of shower gel.

"Did you have a nice swim?"

"Yes, I did, thanks."

"We have to hurry so Wendy can pick up her kids."

I got into the back seat, and we drove back to town with just radio accompaniment. Max and Wendy glanced at each other, smiled, and winked. I couldn't see their hands, thankfully, and went into my own reverie while looking out the window.

As soon as Wendy was out of the car, I let Max know that this couldn't happen again. "Sylvie is my friend. I can't do this to her. Don't ever put me in this position again. You can't. All right?"

"What position?"

"Supporting a lie. Your lie. You owe her better than this."

"Owe her? What kind of bullshit is this? She owes me."

"You're her husband. You at least owe her loyalty. Besides, she supports you!"

"What are you talking about? I give more than anyone."

"She pays the bills."

"Ach. That is so American of you. What I give is far more important than money. This is all you Americans can think about. Don't bother me with this, please."

"Then don't ask me to lie for you. You'll do what you want, but don't make me a part of it."

"I'm disappointed in you. You just want to live like a bourgeois mediocker."

"Whatever that is."

"You have so much to learn."

"That's why I'm here."

When we arrived back at the house, Sylvie met us with an enthusiastic hug. "Did you all have a good time? How was the beach?"

Max was beaming. "It was the greatest! We had such a good talk."

"Did it give you plenty of ideas?" Sylvie asked as I retreated to the back of the house, leaving Max to come up with his own responses.

"The ocean is so nice. You should go." Max disappeared to the bedroom for a nap, so Sylvie tracked me down in my own room to volley questions I had no answer for.

"Did Max go in the water?"

"Not really."

"Did you stay in very long?"

"Yes."

"Was the beach crowded? What type of people were there on a Monday?"

I answered her questions the best I could, avoiding eye contact when it felt like a lie. It was painful. She had to know.

"I need to do some work now."

"Oh. Okay."

For some reason, that line always seemed to create space when I needed it, most likely because that was the reason I was there.

Max didn't ask me to alibi for him again, but he would stop by the editing room after his afternoon excursions with detailed descriptions of his sexual adventures. His life began to change because, as it has happened to so many in so many levels of power, Max was becoming obsessed with something more powerful than work.

The morning after our Malibu trip, Max and I were preparing to leave for the editing room when Sylvie approached with a quivering lower lip.

"Sylvie, what's wrong?"

"I was thinking. You know, you two went to the beach yesterday and had so much fun. I was thinking that maybe I need a day at the beach to have fun myself."

"Sweet thing, I can't do that. I have to work today. Can you go without me?"

"Why don't Terry and I go to the beach? You and he went yesterday. We can go to the same place! I deserve some fun, don't I?"

"Yes, my darling, of course you do. That's a terrific idea. You two go to the beach today," he said, welcoming another opportunity to confer with his "publicist."

Sylvie, meanwhile, pulled together beach towels and the same chairs I had loaded into the car the previous day. "This will be so much fun! Thank you, doll!" She hugged and kissed Max, his eyes beaming over the back of her shoulder.

"Yes, it will. I want you to have a great time!"

Again, I was on my way to Malibu, hoping I wouldn't be asked too many questions about the previous day's excursion. Sylvie liked to talk, and most of the drive was filled with her spontaneous observations about everything from the efficacy of tax laws and dog licenses to the divine reasoning behind sweating palms. Why would God make a human's palms sweat when frightened? What if we lost our grip and fell from a tree?

When we arrived at the same parking lot in Malibu where I had been the previous day, I again started to unload the beach gear while Sylvie remained in the car.

Noticing that she didn't appear to be planning to leave the driver's seat, I walked to her door and eyed her suspiciously, figuring the odds couldn't have predicted this. "What are you doing?"

"Do you mind hanging out by yourself for a few hours?"

"Because you need a day at the beach to have some fun?"

"I'm going to meet William. Sorry, but you can't say a word about this to Max. It's okay, right?"

"Come on."

William was the handsome son of a movie star and a somewhat successful actor himself, though not as big a star as his father had been. Sylvie and William would be costarring in the next film that she, Max, and Otto were planning, which was a passionate thriller. William and Sylvie had been reading lines and rehearsing love scenes, and as often happens in rehearsals, reality blurred, and the characters came to life.

For a committed actor, when the scene is physical and the idea is to sell an emotional connection, it's often difficult to distinguish between playing in love and being in love. The two would have nude love scenes in the film, and it's asking a lot of two actors to make it convincing if they've never been there before.

So, here we were.

"I'll be back at two o'clock." Sylvie had a habit of smiling broadly, no matter the emotions. She would bob her eyebrows for emphasis, as if exaggerating the fact that we were having fun. "Okay?"

So, one more day of jumping in the waves, walking on the sand, enjoying a hot dog. The day was identical to the previous one, a characteristic of Los Angeles that ultimately begins to wear on one's psyche. For some reason, weather, any weather, can become an inspiration. The lack of it makes one feel anxious without anxiety. The need to see a cloud, feel the rain, or breathe deeply after a thunderstorm. Feel the bite of an autumnal breeze, inhale the fragrance of a late spring day, hear the crunch of boots in wet snow. These experiences enrich your soul, and sand is no substitute.

This wasn't how I envisioned my film education. I anticipated an experience where I could learn in a creative environment where, unlike what I was accustomed to, I could be surrounded by my peers, like students vying to make the grade. I had pretty much made the turn in my life when I closed up shop and moved to California. If it didn't work out, I could always go back and restart my company, but that is rarely a realistic option for anyone.

Each day, I learned more about making feature films, and to learn was exciting. Like how to differentiate between decisions made from necessity and those for personal taste. That part of the education was crucial, but finding the right instructor was hard. Max was good in the sense that he was committed to making films, but I questioned his skill as a filmmaker.

I wanted to work with experienced directors who I felt more comfortable with, and I ultimately did, but my time with Max and Sylvie was extremely important to me on many levels. Not only did I learn the fundamentals of making films, but I was exposed to so much that I never would have been otherwise, like the fact that I was sitting on a beach for the second day in a row as a foil for both members of a married couple who were cheating on each other. I was learning little about filmmaking but a lot about the human condition.

When Sylvie's car pulled up, I loaded the gear into the back and shook my head when climbing into the passenger's seat. I said, "You can't drag me into this, Sylvie. I don't want to lie for you."

"You don't understand. Max is always too tired for me. I have needs like anybody else!"

"Don't drag me into the middle of it."

"Okay, okay."

When we arrived home, Max welcomed us with a satisfied grin, having just returned from an afternoon with Wendy. Sylvie assured him we had enjoyed ourselves at the beach. I avoided Max's winks over her shoulder and retired to the bedroom.

"We should get to work early tomorrow," I said, with distant hope.

"Of course," Max cheerily replied. "We are well rested!"

CHAPTER 20
LOOKING FOR THE RING

We were closing in on the first cut of the film, and Max was excited to see where we stood for the first screening on the Kem. I had completed my cut in nine reels and flew back to Washington for a break. After I left, Max asked Barry, my assistant, to assemble all the reels so Max could watch the film from the beginning, which I had not even done.

My second day home, Max called from LA, sounding giddy enough to be thrilled, but he wasn't.

"Fifty-six minutes!"

"What?"

"That's how long the film is! Fifty-six minutes! Can you imagine?"

"What are you going to do?"

"What am I going to do? What are *we* going to do? You have to get back here!"

"What do you want me to do?"

"The film cannot be fifty-six minutes. We have to make it eighty minutes, at least. The very least!"

"I can't pad twenty-four minutes of screen time. You'll have to shoot some more."

"Shoot what? What can we shoot? This is crazy."

"I'll come back and we'll talk about it."

"When? Tomorrow?"

"In a few days."

These phone calls persisted daily, until I agreed to return. When I arrived, Max showed me the cut and agreed that we couldn't put film back; we had to find something new.

Max met with Otto, and they decided that the film would be easier to sell if they cast a name known around the world to play a small part, one which could be shot in a day, with at least twenty-four minutes' worth of usable footage. I was dubious as to whether they could shoot that much in one day, but Max and Sylvie conferred with the director of photography, who had helped them write the script, and they came up with several new scenes. The reshoot was scheduled for a total of four days.

Sylvie's trust management put a cap on her access, so to finance the additional shooting, new investors were found by promising roles to either those who carried their own acting dreams or a love interest with visions of a credit on the big screen.

We wrote scenes for the performers but neglected to buy film for the camera. When the investor or paramour arrived, we would take them to a location where the camera and lights were set up. Hair and makeup stylists would be summoned from their trailers to perform their duties, Max would offer some superficial direction, and the characters would take their places.

The camera assistants had charged the camera battery enough so the red light would appear next to the lens, visible to the talent, and the gears in the camera body would turn. The cameraman would huddle over the eyepiece, Max would yell for camera and sound, the recordist would confirm "rolling," the director of photography would turn on the camera and yell "speed," the assistant would clap the slate, complete with a bogus scene number, and Max would begin with "Action!"

While the gears turned in the empty camera magazines, Max

would sit in the director's chair, watching the boom operator following the actors around the set with the mic hanging from the pole, offering performance notes along the way.

"More, Evan. Louder. That's it. You've got it. This is so great!"

"Yes, Cheri. That is perfect. You are a star!"

Every take would, of course, be spot-on. Occasionally, the investor would ask for another take and be given it. It was painful for the crew, knowing it was a façade, but at the end of the day, checks were written, and the scenes had been financed.

Several of the original actors flew out and stayed in two cheaper motels on a seedy stretch of Sunset Boulevard, with soliciting prostitutes parading in front. An aging actor with a famous name was chosen to play a psychiatrist who would interview patients in his home. Sylvie would become a patient of his, since she was tormented by this pesky mirror piece, and these sessions, along with family scenes with the original actors, would be interspersed throughout the film for . . . about twenty-four minutes. We shot small scenes of different family members and home scenes with expositional dialogue until we felt we had enough to cover the missing time.

This was all part of my education. How to stretch a story to fit a contractual window for theater chains to display so many screenings per day. Five minutes I could understand, but twenty-four? Everyone apparently thought the script was long enough, close to one hundred pages, but it obviously wasn't, and the acting certainly didn't help stretch it—since wooden acting had been the cause for so much of the film being cut in the first place. What happens in a story should come naturally, and if the story is padded, wouldn't an audience notice and leave? I understood ebbs and flows, but too many ebbs must spell disaster, no? All part of the education; every day was a learning experience.

We added the twenty-four minutes, including therapy sessions and dinner discussions, with space for ominous music throughout, until we had achieved a running time of eighty minutes. Our mission was accomplished. Now we needed sound, music, prints, and a distributor to pay for it all.

I once heard a studio executive excitedly describe the rough cut of a film he had just screened as "this isn't maybe a movie. This *is* a movie." The film turned out to be a critical and financial disaster.

Some movies are destined to be maybes.

We met with potential composers, finally settling on Jake, a genially caffeinated, robust son of an Oscar-winning composer. Jake was enthusiastically young and driven, with a harrowing nicotine addiction and unsettling attachment to diet colas and synthesized music. Cheerful but antisocial, he worked alone in his home studio for days, sometimes weeks, only breaking to eat, sleep, and occasionally shower.

I would visit weekly, using the side entrance behind the kitchen, to be hit with a knee-quivering stench emanating from the growing but already insurmountable mountain of drained soda cans filled with cigarette butts and candy wrappers, covering every table and speaker in the room. Behind this landscape, ripe from the body flow produced by days of intensely uninterrupted concentration, Jake would be spread on his piano bench, anxiously gripping his synthesizer keyboard like a cat scoping a ball of string.

"Hey, how's it goin'?" he barked without exception. "Wait'll you hear what I got. You're gonna love it!"

"I can't wait," I always replied, true at the time.

Jake would play his inspiration, and sometimes it was disappointing, but there were moments when it was not. This is, I have learned, a common situation for any two people involved in a creative process. Disappointment follows disappointment. Sometimes it's even hard to tell whether it is a disappointment, but there are inspired moments when it is clearly not, and those are the moments we live for.

"What do you think?" He always called and asked me to listen to something before he played it for Max, and I obliged; most often, it would fall short of excitement.

"I think we should work on it a bit." This was the most common exchange we had at the beginning of our sessions. We would do that, sometimes coming up with music or sounds that felt inspired. Jake had a deft touch for accentuating frightening moments. He provided excellent "zings" and swells. It was a pleasure to host him for spotting sessions, where he would bring a plastic ring full of diet sodas and we would run through the film together, deciding precisely where music was warranted, optional, or forbidden.

On the sound stage, I walked the foleys for the finished cut and pored through hours of different ambient noises and sound effects to create tracks for the mix. Today, this work is done by a team of sound and SFX editors and assembled by their assistants. For our film, it was just Barry and me, working tirelessly to finish within our projected completion date to make the film available for a fall release, coinciding with a new school year, which is when horror films flourish.

Max dropped me at the editing facility every morning, and for months, I rarely took a day off. I had nowhere to go if I did—and no way to get there. I wasn't adventurous enough to take the bus to Santa Monica or elsewhere, and I had spent enough time alone on the beach. Regardless, I would rather work. Finishing the movie on time became a mission of prime importance, probably because I was being paid nothing to do so. The sooner I finished, the quicker I could move on.

I was driven by a compulsion I can neither identify nor justify. It wasn't *my* film, but it became my film, my goal, my mission . . . to complete it as quickly and as solidly as I could, to make it as good as possible. I became a soldier in an unjustifiable war, facing overwhelming odds against victory, knowing there was an end in sight.

When I look back, I try to recapture whatever it was that compelled me to work so long and hard on something I considered unworthy, in often unpleasant and cramped conditions, with no financial compensation. Perhaps I believed that my participation might actually be worth something if the film was successful, but I don't think that was the case. After the time I spent in a dense, emotional cloud, having found my direction was a gift, and it seemed a simple truth to me that hard work becomes its own validation.

I had no car, income, or friends nearby. I was a guest in a house with a married couple, who I could have called employers if I was being paid, but since I was only being housed and fed, indentured servant (but without a clothing allowance) could have been an accurate description. I had no social life, creating nothing for myself other than the knowledge of how to put a movie together. It was terribly lonely, but I had a purpose.

I often saw the sun rise on the intersection of Highland and Santa Monica during that stretch. I would step outside at daybreak to watch the leftover characters shuffle along the stained boulevard, clearing my head for the return to what we called "the brig." I can't even remember if I smoked cigarettes at the time, but it would have suited.

During that period, Tippi Hedren and her young daughter Melanie Griffith would often arrive just after dawn and disappear into the rear sound stage on the first floor. Tippi had starred in Alfred Hitchcock's *The Birds* and *Marnie*, but her career had slowed since. She and Melanie were playing roles in *Roar*, a notoriously dangerous movie being directed by Hedren's husband, Noel Marshall. Nearly ten years in the making, the film was the story of a naturalist living on a nature preserve in Africa but was being shot on the animal rescue ranch where the family lived, northeast of Los Angeles in the community of Acton. The compound was home to, in addition to the Marshall family, over 150 lions, tigers, cheetahs, and jaguars.

Because of the seventy injuries suffered by cast and crew members, *Roar* became the most scandalous movie of its time. Since my arrival in Hollywood, starting with tales from Gary while delivering Kems in his Porsche, I had heard numerous stories of the panic, danger, desperation, and passion on the set of this film.

The director of photography, Jan de Bont, was scalped by a lion. Melanie Griffith was mauled and scalped, requiring facial reconstruction surgery. Tippi Hedren broke her leg, was severely bitten in the neck and head, and was seriously injured after being thrown from an elephant.

As were many of the camera crew and lighting technicians, the assistant director was injured and treated at the hospital so many times that he eventually refused to return to the set. A wound administered by a lion, tiger, cheetah, or jaguar does not heal quickly and very often leads to infection. The director, Noel Marshall, suffered so many deep injuries from animal bites and claws that he developed gangrene.

Roar was a topic of discussion at most every lunch counter and supply house in Hollywood. Every time a crew member was attacked, there was an accident on set, or equipment failed or was damaged, everyone in town knew about it the next day. To complicate matters, the financiers ultimately pulled out, and the family was forced to sell everything to try to finish the movie on their own. This is when the Marshall family entered our sphere at Santa Monica and Highland, where postproduction facilities would be offered to a struggling low-budget production in exchange for a percentage of the film.

Despite the injuries, despair of lost time, property, and bank accounts, and painful trials of a clear creative vision seized by a parade of financiers who proceeded to obscure that vision with a rogue blender of ideas for endless reshoots and edits, the ordeal concluded with no American distribution, and the marriage ended. As a final cruel twist, in 2015, the film was finally picked up by Alamo Drafthouse as a reclamation project, more than thirty years later, and released in just six theaters nationwide.

When I first saw Hedren and Griffith arrive in their Mercedes, they were both in bandages, and Hedren walked with a cane. They came in dutifully to record their ADR and supervise the editing, but the toll of the film on their health, morale, and bank account was visible in the time it took the women to move from their car to the stage door. Every step was a painful journey. Those steps could be emblematic of filmmaking at its most trying. *It's only a movie.*

CHAPTER 21
ASSES IN DECEITS

Otto lived in a sprawling home in the Malibu hills away from the beach, with a fenced pool and patio neatly surrounded by desert scrub. He liked to hold poolside meetings at his home because he felt that potential European clients, particularly northern Europeans, would be impressed by his poolside living, surrounded by cactus and agave, just minutes from the Pacific Ocean.

It was a long drive to Otto's house, nearly in Ventura County, a good twenty miles north of Los Angeles, and Otto only ventured south when he had other motives than to talk business with one client. In our case, it was to watch scenes of the film or have dinner with young actors in order to accurately assess their "star potential."

According to Max, Otto held business meetings at his home not only because he considered his living arrangements impressive to European clients, but he felt it established his notch in the food chain by making them travel the distance to see him. Otto never offered to meet halfway. Maybe a quarter, but he would travel only far enough not to confuse who held the leverage.

I eventually discovered that this method of business was accepted and practiced by more studio executives, agents, and business affairs representatives than I could possibly have imagined. By the time most creative talents amassed this kind of leverage, they had little need for it.

I am sure this gamesmanship holds true in many positions of power. It was something I had seen while working on Capitol Hill, but always in a political context. I never fully conceptualized it until I came to Hollywood because the hierarchies of power were so clearly defined in politics. In Washington, those holding powerful positions were elected or appointed. In Hollywood, anyone can claim whatever title he or she desires, and if some money is spent, actually perform the job, regardless of qualifications, training, experience, or lack of such. I don't imagine there is any other business in the world, with such a high investment at stake, that can claim this to be true.

Someone can be sitting in a theater watching a movie, and if this person decides to become a film producer, the perception can conceivably become reality within days after returning home. First, launch a website as a production company; then find one of thousands of screenplays floating about Hollywood available for option, often free. Option the script, hire a publicist to promote the story, then seduce the writer with enthusiasm for the project. Next, inform the trade magazines that you are casting a film, offer a young, social-media-savvy director fresh out of AFI or USC a guild minimum salary once the film is financed, and then start fielding calls from agents trying to place their clients. Collect several of these and use the actors you assemble to lure a real producer who is available to help raise money; then feel your way by hiring young, talented people who can make creative choices. You are now a film producer.

Over the years, I have known numerous "producers" with no background or experience in screen production, writing, or even analysis but with large reserves of earned, inherited, or borrowed money and connections that they use as collateral to raise enough funds to open a production company. Within a short period of time, once they have produced a film, regardless of the quality, they have become recognized producers. Other than elected positions such as members of Congress, not many job titles can be so easily acquired with no training or experience. The only requirements to give it a go are substantial amounts of money, ego, and ambition.

Aside from determining the distance of travel to a meeting, the leverage could be exercised by determining who picks up the check (the player with the upper hand always determines who pays), what time every meeting is to take place and where, and seating arrangements. The leveraged hand will always make an effort to sit in a higher position, whether it's elevation or slant, with the light at his or her back, forcing the lower hand to squint while trying to focus. Unattractive as well as uncomfortable. A clear advantage for the upper hand.

When we arrived at his house for a meeting, Otto would greet us in his swimming trunks and cabana shirt. We sat on flowered vinyl pillows promoting tourist destinations in California and the Pacific while a Latina housekeeper set cold German beers and frosted glasses on the circular poolside table. Otto would grab a chair on the upper tier of the patio, which felt like a set with a desert backdrop. As visitors, we were seated slightly downhill, facing up at the thorny brush on the hillside.

Otto sat with his bare feet propped on the table, revealing pink and soft soles, as if they had never touched the ground. His toes and fingers were perfectly manicured, like rubber models in the window of a nail shop. He undoubtedly had them attended to weekly, and Otto revealed to us that, though he enjoyed sitting by the pool, he never went into the water because he hated the thought of chlorine on his skin. Resting on the corrugated plastic, his position was high enough to ensure that while talking, we were forced to stare at the bottom of his feet, which was no more appealing than it sounds.

While facing Otto's pink soles and wiggling toes, we would listen to his philosophy and maxims of filmmaking. Most were forgettable, but the one line I remember very clearly from a poolside lecture was one I was hearing for the first time but have since heard hundreds of times, as I am sure Otto heard it from every one of his mentors. The most important aspect in the process of making a film is to realize there is only one job, and everyone shares it.

"Forget about making a goot film. European bullshit! Nobody vants dat. Vut dey vant is asses in deceits."

He paused a moment. We looked at each other, trying to decide whether Otto was being funny or serious, for, with his strong German accent, it was often hard to tell. He nodded again. "Asses in deceits!"

"That is a great expression, Otto," Max offered, with far less affectation. "And, of course, it is so true!"

Otto and Max would raise their pilseners and debate strategy to put "asses in the seats." Sylvie would occasionally interject with her own entertaining view of the world, and I would mostly stay quiet, trying to be, in the words of Elvis Costello, more amused than disgusted.

Several horror films were extremely profitable in the mid to late 1970s, and 1980 was the perfect time to enter the marketplace. Wes Craven's *The Last House on the Left* and *The Hills Have Eyes*, as well as John Carpenter's famously successful *Halloween*, had initiated the wave. Genre movies, particularly horror films, were starting to be produced by major studios.

New distributors had opened offices and were looking for small, independent films with the potential to crack the box office. Otto arranged screenings for several of these distributors, and soon we had several offers for domestic distribution. The decision was which to accept.

When I had arrived in California, while having lunch in a diner, Max had agreed that in lieu of a salary for my services, he would offer me a producer's credit as well as 8 percent of his receipts from the film. As an eyewitness to Max's behavior during the shoot, I was already aware of his extraordinary ability to wiggle, and I realized if I didn't exit that diner with some proof of our agreement, it would never exist.

Just as I had done with Keith Jarrett, I swept the crumbs off the formica tabletop, pulled a napkin from the dispenser, pulled out a pen from my pocket, and hastily wrote out an agreement. Our food had not been delivered, so Max had no escape and no excuse, so he signed the napkin.

I wasn't completely ignorant of how the business operated. I had heard the jokes about what "net points" in a film were worth after "deductions" (nothing), but nonetheless, I folded the napkin and put it in my pocket, in the small chance that at some future date, it just might serve a more valuable purpose than clearing food waste.

With Otto's help, Max sold the worldwide rights to a distributor, who told him, "The first check is in the mail." I was keenly aware of what time the letter carrier passed the house each day, so when the check arrived, I was happy to greet the carrier in front of the house and happier still to deliver the envelope to Max in person. Plausible deniability no longer an option, Max opened the letter containing a cashier's check for $40,00—his first payment—from which I immediately claimed my 8 percent.

I rode to the bank with Max so he could deposit the $40,000 and asked him to write me a check for $3,200 that I could cash immediately. That was the first—and last—money I received from the film.

One of the hardest things for a filmmaker to do is watch a completed print for the very first time. Decisions have been made and the consequences remain. Once the lights go down, there is no stopping for trims and embellishments. It's over—and time for judgment.

Aside from the obvious financial gamble, self-esteem is at stake and many choices left to be reconsidered. The experience is nerve-racking and painful, leading to a sleepless and stressful night that rarely ends well, regardless of the quality of the film.

But the film was finished, and our journey at an impasse. I realized that, according to the strategy outlined to him by Otto, Max would use his debt to me to keep me coming around. Whenever I did, he would enthusiastically talk about "our next film."

But, in my mind, I had moved on. I had learned what I could from our experience, and the connections I was being offered would not lead to the type of films I wanted to make. In some respects, particularly for his time, Max was quite unique in his approach to filmmaking. He adopted what he saw as a European, an "anarchic" style, as he described it, meaning spending very little on production value (sets, locations, and costumes), dispensing with rehearsal, employing a minimal crew, and spontaneously rewriting scenes on the spot and shooting them in quickly accessible locations. All this would be accomplished in as little time as possible with a static camera and actors.

While in New York, Max knew it was appropriate for aspiring filmmakers to learn every aspect of the process, so all those in the business, whether they made documentaries, porn, commercials, industrials, or the smattering of features, were called "filmmakers."

In 1980 Hollywood, filmmaking was an industry with hundreds of job titles. "Filmmaker" wasn't one of them. Producer, director, assistant director, second and third assistant director, production coordinator, production assistant, lead man, rigger, costumer, makeup artist, writer, editor, assistant editor, camera operator, camera loader, focus puller, gaffer, grip, dolly grip, key grip, best boy, transportation captain, teamster, location scout, color timer, negative cutter—these, and so many more, were all job titles recognized by everyone who worked in Hollywood, and each job carried its own union rules. Today, multiple visual effects and postproduction positions have been added.

The film industry was very scant in New York, except for pornography, which moved to the San Fernando Valley in the 1980s, and horror, which also left with Wes Craven around the same time. Filmmaking was far more structured in Hollywood than it was in Europe, and after an initial resistance, Max embraced it. I realized that for me to do so, I had to focus on one job, and only one of those jobs required aptitude in all of them.

I had no more to learn from Max. I needed to seek my own work as a director. I wanted to commit myself to my chosen profession—and my own approach to it.

When I went to tell Max of my decision, he complicated matters by offering to pay me a considerable weekly salary to cut his next film, in a nicer facility with a larger cutting room, with additional compensation as a credited producer. The film had already been financed, and he wanted to start shooting immediately. I didn't yet know how to say no to a film job with creative responsibility, and if I had never learned how to do that, I would arguably have a different set of regrets than those I carry.

Max had learned to dismiss any expectation of fairness as "bourgeois mediocker," and when I initially refused his offer to work on his next film, he surprised me by doing the unimaginable. Instead of accusing me of being "mediocker," he nodded silently, thought a moment, and in a shocking gesture, increased the offer.

This was unprecedented for Max, and I was so dumbfounded, I couldn't respond. I now needed the money, I had the experience to ease the process, and I was at an age where time spent on location with a crew, though exhausting, is like time spent at summer camp. It was fun, and I could bank what I made since per diem covered most personal expenses while on location.

I had no desire to continue to work on Max's films, but there was one truth I just couldn't ignore: I owned a percentage of the last film. If I stopped working with him, it was guaranteed that I would never see a penny. If I was around, I would at least know when money came in, and I could stake my claim.

That is when the realization hit me. Though I would have been pained to admit it, Max's philosophy worked. I had stepped into the trap, and for fear of losing what I was owed, I refused to step out. *The risk of losing what I had already earned but not yet been paid.* It is a trap that, without a court order, and most often with, is impossible to escape. Max had won.

I went back to see Max and agreed to work on the film. Max suggested we immediately leave for northern Arizona. He was very excited about his new inspiration; he had chosen a location, written a script with Sylvie and a young American assistant he had found, and wanted to talk about the story.

CHAPTER 22
BECAUSE IT IS

Germans tend to be fascinated by the American West, and Max was no exception. He loved the idea of shooting among the cactus and desert growth that he marveled at as a child watching American movies.

While flying to Los Angeles from a fundraising trip in New York, Max read a feature article in the airline magazine about the quirky history of the famed London Bridge. He learned that in 1964, the 133-year-old structure was determined to be sinking into the muddy bottom of the River Thames. To avoid demolishing the storied antique, the city of London had put the bridge up for auction, hoping some wealthy eccentric might find the relic a "fun" collectable.

When Max McCulloch, the notoriously flamboyant Missouri-born chainsaw magnate, got wind of the auction, he had a wild inspiration. McCulloch would develop a town filled with English pomp and ceremony in the middle of the Arizona desert and invite tourists around the world to experience what they couldn't anywhere else. The opportunity to enjoy afternoon tea and crumpets in a quaint English garden, catered to by costumed servers while guests strolled through the village, sporting Justin riding boots and Stetson ten-gallon hats. All in view of the famous London Bridge, spanning a cactus-lined desert waterway.

With a bid of $2.46 million, McCulloch purchased the bridge in 1967, spending an additional seven million to disassemble it brick by brick, number each individual stone, and have each brick stored and shipped through the Panama Canal to be unloaded in Long Beach, CA. There, the bricks were packed and trucked from Long Beach to the Arizona side of the Colorado River, where McCulloch had founded a town on the shores of a recreational lake, created by the Parker Dam.

McCulloch hired engineers to dredge an inlet leading away from the lake. After the runoff filled the inlet, McCulloch imported European city planners to design a British-themed community with shops, pubs, and condominiums on the lakefront, all with an unobstructed view.

Before the bridge could be reassembled over the water, engineers were required to match the portion of water under the bridge to the River Thames. A team dredged the extra yardage to accommodate the span of the bridge, the numbered bricks were reassembled from shore to shore over the inlet, and the London Bridge had been moved to Arizona.

The work was completed in 1971, and the town of Lake Havasu, Arizona, founded by Robert McCulloch, with an English Village featuring residential condos, pubs, and gift shops with costumed hosts and hostesses, was open for business.

By 1979, the town's population had risen from 400 in 1971 to over 10,000, and annual tourism was estimated by the Chamber of Commerce to be over two million visitors per year.

As a European who was fascinated with the American West, Max loved the idea of combining old Europe with the new frontier. His idea was to tell the story of Olivia, an English girl who grows up alongside the River Thames in the shadow of the London Bridge, listening to footsteps and foghorns at night, though the source of those steps and horns would be questionable on the Thames.

One night, six-year-old Olivia witnesses her mother being brutally beaten to death by an American soldier, somehow stationed in London in the 1960s. Olivia is traumatized, and as a method of revenge (unclear how), she emerges into womanhood as a prostitute, walking the same streets under the London Bridge.

When the bridge is moved, Olivia "follows" it to Arizona, where she has a change of heart as well as profession, deciding to sell English Village condos on Lake Havasu.

The notion of "following" a bridge was something Max could understand himself, but not a concept easily explained to the rest of us. The idea of applying for a green card with the explanation being that one is compelled to "follow" a bridge across the Atlantic like a dependent child, was amusing to many, but when questioned about this logic, Max would, of course, dismiss his interrogator as "bourgeois mediocker."

It is the movies, and movies don't need to be explained, Max would point out when I would confront him over story logic. "It is because it is; that is enough" was his thinking, and whoever could not understand was simply bourgeois mediocker.

We shot the movie in Lake Havasu in the fall and winter, and none of us realized how unforgiving the desert can be at night. I had always envisioned Arizona as dirt and saguaro cactus baking in temperatures over 100 degrees. Perhaps this was true in July, but after sunset in November, the cold was numbing. All of us from the East were completely unprepared for the frigid desert nights.

Generally, the crew found it difficult to process the notion of someone dismantling a bridge, a sinking bridge at that, brick by brick, to move it halfway around the world. It has never been published what McCulloch actually spent to do this, but it has to be one of the most expensive follies ever. We felt as if we had been transported into an imaginary theme park in the middle of nowhere, with costumed guides refusing to let on it was all fake.

We had an endless supply of willing free extras in the form of tourists who loved the idea of appearing in a movie. Maintaining continuity with volunteers who were unaware of the impending boredom of waiting for setup changes became a problem, but Max's philosophy was that most audiences would never notice, and he was certainly right with this film.

The setting gave the movie a bizarre atmosphere and offered a dose of macabre credibility, but in the end, the obstacles were too great to overcome. Like its predecessor, the finished picture was far more amusing than scary, and it was emotionally flat. Not a good start for a tragic love story.

Not long into the shoot, I realized I had made the wrong choice in taking the job because it had become just that, and a job is not what I was looking for. I didn't believe in the value of what we were doing, found that I wasn't prepared to work for a salary, and was extremely anxious to pave my own way, regardless of the outcome. It soon became apparent that most everyone involved would exchange any part of the experience for the opportunity to work on something that was clearly a worthwhile effort. Everyone had read the script, and even though it is true that most people, including those who work in movies, don't know how to recognize a good script in terms of the story structure, conciseness, language, and character depth because each specialist mostly focuses on a particular aspect and ignores the rest, everyone seemed to recognize how bad this script was.

But like so many on the fringes of the business, we all hoped there might just be something eccentric enough, strange enough, incomprehensible, ethereal, or just plain "different" about this picture, that, with some otherworldly aid, it could stand on its own. When filmmakers wrap a picture, nobody knows how successful it will be; no matter who the director or stars are, there is no guarantee for anything. So many legendary films were assumed to be flops when they were wrapped or released and, often, lambasted by critics. Sydney Pollack's *Out of Africa* is one example. It opened in 1986 to a tepid critical reception yet went on to win seven Oscars, including for Best Picture. *The Wizard of Oz* was famously ignored by audiences and critics when it opened, yet once the magic took hold, it became a classic. That's why filmmakers always maintain hope, no matter the circumstances.

In the meantime, I utilized the skills I had learned from the first experience, and the process was far easier and quicker this time, and I was sure to be paid each week. But I couldn't wait for it to end and liberate me. I knew instinctively the film would never see the light of day, no matter how much I wanted it to, so I made plans for myself when the film ended. I submitted the final cut, told Max I was moving on, and went back east to marry Pam in Rhode Island. Pam quit her job in Washington and drove west to join me in Los Angeles. We sublet an apartment in the famed Montecito on Franklin Avenue, got California drivers licenses as everyone here must, and became official Hollywood residents.

I only saw Max one more time, which was to collect my final check, and it was a fitting end to the relationship.

CHAPTER 23
THE MUGGING

Sylvie appeared to be done financing films, so Max followed the example set by his German New Wave counterparts and began selling distribution rights to different territories and using the advances he received to not only finance the film he was making but also his lifestyle. He learned how to do this both from successful German directors cajoling money out of private investors and Otto's methods of supporting a comfortable life in the Malibu hills by preselling distribution rights to foreign territories. Using both these methods, Max could raise $300,000 to $500,000 to produce a film, pocketing half and financing the film with the rest.

Max opened an office in the Sunset Gower studios, the old Columbia Pictures lot that had been refurbished as an independent studio with offices, sound stages, and editing suites for rent. I finished the Arizona bridge movie in one of those suites, and when I returned from my trip east to get married, Max had incorporated and opened an office in the main building in which to hold meetings with potential employees and investors.

When I arrived back in LA, I called Max's office to make an appointment to come collect my final week's paycheck. Having learned most of Max's evasion methods, I knew that physical presence with a refusal to leave until paid actually worked. Max was a cunning man, but he was slight, unimposing, and easily cowed.

I expected to be the only one there, but I was greeted by a waiting room full of people—a few actors looking for parts, but mostly potential investors and distributors from around the globe, all waiting to see Max.

The receptionist was on the phone when I entered. Spotting me, she waved me over to her desk.

"He wants to talk to you."

"Who?"

She handed me the receiver, and Max was already talking by the time I held it to my ear. "You have to come get me right away. It is life and death here. Please!"

"What do you mean, life and death? Where are you?"

"I'm at McDonalds on Ventura Boulevard in Sherman Oaks. Come get me right away. I'm in danger! Please!" He hung up. I looked at the receptionist, who shrugged, clueless as I was. I handed her the phone and left a waiting room filled with frustrated people, some who had been there all morning.

When I arrived at the designated McDonald's in the Valley, I pulled into the parking lot. As soon as I stopped, the door opened, and Max suddenly appeared in the passenger seat. He was naked save for a pair of white jockey briefs, his hair was sticking straight up in all directions, and his chest, back, and arms were covered with bloody scratches.

His eyes were wild and frightened, darting in all directions. "Go, please go. Get out of here, quick!" he pleaded. I started to drive back to Sunset Gower, and he explained why he was hiding in the McDonald's parking lot in his underwear.

Apparently, Wendy, our beach companion, lived in an apartment building just down the street. For the past few months, Max had been visiting her regularly for sadomasochism and bondage sessions. This morning's frolic was supposed to end in time for Max to keep his appointments at the office, but Wendy had other plans.

When Max was naked and handcuffed to the massage table where

Wendy would tease and pleasure him, she suddenly got rougher than usual and began drawing blood with her nails. When he asked her to stop, she pulled a pistol from a drawer and held it to his head. She threatened that since he hadn't come through with his promise to divorce Sylvie and marry her, she was going to kill him. He begged for his life, but she told him she was finished listening to his promises. If she couldn't have him, no one would. She would shoot him, then shoot herself.

At that point, Max told me, the doorbell rang. A FedEx package Wendy was waiting for had arrived. Figuring she could delay her murder-suicide until after she retrieved her new cosmetics, she left the room to answer the door.

While Wendy was at the door, Max was able to reach the key to the handcuffs on a nearby table and free himself. Unfortunately, his clothes, wallet, and car keys were in the living room with Wendy, and the love-play sessions were held in a back room off the kitchen by a window leading to the outdoor walkway. Only Max's underwear was available, lying on the floor by the table.

Max pulled on his jockeys, climbed out the window, and ran down the walkway and stairs leading to the driveway, then out to the street toward Ventura Boulevard, where commercial businesses offered at least a bathroom to hide in.

Scratched and bleeding, Max ran into McDonald's and took shelter in the men's room. He pleaded to the first customer who entered that he had just been robbed and needed a dime to call his wife. The customer obliged, and Max scooted out to the pay phone to call his office, where I was walking in the door.

Max hid between parked vehicles until I drove into the lot, scurrying away as people returned to their cars. This was a period long before mass homelessness and seeing a nearly naked, bleeding man running wild-eyed in a parking lot would cause most people to panic. Fortunately for Max, no one called the police on him, or at least no police had arrived before I did.

Max had to get to his office and meet with the investors. Could I please stop somewhere and get him some clothes to wear for these meetings? He couldn't go home looking like this. I told him I didn't have time to take him to a store, but I would stop at the drugstore in Gower Gulch across from the office and buy whatever was available. He could reimburse me in addition to my owed salary when we arrived at the office.

Max agreed to this and waited in the car while I went inside the Rite Aid, which sold children's budget clothes. I bought him a robin's-egg-blue boy's T-shirt with a large yellow smiley face on the front, some green polyester boy's pants, a pair of plastic boy's loafers, and a polyester baseball cap to cover the cuts on his head. The boy's trousers fit Max's slight waist and hips, but they resembled what Southerners would call "high-water britches," riding an inch or two above his ankles. Dressed, he really did look like a dopey kid, but his face never betrayed the reality. He asked me to wait for him to take two meetings and then drive him home afterward, which I agreed to. He would pay me at the end of his meetings.

We walked into the waiting room. Everyone stared as we passed, but there was no sign of surprise or amusement by his appearance. I followed him into his office, and the investors were called in one group at a time.

I took a seat by the wall in the back of the office. Max sat at his desk, and the investors took seats across from him. My view was the back of their heads, Max sitting across from them in his new costume, the giant yellow face smiling at all.

The first group of investors were three Filipinos. Once they were introduced and seated, Max began to make up a story and perform it, which was memorable. He stood and acted out each part as he invented it, and the audience watched him, enraptured. The adolescent boy outfit seemed to have no effect. These people had no real idea what Max was like. Maybe he dressed like this every day? I mean, it is Hollywood, the land of eccentricity, right? They all sat quietly, watching his every move.

When Max clearly got tired of the performance, he closed out the story by saying, "And from there, it gets even more sexy and exciting!"

The Filipinos applauded. Max shook their hands and told them he would call tomorrow, and they left. The next group entered, and the show began again, this time with changes as they occurred to him.

I was mesmerized that Max had the poise, or perhaps cold-bloodedness, to put on this show, considering what had to be going through his mind. He had been threatened with his marriage and then his life, had lost his wallet, clothes, and car, and now had to somehow explain this to his wife. Yet, he could take refuge in an improvised story about nothing—one that he could make interesting solely with his commitment to the intensity of the character he was creating. This was his greatest skill—his genius, this perhaps sociopathic ability, even desire, to fully remove himself from reality and enter an imagined truth. It was like nothing I had ever seen, but once I was paid for my work and expenses, I planned on never seeing it again. When the meetings were finished, he paid what he owed me, I took him home, and Max was out of my life.

I did stay in touch with Sylvie, who explained that police had recovered the car, wallet, and clothes stolen from Max when he was mugged by a street gang.

After they divorced, Sylvie gave up acting and moved away from Los Angeles to be closer to her family. Max continued to make the same types of films for years; securing a deal with a notable home video distributor and using his practiced charm, he was constantly able to find new recruits to help him until he moved to Brazil, then ultimately back to Germany, where he succumbed to heart failure.

Max died with sixty-six credits as a director, ninety-five as an actor, and sixty-four as a producer. Our venture together in Maryland with the Styrofoam and Karo syrup brought us both to Hollywood, and it became his most successful and recognized film. Mostly panned by American critics, it was a genuine international hit. With a budget of $300,000, it grossed over $35,000,000 worldwide according to Worldwide BoxOffice.com, and today it still maintains its own cult following, which grows each year. In addition to the film, Max developed his own cult following among specialty cinephiles.

I was recently asked to do an accompanying commentary for a 4K restoration of the film. After I did so, the owner of the distribution company, which specializes in cult films, excitedly told me, "This was my absolute favorite film growing up. I can't tell you how surreal it is to have you here now doing this."

In Hollywood, there is always room for hope, no matter the circumstances.

CHAPTER 24
THE MAGIC HAPPENS

To finish the Arizona movie, I directed the second unit work in Los Angeles and London. These are scenes with or without the primary actors, often involving action, which capture the visual personality of a secondary location.

While doing so, I met some technicians who I established a rapport with, and several months later, when I returned from getting married, I discovered that one of my closest friends from the Max and Sylvie projects had recommended me to a camera operator working in an equipment rental house. The operator had been enlisted by a producer to help him find a director for a film about a youth soccer team. The operator described the project as a "family drama," which I considered fresh air after so many grisly efforts trying to make condiments and food coloring believable as blood.

I drove two hours north to meet the producer. He was a cheerful but anxious man with a prematurely lined face, bright-blue eyes, and the unnerving habit of displaying unwarranted enthusiasm over every unexpected development. Later in our relationship, he would respond to the news of a nettlesome lawsuit being filed against the production by enthusiastically proclaiming, "That's the best thing that could have happened to us!" This, despite the fact that the suit could delay the film's release indefinitely and thereby cause him serious financial hardship. When I questioned the logic of this, he implied that a major quest in his life was to accept every development, no matter how dire, as "the best possible outcome" and proceed from there.

The producer had zero filmmaking experience, but he loved watching movies, particularly family films. His own family owned a successful business, and along with some partners, they offered to invest in the movie. It was from these investors that he raised enough money—or so he thought—to film what he considered a commercial script written by a young man from his neighborhood. The writer was also a novice, whom the producer had originally hired to paint his house. Together, they had teamed up to write a screenplay about a youth soccer team.

After we spent two hours together, the producer handed me the script and told me if I was interested, I had the job. I was stunned to be offered the position so quickly, but as I later learned, that was how things often worked in Hollywood at the time.

I raced home, Pam and I celebrated with a ribeye steak and fine Bordeaux, and I settled in to read the screenplay, which quickly tempered my enthusiasm. The story lacked discernible heft, and the dialogue was no more than information. Did the producer not see it, or did he see it and not care?

I slept on this sad choice and called him in the morning.

"I think this script is lacking in drama."

"I know it could use some work, but what exactly?" he responded.

I laid it out and he listened, or at least he didn't make any noise.

"So, you don't want to do it?"

"Not this script, but I'll rewrite it for nothing. I think I can make it better." I knew it sounded brash, but I had no doubt that if nothing else, I had enough of an opinion and hands-on experience to recognize bad when it presented itself.

"All right, tell you what. We start shooting in five weeks. If you can rewrite it in a week, and we get who we want with it, we'll use your script."

"Have you already gone out to actors?"

"It's fully cast, except I would like to do better in one role, if we can."

As it happened, the story was about a priest who runs an orphanage and coaches a youth soccer team. For the big match against the privileged school, a professional soccer player comes and coaches the team to victory. The producer had approached Pelé, the legendary Brazilian World Cup champion, to play the professional, and Pelé had turned him down because he, or most likely his agents and advisors, didn't feel the script was good enough. If Pelé would agree to do my script, we would go with it.

I had only written one screenplay, a psychological thriller called *The Dark Side*, set in a cabin in the woods. It was inspired by Roman Polanski's *Repulsion* and is the story of a man losing his grip on reality, which I considered to be every person's worst nightmare. While learning how to cut a movie with Max, I had also learned how to pace it, massage it, embellish it, and most important, tell a story on screen. It's true that I learned most of this by recognizing what to avoid, but my experience writing *The Dark Side* was rewarding, and I got excellent feedback from professionals. If I had been willing to let someone else direct it, I had offers, but I had other plans. This was my chance to bring those plans to life.

I set down to work, completing the full rewrite in a week with a part designed exclusively for Pelé, so he would be able to play himself. I then flew to New York to meet him. The producer had asked Pelé's office to arrange a meeting with a new director, with a new script, and Pelé reluctantly agreed.

Pelé was hospitable and charming, displaying a warm humility and open smile that would clearly light up a screen. We met at his office, had dinner at his favorite club, and he retired to read the script the next day. I got on a plane to fly home. By the time I landed, the producer had called three times. Pelé had agreed to take the part.

This was a major achievement for me. My biggest test to date—and I passed.

The first lesson I learned as a director was that luck must be summoned in order to be found. This is done simply by creating the opportunity and accepting with all manageable grace both good and bad luck when they appear, which both will.

I met the rest of the cast and was discouraged that many of them had very little professional acting experience. The "name" star of the movie, who was the most experienced actor contracted, had a long and varied career in television and film, but in my opinion, he lacked gravitas and emotion. Most important, he was clearly uncomfortable around children.

Wanting to cash in the currency I earned with my recruitment of Pelé, I asked the producer to replace the star. He initially wouldn't listen to my reasoning but eventually came around to hear me out and ultimately became supportive of my efforts, a condition that is often short-lived in the film business. It is a passionate endeavor with a lot of money, time, and ego at stake for everyone, so friendships often dissolve in the fire of battle.

The producer asked who I would suggest as a replacement.

"What if I can get John Huston?"

Serious as I was, the producer first looked perplexed, then amused, then somehow enlightened. He laughed nervously, wrinkled his cheeks, and looked at the sky, returning to perplexed.

"How will you do that?"

I started to think, then immediately stopped, deciding it was too soon to risk that. "I don't know, but if I can get him, will you go with it?"

At the time, Huston was one of the most iconic directors, and an occasional actor, working in Hollywood. An unthinkable catch for our modest enterprise. The producer lowered his eyes and smiled.

"Okay."

"You'll do it?"

He looked at me for the first time. "Only if it's the same rate."

"But if I can make it happen, you'll pay for the switch?"

"I'd be a fool not to, right?"

I didn't want to answer, but I offered my hand, and he took it.

In 1982, access to power, even for the hoi polloi, was much easier than it is today since the gates to an agency were normally the only gates one had to traverse to make an offer to talent. Today, there are steps one must take just to talk to an agent capable of deciding whether a client can even submit material. Then another process begins.

I phoned the Directors Guild and learned that John Huston was represented by Paul Kohner, an Austrian immigrant who came to New York in the 1920s, founded his talent agency in the 1930s, and now represented a stable of some of the most prestigious actors, composers, writers, and directors in Hollywood, including nearly all the European artists working in town.

Upon researching the agency and learning it had a reputation for civility and discernment, I purchased a new navy Brooks Brothers suit and tie, a matching pair of wing tip dress shoes, and an elegant dark leather document briefcase. I would not appear unprepared. Realizing an appointment would be an impossibility for an unknown, I dressed the part and drove to the address on Sunset Boulevard listed as the home of the Paul Kohner Agency.

The current star had agreed to a mere $25,000 to play the lead role, but I had the blessing of ignorance working in my favor—and no history of failure to discourage me. So, wearing my suit and wing tips and carrying my briefcase containing a screenplay and a pen, I entered the Sunset offices of the Kohner Agency, prepared to offer that same sum for John Huston.

Unlike other talent agencies, this office building was a converted home, with individual offices carrying the warmth and personality of a living space. On this Friday afternoon, hot tea, coffee, and cookies were being served in the waiting area. As I later learned, this occurred every Friday at 3 p.m. I noticed the trays as I approached the reception desk, charmed by this gesture of civility absent from the Hollywood I'd been exposed to thus far.

"Good afternoon. May I help you?" A greeting delivered with a welcoming smile that felt unrehearsed. I wasn't sure if the receptionist's amusement was a reaction to my painfully novice appearance, but I played the hand I was being dealt.

"Hello. I'd like to talk to someone about hiring John Huston to act in my movie."

She clearly had not heard this approach from a walk-in, and her smile broadened.

"Oh? When you say your movie, are you the producer?"

"I'm the director."

"Oh," she said again. I was learning the director declaration always resulted in a shifting of gears, no matter where delivered.

"Please take a seat and help yourself to some tea and cookies. Someone will be right with you."

I did as I was asked, surprised to discover the European cookies being served on sterling silver trays were genuinely European, this being a time when imported foods were still a delicacy. The tea and coffee were also European, served in silver pots, resting on silver trays. A touch of class in a proudly impudent business, where politeness was often construed as weakness.

After several minutes, a graying man in his sixties, wearing a navy suit nearly identical to mine, came into the waiting area and introduced himself. He smiled, seemingly delighted to find a younger man who shared his taste in clothes, enjoying the Agency's European hospitality. This was Walter Kohner, Paul's brother and partner in the Agency.

Walter led me into his office, where I immediately noticed a full grand piano by the window, nestled among exquisite antique furniture. After I sat, he asked me about my background, and when I mentioned I had been a musician, Walter told me about his own musical aspirations, then took a seat behind the grand and began to play, engaging me with a lovely and solid rendition of "Swan Lake." To this day, I can't imagine a talent agent in Hollywood who would put a grand piano in an office, much less play it for a walk-in.

He finished the piece, then asked how he could help me, and I told him. From my entry into the lobby, there was never an uncomfortable moment in that office, which, considering my obvious inexperience, was shocking. The conversation was more about who I was than the part I was asking his client to play, and after he hosted me for an hour, Walter politely suggested I leave the script, and he would call me.

I did as I was asked and returned home to wait, having no idea how long this could take. I was assuming several days, or perhaps a week or two. Walter would probably have an assistant read it, who would make a recommendation, and then we would see where it went from there.

The next morning, a Saturday, the phone rang at 8 a.m. It was Walter. He thought the part was a "tour de force" for John, and he would be happy to recommend it. He then raised the question of money. When I told him what we were offering, he apologized and said that Mr. Huston would never consider playing a lead role for $25,000, no matter how much he liked the material.

I asked Walter to not say anything to Mr. Huston about the size of the offer, and please give me the opportunity to talk with him before making a decision. I figured I could at least present it in the best possible fashion, let him see who he would be dealing with, and let fate take it from there.

Walter said he would do this, and within two hours, he called me again. "I have good news. John has agreed to meet with you before reading the script. Isn't that great?"

I agreed that it was. "I can meet with him today if he's available!"

"Well, that's not possible. If you want to meet with John, you'll have to go see him."

"Okay, I can do that. Where does he live?" I said, hoping he was free that afternoon.

"He lives in Mexico."

"Okay, let me talk to the producer and see what I can arrange. I'll call you back."

"Just know that it's difficult for me to talk to John because I have to reach his secretary first, then she has to patch me through a short-wave radio, which only works on limited hours when his generator is running."

The reference to short-wave and generators confused me, but I figured to shelve these questions for the time being. The issue at hand was convincing the producer to finance a trip to Mexico so I could meet with John Huston.

I enthusiastically called the producer but neglected to mention the problem with the fee, hoping that could take care of itself in time. The first step was meeting Mr. Huston and hopefully bringing him on board. The producer quickly agreed to fund the trip, so I called Walter to set it up and sat back and waited.

The next day, Walter called to let me know that I would have a day to meet with John, spend the next at his house, and return home the third day. Excited to know I would meet him alone with no agents present to provide discouragement, I didn't ask about the generator and short-wave radio. At least we had a shot.

Misfortunately, as it came to be, I prepared my briefcase, navy suit, and wing tip shoes for the trip. I flew to Puerto Vallarta the next day, where John's affable secretary, Joanie, picked me up in her VW bug, and we began our journey south through the jungle toward Manzanillo.

Joanie explained that John lived on a peninsula south of Puerto Vallarta on land he leased from the Huichol Indian tribe. The only access was by panga, a twenty- to twenty-five-foot open-hulled high-speed boat, slightly wider than a rowboat and used mostly for fishing or ferrying small groups across open water. Joannie would drop me off at a small dock in Yalapa, about an hour south of the airport, where I would board the panga, which would take me to see Mr. Huston. Now I was remembering the reference to short-wave radios and a generator, and more was coming into focus. I looked down at my suit and shoes, and for the first time since I began this venture, I was unsettled.

Having no idea where Puerto Vallarta was on the Mexican coast, I hadn't fully considered the fact that I was flying into the tropics, where the average temperature even in winter hovered around ninety degrees, with nearly 100 percent humidity. Wedged into Joanie's VW in my navy suit and dress shoes, I was sweating heavily before we were out of airport parking, and I realized that this could easily become a serious test of both my endurance and sense of humor. I began thinking that a large part of Joanie's smile when we met was most likely a reaction to my ensemble, now ironically capped with an Armani necktie cinched with a double Windsor knot.

We drove with the windows lowered to accommodate the lack of air-conditioning in Joanie's aged and struggling vehicle, an appropriate description for nearly all the cars sharing the road to Manzanillo. After an hour and a half, we turned off the highway onto a small dirt path leading into a thick clump of jungle. From there, we edged our way through the vines for an achingly long twenty minutes or so, ultimately reaching a clearing where before us lay the enormous azure expanse of the open Pacific.

At the end of the path was a small wooden dock, where a single panga was moored. Sitting on the edge of the dock was an older man wearing a baseball cap, white T-shirt, and khaki pants soiled from what was clearly a day's fishing. He stood up and welcomed Joanie, then broke into a grin when he eyed me.

By now, even I understood. I was a greenhorn. I smiled, trying not to look embarrassed, and turned to Joanie as the man climbed into the boat. She told me she would pick me up in three days and waved goodbye.

Holding my bag in one hand and briefcase in the other, I carefully made my way to the edge of the dock, down the wooden steps, and, balancing my gear as I stepped off, boarded the boat with one long step.

It wasn't pretty, my leather soles hydroplaning on the standing water in the bottom of the boat, and sitting down required an uncomfortable dance on my part. I didn't look at the VW because I never heard it start, and I knew Joanie was far too amused to leave just yet.

The humor also wasn't lost on the boatman, who smiled and nodded at me as I stowed my gear and nodded back. As if cleared for takeoff, he sucked gasoline out of a tube inserted into a five-gallon plastic milk carton with the top sawed off, spit out the fuel, inserted the tube into the engine, and pulled the cord. The engine roared to life.

The boatman waved to Joanie, who returned the gesture and climbed into her car as we pulled away. Within seconds, the panga was flying across open water, bouncing with the swells, gushing spray, salt, and ocean detritus over me, my confidence, and my new navy suit, which, after two minutes on the open sea, could never be worn again.

An hour later, we closed in on the peninsula supporting Mr. Huston's compound, which contained a main house, guest house, and several outbuildings. Water was pumped from a well and electricity furnished by generator, powered by gasoline delivered by the same panga I was bouncing on, when weather and the boatman's whimsy allowed. There were no roads on the Huichol reservation, and no land access through the Jalisco jungle south of Yalapa. The only way to find Mr. Huston was over water in a small craft—though best done without the suit.

He was standing atop a cliff face as we approached, dressed in a linen tropical day suit, hands on his hips, and one foot propped on a rock seawall providing protection from wind and spray. Next to him was a segmented stairway leading down the cliff to the water.

The boatman approached to within thirty yards of shore and pulled parallel to the beach, where he idled the engine and gestured to me.

"You jump." These were the first words I heard him speak.

I looked back in bewilderment. The water was at least three feet deep, and I was clearly not dressed for a dip in the ocean. "Can't you pull up to the beach, at least?" I asked him.

His expression never changed, nor did the position of the boat. "You jump. Now." A lit cigarette dangled from his mouth, hovering over the open gas container at his feet. Another enticement to jump.

I collected my briefcase and overnight bag, looked up at Huston on the clifftop, who also hadn't changed his position, and jumped into the ocean.

It was a unique moment—with an unprecedented mixture of humiliation, fear, astonishment, exhilaration, and bewilderment as my wing tips settled onto the ocean floor and immediately filled with salt water, sand, and seaweed. My suit clung to my legs and waist as I started ashore. Each belabored step became its own performance as I kept my eyes on Huston, who made no effort to hide his amusement.

It was only thirty yards or so, but it seemed the length of an airfield before I no longer had to trudge through the waves. It got only slightly better when my wing tips started digging through soft sand in the direction of the wooden stairs. The sound of my feet squishing with each step was excruciating. My briefcase and bag were soaked with salt water by this point, and I was struggling to think of something to say when I reached the top. I had plenty of stairs to climb, and too much time to think about it, but there are no perfect lines for moments like these, no life lessons to prepare one for humiliation.

Lacking both the wit and experience to come up with something humorous or beguiling, I went into default, which was simply the truth. "I hope all your guests aren't as embarrassed as I am," I said with a smile of resignation.

He smiled in return. I later decided that my nearly vaudeville entrance, as compromising as it was, was the best approach I could have possibly invented, for he was ready to accept me at once. "Your quarters are right there," he said, pointing to a small house at the edge of the cliff. "I'm over here." He pointed behind him. "Why don't you get cleaned up and come on over and we'll talk?"

"Yes, sir."

I did as I was told, and within minutes, I arrived at his screen door, freshly showered and comfortably dressed. He welcomed me, and having witnessed my experience, he offered me a drink. It was early afternoon, nearly two o'clock. By six, we had finished lunch and a bottle of Jack Daniel's. By midnight, we were done with dinner, dessert, and part of a second bottle. By this time, I had met his companion and muse Maricela, their adopted four-year-old daughter Graciela, their young chef Archie, and their very young Rottweiler Diego.

We talked mostly about me, but not the script itself. He asked most of the questions, which were pointed. He nodded and smiled at the majority of my answers, clearly pleased that I had not been to film school, a path into filmmaking that he found was homogenizing the industry. Particularly in his early years, he had known so many great filmmakers from varying backgrounds and, presciently as it turned out, was concerned that young film school graduates with great enthusiasm, technical skill, and energy, but little life experience to draw from, were choking the business like a young, insatiable weed.

I left the script with him, which he promised to read first thing in the morning, and retreated to my guesthouse, falling asleep to the embracingly slow repetition of ocean waves on a calm night. Possibly the most welcome sound in the world.

The next morning, as I was working on the terrace outside my casita, Graciela came up the steps and called out over the divide. "John says you should go for a swim."

"Thank you, Graciela," I replied. "I'll do that as soon as I'm finished working."

She didn't move. "John says now."

When a four-year-old speaks, it is often an order, and you better listen. I put my work away, donned a bathing suit, and stepped back down the segmented stairway leading to the beach, where Huston was sitting on the bottom step. He gestured for me to sit.

"Have a seat. We'll talk, then go for a swim."

As I sat, his eyes nearly closed with the creasing of that well recognized grin, one he often mustered. "I read the script. It's a good script, and frankly, I don't see how you can lose."

He paused, as if that was all there was to say.

"Thank you very much."

"Now let's go for a swim."

"Wait, does that mean you'll do it?"

"Sure, I'll do it."

"Did Walter tell you what we are paying?"

"No, how much?"

"Twenty-five thousand dollars."

He shrugged and stood up. "What the hell. I like it. Now let's go for a swim." He removed his T-shirt and walked into the ocean.

I remained on the stairs, astonished. He was committing to both the project and to me. It was so easy, which, as I later discovered in trying to put together films, is often the case when everything works but nearly impossible when it is not. Within the past three weeks, I had gone from unemployment to being offered a directing job, rewriting the script, and securing first Pelé in New York and now John Huston in Mexico. And as my good fortune continued, I was soon to be stranded in Huston's compound for an additional three weeks by an airline strike. During that time, I received an impromptu education from one of the all-time masters of the industry, covering all aspects of filmmaking, a personalized class conducted in the most desirable of conceivable settings, preparing me for the task ahead. At least I felt prepared at the time.

When I met John Huston in Mexico, I was a first-time director. Huston had taken the part because, he told me, he believed in the story he had read on the page and had an instinctive confidence working with me. He believed the best directors were writers. I don't know if this is true, but I know why he believed that.

Huston felt that in Hollywood's glory days, directors came from all walks of life. They were raconteurs who had developed a point of view about the world, wanting to tell rich stories about love, greed, justice, pride, guilt, and consequence, visionaries who wanted to tell not just their own stories but those of great novelists as well. Film could do this. Film could express this point of view on a scale only imagined by a novelist, so a director was capable of expanding the writer's reach.

So many of the directors who became legendary during Huston's time were writers first. Some started in other creative areas of filmmaking, but not one learned the craft in a classroom. Huston felt that the best film education was to participate in making films, in any capacity. He bridled against the notion becoming the focus in many film schools, that marketing, dealmaking, and understanding the "business" of Hollywood was essential to the craft and films should be conceived with that in mind. In fact, he thought such a focus would signal the end of filmmaking as we knew it.

I believe he was right. Sure, getting a film made requires an understanding of how the film gets financed, promoted, and sold, but when making a product is secondary to selling it, does anyone really care about what they are making? Does a songwriter think about how a finished song can be promoted when writing it? Storytelling must come from the heart. Otherwise, it will have no life.

This was part of Huston's lament to me during that magical time in his Mexican compound. He clearly loved the industry but feared for its creative future. He complained that studios were already being absorbed by multinational corporations, and as corporate interests expanded, they would take over all film production and agency representation.

He feared it was the death knell for Hollywood as he knew it because the only films getting made in town were those most likely to make over one hundred million dollars. That meant only expensive movies, with the most recognizable elements (stars in the 1980s, comic book heroes today), would be made.

This figure would be considerably higher today, the average

marketing budget being over forty million dollars per picture, but the point was that small, story-driven films would disappear. This hasn't happened entirely, thanks to the advent of cable, streaming, and private investors, but without either star power or a rich uncle, independent filmmakers continue to struggle.

It began with *Jaws* and *Star Wars* and just got bigger and more encompassing. Steven Spielberg and George Lucas never planned to change the landscape, but they did. Now a studio won't plan a picture that it doesn't believe can "open," meaning create a big box office return the first weekend. Huston bemoaned this change; he felt the movie business "just wasn't fun anymore. Agents are getting too damn powerful, and there is no humanity or humor in these people. I'll be glad to get out, even if dying is the only way."

CHAPTER 25
THE BLACK LIGHT, THE WIZARD, AND ALL THE MAGNIFICENT CHAOS

The shoot was scheduled within two weeks of my return from Mexico. Elated over Huston's signing, the producer and I were eager and united in our plans to get rolling. This collaboration, as with so many in Hollywood, didn't last long.

We planned to film in San Diego, arranging to house cast and crew while securing the necessary locations. The producer and I ping-ponged between Los Angeles and the San Diego area, choosing the right spots, and soon the producer hired some help and began on his own. I became a little concerned when I learned that several of the key positions, including production and even cast, were being filled by family and friends with little or no experience in these jobs.

When production began, I decided to ride to San Diego with Pelé's entourage in his stretch limo to spend time getting to know him. The group included his manager, his assistant, his chiropractor/"personal advisor," his bodyguard, and his girlfriend.

We were traveling midday, and everyone became hungry halfway through the trip, so it was suggested we stop for lunch. I had no knowledge of any notable restaurants on the I-5 leading to San Diego, and I couldn't take Pelé just anywhere. As we were discussing the options, Pelé suddenly pointed and shouted in his heavy Portuguese accent, "Chart House!" And sure enough, we were passing a Chart House restaurant not far off the highway. As it happened, the Chart House chain was one of Pelé's favorite American restaurants, and there it was, right in front of us.

The moment we entered the restaurant, Pelé was recognized. Within minutes, busboys, waiters, and diners were not so casually strolling by the table to get a closer look at the man *Readers Digest* had declared to be the second most famous person in the world, slightly behind the Pope.

This was decades before the internet and cell phones and remarkable for a man who later told me the story of his childhood in the mountains of Brazil, where every room in his family home had a dirt floor. His family was so poor that, when he was fifteen years old and offered a contract to play for the professional soccer team Santos, his mother sewed two pairs of short pants together to make a mismatched long pair for him to wear to the signing. She didn't want him to be embarrassed because pictures would be taken, and the family was too poor to afford a pair of long pants only to be worn for a ceremony.

While we were eating, a busboy edged his way to the table and, while refilling the water glasses, shyly asked Pelé if he would mind coming to a pay phone near the kitchen to say hello to the busboy's mother, who lived in Guadalajara and was waiting on the line.

Pelé, whose native language was Portuguese, spoke passable Spanish but very little English. He brightened and told the busboy he would be happy to accommodate him. He got up, with his Cuban bodyguard Pedro, who followed him everywhere, left his lunch, and went to the bank of pay phones near the kitchen, where the receiver was dangling from the wall booth.

Constantly interrupted by workers stopping to shake his hand, Pelé talked to the young man's mother for at least ten minutes, learning the names and ages of her entire family, including pets, before returning to the table and resuming his now cold meal. The busboy was thrilled beyond measure.

When we were finished with lunch, Pelé asked his assistant to bring promotional photographs from the limo so he could sign them for the staff of the restaurant, which he proceeded to do for the next fifteen or twenty minutes, until every employee and customer received a signed photo.

I later learned that this was standard behavior for Pelé, who, during the making of the film and beyond, proved to be generous, open, and kind of heart—a man John Huston described as framed by a "black light." When I asked what he meant by that, Huston looked up with wet eyes and offered the perfect definition of the man: "Purity."

We arrived in San Diego, settled into a motel, and went straight to work. The first days shooting a movie are emotional chaos for nearly everyone with responsibility, and it was soon clear to most of us what needed to happen to ensure the film was completed.

I had answered questions but unfortunately asked very few when interviewing for the job. I soon became aware of how little exposure the producer had to actual filmmaking, as in none, and this would become costly. Experience, at this stage, is arguably the most valuable asset on a film set. The lack of it in any department is expensive to some. When the producer lacks it, it can be expensive to all.

Without specifics, the producer was overly optimistic as to what our budget would provide, with no immediate access to additional resources. He had no experienced production heads to turn to for counsel, and when the shortages became obvious, his frustration boiled over. This is not uncommon for movie sets since emotions are on the surface, conditions are constantly changing, and cash can easily fall short of mounting invoices.

The producer's anxiety manifested itself in temper tantrums that would come close to derailing the production. More than once during the first week, silence in the motel was shattered by the resounding crash of a slamming door, followed by the tinkling of glass and splatter of stucco onto pavement. On the motel walkway, small piles of broken plaster collected outside the doors to the producer, production manager, and department heads' rooms; trails of rage debris were left behind as the producer exited, furious because some mistake or miscalculation had resulted in yet another unanticipated expense.

It soon became apparent that we were woefully unprepared to shoot the script I had written, with neither the financial resources nor collection of talent necessary to pull it off. I did my best to stay positive. The producer would deflect my concerns with the common assurance that "I'm not worried. I know we can do it!" He would bravely, yet I feared blindly, face our growing list of calamities with unflagged optimism. "This is the best thing that could have happened to us!"

These head-scratching declarations were eye-rolling at face value, not to mention uniformly inaccurate. They are also, more often than you might reasonably imagine, uttered by blindly optimistic producers or directors on film sets. I wrote what I thought was a good script, and John Huston had agreed. I figured his opinion would count, even if no one else's did, including my own. I didn't know what it would cost in real terms, but I assumed the producer did.

The reality was that the producer also didn't know, and he had hired a production manager who was not only new to the job but had never created a film budget. She, in turn, had hired friends as assistants, with little if any experience. When I expressed my concern over this to the producer, his response was "Oh, don't you worry about her. She knows her way around a movie set."

This turned out to mean that she had a good deal of experience working as an extra. This is professionally known as "atmosphere," which makes for an interesting occupation noted on a tax return, but not a useful background for producing movies.

Since most of us were relative amateurs, it didn't take long for the entire operation to develop into an undisputed catastrophe, with one mistake collapsing onto the heels of the next, building momentum until cost-cutting decisions alienated not only the providers of physical equipment, housing, and shooting locations but much of the cast and crew as well.

After one week, it became apparent we needed an overhaul. Realizing he had made a mistake in selecting personal friends and family members over professionals, the producer stopped production, got a loan to pay for what had been spent, and replaced the inexperienced department heads. We took a week's hiatus to reboot.

Everyone returned home, the producer borrowed more money, and we hired an experienced production manager who replaced most of the department heads and enlarged the crew.

Things went much more smoothly after that, but we were still in a financial hole from which extrication seemed impossible. That's when I realized as a director that making a movie produced its own unique series of nightmares—it becomes a magnificent chaos, and the worries, concerns, fears, regrets, and all the countless anxieties keep a director up at night. And the hollow encouragement offered by investors and producers is just that.

After a two-week delay, the cast and crew returned to San Diego and resumed shooting with mostly new department heads. Save for the continuing mishaps and roadblocks created by budget and scheduling miscalculations, things seemed to be looking up.

But that turned out to be misleading. The producer and I differed on the approach to making the film, as often happens with producer-director relationships. Essentially, he wanted a heartwarming, Disney type movie, and I wanted something more quietly ambitious. This dispute was magnified by my relationship with the cast and crew, who mostly sided with me over creative decisions demanding complicated camera setups, which admittedly took longer to film, thus more expensive. This created a gulf between me and the producer, which turned toxic in a way I had not fully anticipated.

Pelé relayed a story to me about an afternoon in Jack Murphy stadium, where we were preparing to shoot some soccer scenes. I was on the field with the director of photography devising a shot list for later in the day when the light was optimal. The boys on the team were gathered around Pelé in the visitors' locker room. He was sitting on the trainer's table, describing how to choreograph the action once on the field.

The producer entered, carrying his hard briefcase as he always did, his face agitated. "Why aren't you out on the field shooting?" Pelé explained that he was waiting for the assistant director to bring word for them to take to the field. The producer's face reddened, his voice rising. "You should be on the field! I'm the producer, and I say when we shoot!"

Pelé bristled at this. "The director tells us when we shoot. You are not the director." This did not sit well with the producer, who began to shout. "You listen to me! He's not the boss. I am! Understand?"

According to Pelé, even with the multiple problems we faced during the production, this was the one incident that made him angry. The man had the lightest, calmest disposition one could imagine, but he was a legendary figure around the world, and being ordered like a boot in basic training was not acceptable. He hopped off the trainer's table and stepped up to the producer, his voice tense. "You want me to understand, you don't shout like a child! You talk like a man! Do *you* understand?"

The producer's face reddened to a propulsion point. This was in front of the boys and several crew members, who remained still, watching. He turned to them. "Who's going on the field?"

No one moved. Still holding his briefcase, the producer looked around the room. Silence. He reared back, wound up, and threw his briefcase as hard as he could, straight up into the air, where it hit the light fixtures running across the ceiling and broke open. As if in celebration, the cloud of agreements, notes, and legal papers floated down like confetti into the locker room as the empty case tumbled onto a training table, splitting apart before it hit the floor. The producer walked out, leaving the floating papers to land where they may.

When I heard about the confrontation, it sounded funny because it ended in such a flourish. I thought even the producer would agree because these contretemps, common on movie sets, normally dissolve and become humorous in time. Everyone has lost their temper on a film set for one reason or another, and we mostly learn to laugh it off. But I should have known that would be the end for me. As a rookie, I was ignorant.

I had naively assumed from the beginning that filmmakers needed to be driven by the quality of the script, crew, and actors. I had a conversation with Huston on the first night I met him in Mexico, where he asked me, "Directing a movie can be difficult. You've got actors, producers, money people, budget, crew. . . . It's a considerable job. What do you think is the most important part of all that?"

My response? "Tell the story."

He smiled at that, seemingly pleased, which pleased me as well because I felt I was being tested—and I was convinced I had passed.

In truth, I realized later that yes, he was pleased by my uncorrupted spirit, but he was also amused by my naivete. He was interviewing an incoming freshman and enjoyed my will and determination, but he knew how much more was necessary to succeed. I later decided the correct answer was "all of the above."

When I met Pelé, I was concerned about his poor English interfering with the story. He had a very pronounced accent and would struggle to deliver lines easily understood. It required a lot of rehearsal.

There was a scene where Pelé enters the bedroom of a young priest played by Peter Fox, who is clearly distraught and conflicted about his faith. When Pelé enters, the line he is to deliver is "you're up late tonight, Father." But Pelé could only manage in his heavy accent "you a plate fodder." We tried numerous times, to no avail. But when I looked at the footage in the cutting room, I realized that even though the line seemed humorous and wasn't that understandable, it didn't matter—because Pelé had the magic onscreen. What makes a star. He lit the room and was inescapably charming no matter what he said. Without question, when Pelé first appears, the entire movie comes to life. All because of his smile, and his overwhelming spirit shines through. The black light.

Late in the film, Pelé enters the boys' dorm room and is supposed to give them a pep talk for their game the next day. With his language limitations, he couldn't really do that, so he brought his guitar and sat down.

"Are you ready, boys? We sing now. Everybody!" And he played guitar and sang a song he wrote in broken English about being a decent man. You must be strong, kind, and work hard. That simple. The words are mispronounced, but the intention is clear, and the innocent tune is as charming as the lyrics. The boys gathered around him and began to sing. His smile, his voice, and the unfiltered adoration of the boys were all the scene needed to accomplish what no dialogue ever could.

It helped me understand what created a true movie moment. A grace note that people remember.

In the movie, Pelé first appears when he joins Huston's character at his deathbed. They hadn't seen each other since Pelé was a boy and Huston's character was a priest in Brazil who coached his soccer team. I had written a long exchange between the two where we learn about the history of their relationship and how much they meant to each other, but it soon became clear that Pelé was not going to be able to pull off the dialogue. We tried for some time, then took a break. I was at a loss for what to do. I went onto the set alone and sat down to come up with something that could work.

Huston retired to his trailer, and minutes later, he returned to me with a small piece of notebook paper torn from a spiral where he had handwritten a short exchange of dialogue in pen. It read as follows:

John is in bed with his eyes closed, near death. He opens his eyes and sees Pelé above him, who he has not seen in over thirty years.

"Pelé! Is it really you?"

Pelé: "It's good to see you, Bud." (The nickname of John's character.)

Huston: (tries to smile through his illness) "What do you say?"

Pelé: "I say it's been a long, long time."

Huston takes him in and tries to smile. Shakes his head. "Look at us. You were a boy; I was a young priest . . . and all of a sudden . . . here we are!" His eyes twinkle.

Pelé: "I've missed you, Bud."

His eyes water because he feels it. He breaks into that heartwarming smile, and they embrace before Huston dies. It was a brilliant moment. As simple as it could be—and one of the strongest points in the film. I was so concerned that Pelé would struggle with his lines. I wrote and rewrote, hoping I could capture something that Pelé could deliver. What I needed to connect to, and what Huston understood, was that the lines were secondary. It was Pelé's presence and spirit that would express what we needed, and it did. John was a wizard.

After I delivered my first cut of the film, the producer silently banished me. This is not uncommon in Hollywood, but I was shocked. I was never shown his cut of the film, nor invited to the premiere in New York or to the reception at the Cannes Film Festival.

When I went to see John to tell him about my unceremonious firing, he sat across from me and looked me in the eyes. "Put it aside and move on to the next," he said. "I have countless stories like this. I'm a good judge of talent, and I hold high expectations for you. You will find people who appreciate what you bring. More likely, they will find you. You're going to go places. Move on."

I held those words close, and I still do. John asked if I was still going to the premiere in New York, and I told him I had not been invited by the producer, who apparently planned to present the film without me.

He nodded, as if expecting it, then told me he would not be

attending either for he was leaving for Mexico to shoot *Under the Volcano*, a book he had always admired. He was very excited to work with Albert Finney, whom he had great respect for as an actor. Finney, playing a dissolute alcoholic amid the breakup of his marriage, won an Oscar for his performance in the film.

Huston gave me one last piece of advice as a director, which I now realize was the most salient of our visit. "You will direct more films, but remember, as long as you are quick on your feet, the actors and crew will back you up. But don't exclude the producers. Invite them to every meal with the stars. The moment an insecure producer feels conspired against, it's over. That's what happened here."

I thanked him for his thoughts and wished him good luck with the film. He stopped me as I was leaving.

"One more thing. Do you have representation in town?"

I told him I did not, and he shook his head. "I'll call Paul Kohner. We all need someone like him." He did, and I had the first of what would ultimately become several agents.

One week later, Pelé called and asked when I was coming to New York for the premiere. When I explained that I had not been invited, he responded, "So, I'm inviting you. Where would you like to stay?"

I was messengered an itinerary with first-class airfare, car service, and five days in a Midtown hotel. Pelé hosted me before and after the screening, and in a final display of kindness, he took me and his costar Peter aside and told us that since he started playing professional soccer, he had been surrounded by people who always wanted something from him. He told us how much it meant to him that we had never asked him for anything and only offered to help him play his part. For that, he was offering us half of his ten points (a percentage of profit participation) in the movie. I knew that as net points, they would probably be worthless due to questionable bookkeeping, but Pelé didn't know that, and we were touched.

Unbeknownst to me, the producer had told Pelé he could not afford to finish the movie and asked Pelé to return his substantial salary in exchange for ten net points. Pelé didn't know how the business worked, so as far as he was concerned, ten points could be very valuable. So, believing in the movie, Pelé agreed to this, and he was now willing to give up half of what he had negotiated for himself—only because he'd concluded that Peter and I weren't opportunists. That is the type of man he was.

I think it highly probable that John Huston contacted Pelé and suggested he invite me to the premiere. But nothing about that diminishes Pelé's generosity in doing so. I realized how lucky I was—to have the experience I did with these men on the set of my first film as a director. The advice Huston had given me proved as true and valuable as any life lesson I could learn.

I later came to accept that the producer was simply overwhelmed by the size of the hole he found himself in and lost his clarity. I never had a conversation with him after he locked me out of the editing room. As time provides, I'm sure his memory of the experience differs from mine, or perhaps it has been blocked completely. As in most every film, we feel remorse over decisions made or not made and behavior too easily checked or left unchecked. But panic is a cruel state, creating damage that often can't be undone.

CHAPTER 26
YOUR MEALS IN LIFE ARE NUMBERED

Shortly after my experience in San Diego, Pam and I moved to a duplex apartment off La Cienega, south of Olympic, where everything seemed to get stolen, including Pam's car, which was parked directly in front of the house.

The duplex was broken into and robbed less than a week after we moved in, with Pam asleep in our bedroom while the burglars went through the house, including lifting her jewelry from the dresser not five feet from the bed she was sleeping in.

Pam awoke, not knowing why, only discovering when she went to the kitchen for water that the front porch light was out, which she had left on for me upon my return home from a poker game. When Pam went to turn on the light, she discovered the front door was wide open. She did the right thing. She ran outside and down the steps to an apartment building next door, where she pounded on doors until someone called the police. No one would let the woman in her nightgown inside, but at least they called the police.

Pam stayed in the building's lobby until the police arrived, and when returning to our duplex, she found that the thieves left all heavy items on the steps as they escaped—items that were not there when she ran out the first time. That meant that at least two burglars were in the apartment while she slept. Her sleeping habits were never the same.

It was a traumatic beginning for our time there, but the apartment was large and comfortable, with a bedroom I could use exclusively for writing. I pored over books and articles that I found interesting and perhaps cinematic, and I rediscovered my fondness for the stories of Jim Harrison, a Michigan author who had spent time in Key West.

Harrison was a highly distinctive writer, poet, and person. I had been determined to ultimately track him down and get the film rights to one of his books, realizing the potential in his body of work. I had read all of Harrison's books as of 1983, including one that begins in Key West and had been mentioned by the writer Thomas McGuane, Harrison's friend whom I was also a fan of, in an interview in *Playboy Magazine*. Written in 1973, it was called *A Good Day to Die*, and Harrison claimed it was "the first real book about Vietnam," though the book doesn't take place in the war-ravaged country. This was the book I focused on as a film.

It's the story of a young, damaged Vietnam vet who can't keep away from pills regardless of which direction they take him, his young and spirited girlfriend whose thirst for adventure is both intoxicating and dangerous for the men around her, and an older, hard-drinking poet who" longs for the life unlived."

The three set out on a road trip from Key West, destined for the Grand Canyon, to sabotage what they believe to be the construction of a hydroelectric dam that would create an environmental catastrophe. In addition to the three travelers, the car includes boxes of uppers, downers, weed, beer—and a large case of dynamite. A triangle develops, culminating in the inevitable disaster, which is not that predictable, involving drugs, love, and of course, the dynamite.

I outlined the book as a screenplay and began to write it out, figuring when it was finished, I could approach the publisher and find a way to secure the film rights.

While working on this outline, my friend Peter, Pelé's costar in the San Diego film, invited me to attend a Lakers game. It would be my first professional game in LA and my first visit to the Forum, the legendary venue that I had only previously seen on television. The Lakers were a great team, with generational talent, so I was excited to see them play live.

Our seats were midway up the first level, with a good view of the court, though from a distance. Peter was telling me about the team, which I was just starting to follow, and he mentioned that Jack Nicholson had seats on the other side of the court near the visiting team's bench. Peter pointed to the courtside seats, disappointed that "he's not there tonight. Don't recognize anybody in those seats."

When I glanced down across the court, two of the occupants caught my attention. I asked to borrow Peter's binoculars to take a closer look.

As I suspected, the man on the end was Lou Adler, who, as a former musician, I recognized as the famous producer of Carole King and the Mamas and the Papas. I knew him for his notable cap, colorful clothes, and signature white beard.

Next to him, also easily recognized from any of his books' dust jackets, sat Jim Harrison, wearing one of his trademark Hawaiian shirts. Knowing he lived in Michigan, I was stunned by the serendipity of the two of us simultaneously sharing this unlikely setting. I mentioned this to Peter, who, aware that I was outlining the book for a screenplay, suggested I go down and reach out to Harrison.

I considered this, and at halftime, I stepped down to the courtside area where Harrison was wandering about by himself. I called out his name and gestured to him. Since my tickets didn't allow me on the court, he walked over.

I introduced myself and told him I was a director who was a big fan, and I was very interested in making a movie out of *A Good Day to Die*. He listened and told me I would have to talk to his agent about the money part, but he would be happy to get together to talk about the proposed film.

So, a friendship was struck, and I went to see him the next day at the Westwood Marquis, a hotel he liked because he could walk around the nearby arboretum, which we did.

Harrison's physique seemed to match his larger-than-life literature. He was solidly built, though he appeared heavy, with a rounded, hard torso like a medicine ball. He had exceptionally muscular shoulders and arms normally garbed in colorful Hawaiian shirts. His neck was round and dense as a tree trunk. He sported an overgrown, dark, drooping mustache, reaching below his chin, thin, brown anarchic hair that, although straight, managed to grow in every direction, and eyebrows that angled in the same fashion over a wandering left eye that never matched the sight path of his right.

Harrison lost the eye when he was seven, he told me, when he and a neighbor girl were playing with a stick. The way he looked at you could be somewhat off-putting when you first met him, and Harrison himself said it gave him an advantage—because no one knew exactly who or what he was looking at while talking. As Jim put it in his uniquely Midwestern nasal growl, "One eye looks for fish; the other watches for birds."

We talked about the book and the film possibilities. He told me he was in LA to meet with director Bob Rafelson over a proposed project called *Samba*, to be shot in Brazil, starring Sonia Braga. It was being produced by Adler and would be directed by Rafelson, director of *Five Easy Pieces, King of Marvin Gardens*, and *The Postman Always Rings Twice*, who was returning from Brazil, where he was scouting locations. Jim was writing the script, though he had never written a script before, and was happy to discuss the process with me.

I told him about my approach to his book, my outline for the story, and we discussed some of my casting and music ideas. These were all concepts he had never considered, but he liked them all and wanted to talk further. But I first had to settle the financial side of the deal with his agent, Bob Dattila.

I called Bob, and we worked out an option agreement, with a

buyout figure if it came to that. The money wasn't something I had access to, but I still had a relationship with Herb Taylor, an investor in Max's Arizona bridge movie, who I thought would like this story.

Herb was an oil-and-gas distributor in northern New Mexico. He loved the West, loved to read, and was always curious about what I was writing, attributes I thought would be helpful in the production of this film. If he liked the idea, he might also be interested in investing in the production.

Herb devoured the book and was happy to put up option money so I could write the script. We put together a deal, and Jim and I began a series of nightly phone calls, originally designed to discuss progress on the script, but I soon realized Jim was a voluble soul who just liked to talk.

He lived in Lake Leelanau, Michigan, close to Traverse City, on the banks of Lake Michigan, but he also owned a cabin outside of Grand Marais, a seaside town at the top of the Upper Peninsula nestled on the banks of Lake Superior. The cabin was his writing retreat, where he would spend weeks at a time while working on a book.

While staying at the cabin, Jim would drive into town after dinner and spend evenings perched at the bar of the Dunes Saloon, a local hangout with a few tables and chairs, stools, and pool tables hosting pretty much the same clientele every night.

Later in our relationship, I spent time with Jim at his cabin while working on an adaptation of his book *Sundog* for director Hal Ashby, and I accompanied him to the Dunes Saloon each night, where I quickly learned that the bar pretty much became Jim's clubhouse and office. He and I consumed a full hotel's share of the local specialty, Lake Superior whitefish, during our nightly visits.

The day we were scheduled to return to Lake Leelanau, a blizzard hit the Upper Peninsula; six deer hunters died of exposure. We started across the peninsula at the height of the storm, with visibility not much further than the front bumper of Jim's Subaru. We were essentially driving blind, but Jim carried on because "We said we were leaving today, so we're leaving today!" He explained it is Midwestern tradition to always follow the plans you lay. Changing plans creates confusion.

Certain we would end up stranded and probably dead in the bleak landscape, I begged him to turn around because I didn't want to die in this godforsaken terrain littered with scraggly pine and timber wolves. Either that or let me drive, because he can only see out of one eye and wasn't a particularly gifted driver either. Finally, after he admitted that he had no idea where the road was, he said, "We've already locked up the cabin. Where would we go if we turned around?"

The answer was simple. "Dunes Saloon. We'll wait it out all week if we have to."

"Good idea."

So, we made it back to the bar, which harbored an animated crowd of frustrated deer hunters locked into the same plan. Jim and I found rooms to rent at a small hotel at the end of the block by the shoreline, and when not gorging on saloon whitefish and bourbon, we spent the next day and night listening to the fierce and relentless roar of gale-force winds and crashing waves pounding the rocky cliffs beneath us. I had been in ocean storms on sailboats, though never a hurricane, but this was a unique sound of power unleashed, alarming yet mesmerizing, somehow otherworldly. The volume and intensity made it hard to conceive that all this noise emanated from a lake, even one called Superior. In the last verse of *The Wreck of the Edmund Fitzgerald,* Gordon Lightfoot wrote, "Superior, they said, never gives up her dead when the gales of November come early." Understood. When the weather eased, we drove home.

Jim was becoming a revered author in Hollywood, but at the Dunes Saloon, no one cared, which is how Jim liked it. He called from the saloon most nights while he was writing at his cabin. The bar phone had a long cord, and the bartender normally perched it right next to Jim's reserved seat so he could talk to his friends around the country.

I think Jim had a nightly call list he went through while sipping glasses of bourbon. He was one of the more entertaining people you could hope to talk with, and at least during the get-to-know phase, a phone call with Jim would at minimum educate you about at least two topics you knew very little about, make you laugh several times, and leave you with at least one memorable insight locked into your brain.

His knowledge was extensive, his memory beyond anything I had previously been exposed to, and his humor, humanity, and ability to spontaneously concoct fresh and laser-accurate metaphors—these were like sitting down to the perfect meal.

I finished the script and was proud of it. I could see this film from start to finish, convinced it was one I would love to see in a theater, which was the gold standard. It had a good pace, the characters were interesting and original, and the parts were strong enough to attract some excellent actors—stars, I hoped.

At the time, my friend Peter was acting in an episode of the Universal Television show *Simon and Simon,* a major hit on CBS. While in the production offices, Pete noticed a copy of Harrison's most recent book, *Legends of the Fall,* in the bookcase of the show's executive producer, Richard Chapman.

Peter asked Richard if he had read *A Good Day to Die.* It turned out that not only was Chapman an avid Harrison reader, but he was also a fellow Midwesterner, and yes, Richard had read it and was an enthusiastic fan.

Pete told him about my script. Richard read it, decided he wanted to produce the movie, and agreed to let me direct. He had an investor in Chicago, the owner of a broadcasting company, who agreed to pay for the film, with a budget ceiling of five million dollars.

That was plenty as far as I was concerned, if the stars didn't ask for too much. That turned out to be more than wishful thinking. I began the casting search, which was eye-opening for me because my experience with the Kohner Agency had been so congenial.

I first approached Sue Mengers, who was a notoriously tough

agent for filmmakers to negotiate with. I was interested in Nick Nolte to play the poet and John Malkovich to play the young vet. I was able to get Mengers on the phone, who gave me an early lesson in Hollywood powerbroking.

"Okay Tuy-rell, I read your script. You want Nick for the mopey guy?"

"I believe he's perfect, and if anyone can elevate that part, he can."

"Does he fuck the girl or not?"

"What?"

"I said . . . does he fuck the girl . . . or not?"

Ms. Mengers had intentionally butchered my name to gain some immediate leverage, and Nolte's character certainly didn't seduce the young woman in the script, but he fantasized about it, which was a significant contribution to the character. It was, after all, the life unlived, and consummation here would have been some serious living for our depressed character.

"Not in the script, he doesn't. No."

"Listen, Tuy-rell. Let's not jerk each other off, okay? You want Nick, he's gonna fuck the girl."

It wasn't just the language that blindsided me but the crude, aggressive manner that I had never seen in a professional woman close to my mother's age. Also, people had mispronounced my name before, but not this badly, and they always asked what the correct pronunciation was.

"Nick says this?"

"I'm saying it."

"I'll talk to the producers, but I don't think it would serve the story."

Her volume shot up. "Gimme a break, Tuyyy-rell! He's gotta fuck the girl. Figure it out!" This time, she exaggerated the mispronunciation, extending the first syllable as an exclamation of purpose, before hanging up.

We all decided to move on with the casting. I felt unprepared for someone like Sue, but I knew there were plenty more like her, though that is certainly in dispute since her death in 2011.

As we collected quotes from stars we were interested in, it became clear soon enough that the parts needed name actors, but our budget wouldn't afford it, so we had to look for more money. Much more than Herb or Chicago could contribute.

In the meantime, Richard asked me to write some episodes of his television show, which I did, leading to a deal with Universal to work as a contract writer for one year.

While I worked on the script and wrote for Universal television, Harrison would come to LA to meet with producers over various projects, and we would meet for dinner whenever he was in town.

A better dinner companion, one could not ask for; Jim was not only entertaining to dine with, but he had a very generous studio expense account and wasn't shy about testing its limit. Over the next few years, we ate at some of the best restaurants in LA.

I clearly remember my first dining experience with Jim, at an exclusive French restaurant on Westwood Boulevard. He had the studio make the reservation, and as soon as we were seated, Jim took out a cassette recorder (which he did at every restaurant) and sat it upright on the table. He then called over the waiter for questions about the entrees.

Noticing the recorder and the open menu, the waiter leaned over to Jim, careful to keep clear of the starched white tablecloth. "Would you like another menu to take with you to refer to our offerings?"

"Why don't you just bring us all your appetizers and these six entrees. I'll make notes as we go."

"Absolutely, sir. May I ask what publication you are with?"

Jim arched his chaotic eyebrows as he looked up at the waiter. "Most all of them. *New York Times, LA Times, Paris Review, Esquire, New Yorker*. I write a lot about food."

"Very good, sir! Would you like a larger table for your dishes?"

Indeed, we would. We were immediately moved to a table for six that could hold all that we ordered.

The procession of appetizers began, followed by the entrees, then every available dessert until the table was full. Jim would occasionally make comments into the recorder, just for credibility's sake, but they rarely concerned the food, more likely whatever observation had popped into his head at the time, often quotes from his favorite poets.

Dinner with Jim was an adventure in a gastronomic sense, but with intellectual and emotional discovery. His New Yorker essay titled *A Really Big Lunch* detailed a meal prepared by French chef Marc Meneau that Harrison shared with Mario Batali and other guests. It included thirty-seven courses consumed over a period of eleven hours. That was extreme, but the man liked to eat and then talk about it. As Jim said in his essay, "Your meals in life are numbered, and the number is diminishing. Get at it."

The critic Ann Levin wrote of Jim Harrison's essays, "Nearly every piece has a saying wise enough to carry in your wallet."

That was true of meals shared with Jim as well. He also enjoyed driving around drinking beer and talking, a pastime I had developed a fondness for as soon as I owned a driver's license, but it's hard to describe the appeal to the uninitiated.

A destination spoils the adventure. The goal is to drive, drink, and talk, with an occasional pit stop, until the nuggets appear, like mining for gold. To find it, all you need is beer, time, country, and a car, in an era when even a teenager could afford all of those. Jim understood this, which is part of what made him so prized among those of us who shared this love of aimless expedition with a storyteller and a six-pack.

I did this regularly throughout my youth and beyond. The popularity of this pastime faded by the end of the twentieth century, of course, and rightfully so, but I had no friends in Hollywood who shared my fondness for beer and bonhomie in a car. Jim did, and I was richer for it. Those were times to put in my wallet.

CHAPTER 27

IT'S A COMEDY

In nearly the time it took for Pam and me to grow accustomed to LA, our marriage ended. Once the patina faded, she grew disillusioned with Los Angeles and wanted to move closer to her family. Pam hated the movie business and said LA made her feel lonely, which was a given for me because I assumed the insubstantial nature of the industry made everyone feel adrift, but I accepted my own loneliness as a fringe of the trade I had chosen. One where your colleagues change with each project, and often your friends as well, until the projects stop and both diminish.

Pam didn't choose any of it, so I felt responsible for her distress on top of my own, only magnifying what already existed. There is so much to be written about divorce, but not here. All that is relevant to this is that it was an effort that fell short, with good company. She moved away. It was an amicable split, with an implosion of the heart that is permanent.

When my contract expired at Universal, I decided not to renew it. I felt television in that time period was a trap for writers, who would just create massive monthly nuts for themselves and become dependent upon the sizeable annual income that just isn't available to writers in any other world. Writers are accustomed to earning next to nothing, but they do it because writing is what drives them, and normally they plow on without asking questions and are happy to accept whatever measly payment becomes available.

With a network television show, writers suddenly find themselves being offered what they would earn in a year for one hour-long television script; then, if it is a popular show, they get paid that amount again in the summer when the show reruns.

Not accustomed to earning this kind of money, writers are tempted to celebrate and start spending. That's when the danger begins. Many writers and producers on the shows I worked on at Universal lived in inordinately large houses, drove expensive cars, and sent their children to the toniest private schools.

Giving up that life is difficult, particularly for a family, most particularly for someone who never really sought it and suddenly discovers a pot of gold, there for the taking.

Writing an hour-long drama for network television normally required developing a forty-eight-minute-long story, around fifty to fifty-two pages, in four acts, which, once the story was approved, needed to be scripted in one week. A writer, or team of writers, would usually write one act a day for four days, each act leading to a commercial break, then rewrite them all on the fifth day. Review and revise over the weekend, turn it in Monday morning, and start meeting about the next story on Tuesday.

Every writer was paid the same sum mandated by the Writers Guild, to be repeated when the show was rerun for the first time, decreasing with each broadcast. A contract writer, like I was, received a substantial weekly salary as a base, with additional fees for writing credits—determined by an arbitration panel with the Writers Guild of America.

Every staff writer at Universal who gathered some credits on a hit show earned serious six-figure incomes (when it was still considered sizeable), and many decided to position themselves as show runners with new ideas. If one of these ideas became a pilot and was picked up by a network, the earning potential skyrocketed well into seven figures annually, with the realistic potential for one hit show to provide a lifetime annuity.

Universal could place a contract writer on any show they found appropriate for one's particular style or talent. After working on staff for *Simon and Simon* for several months and doing assignment work on other Universal shows, the studio attached me to a new show called *Dalton*, which was the story of a Vietnam Special Forces vet who traveled around the country offering his unique skills to those in need of help, often victims of criminal opportunists. The show was created by Robert Foster, the executive producer of *Knight Rider*, and the lead writer was Herman Miller, who had written the Clint Eastwood movie *Coogan's Bluff* in 1968 and created the *Kung Fu* series of the 1970s.

The writers I met at the studio were intelligent, talented, and (for the most part) extremely collegial. I did feel, however, that many had become dependent upon the money, which became the fuel for their ambition, not the work itself. I wanted to avoid that, so I quit.

Leaving TV was an easy decision for me. Since the advent of cable and streaming, things have changed significantly in the television universe, and the quality, for the most part, exceeds that of many theatrical films. At least the writing, and possibly direction. But in 1986, there was no comparison, and I wasn't interested in writing TV shows that I would never watch, which described nearly everything on network television.

An interesting comparison I made when I first arrived in LA was that when I lived in Washington, I didn't know anyone who watched network television, and therefore no one I knew had any idea what the shows were, who starred in them, and who won Emmy awards. This included me.

The same held true for Grammys. All my friends and I listened to an alternative radio station that didn't play commercial music, and aside from the most famous ones, none of us heard the popular songs that won Grammys, so when the winners were announced, few of us even knew who many of these artists were. This was a time before social media existed, and advertising was targeted, so it was still possible to have boundaries as to what you were exposed to.

When I moved to LA, however, I learned it was a stigma not to watch TV, not to know who the stars were, and most damning to have no clue who has ever won an Emmy Award. I tried watching to lose that stigma, but it didn't take, and it still doesn't.

I was still represented by Paul Kohner at the time, so using my screenplay for *A Good Day to Die* as a selling point, the agency procured a few rewrites for me, which landed me an introduction to a small company that had secured financing to produce a series of $750,000 films based on the titles of hit songs from the 1960s and 1970s.

The development head asked me to choose from a list of titles and come up with a story idea based on such. If the producers liked it, I could write and direct the film.

I chose "Riders on the Storm," the Doors song from 1971 that I saw as being evocative, intriguing, and potentially cinematic. I invented a story and pitched it to the development head, who was excited by the idea and quickly bought it.

I wrote a black comedy about an obsessively delusional clerk, Thelonius Pitt, stuck in a monotonous job, who escapes his boredom by losing himself in the fantastical poems he writes.

Thelo takes a week off to retreat to the mountains and write. There, he meets a beautiful young woman, Melanie, who enters his life as a figurative and emotional mirage. Thelo falls madly in love, but with the covert aid of her boyfriend Earl, Melanie proceeds with wince-inducing skill to artfully twist Thelo into knots.

My inspiration was *Lolita*, and I wanted, in a perfect world, to capture the ironic humor and cold impact of the Kubrick film, but in rich, warm color, using all 1960s and 1970s songs, with a subtlety not often found in the films of the mid-1980s. It was a tricky goal, not attained.

I wanted to cast Joe Mantegna as Thelo, Jennifer Jason-Leigh as

Melanie, and Michael Madsen as Earl. The producers agreed to cast Michael, who had the right look and sense of humor, but they would not accept Jennifer because they found her too serious, nor Joe for a more classically Hollywood reason.

The lead producer was a student of transcendental meditation whose instructor was married to Ned Beatty. The producer admired his instructor, who thought it would be a cute part for her husband to play, so, as logic would, of course, dictate, Ned Beatty became perfect for the part and was cast.

I argued against this casting, not because Ned, an Oscar-nominated, accomplished actor, wasn't capable, but I felt he was too large a presence to play this internalized, timid man who is dazzled in the company of a man-eater. Joe had that capability, as well as an understanding of the subtleties, and he more than demonstrated it when he read for the part. But the quiet power of transcendental meditation won out, and I was overruled.

We shot the film at Camp Nelson, in the Sequoia National Forest among the redwoods, a suitably enchanting spot that became a quiet but stressful home for the summer.

As in my first film, the producers' money ran out, and crew started going unpaid. This led to massive resentment, with no producers on set to try to assuage anyone, and not much phone service outside of the local bar. This was decades before cell phones, but having no phone service was a situation that most everyone had encountered many times, and no one panicked.

It culminated with Ned throwing a tantrum and destroying the screen doors to his cabin, then walking off the set in the middle of a scene due to a disagreement with me regarding his positioning in a shot. As happens more often than anyone would care to admit, it was a call for attention, and once he got it, shooting resumed, though we lost three hours, which is a lot of money on a film set.

Ned had walked to the local tavern, and I was bound to follow him to talk him down. While doing so, I noticed on the television behind the bar that John Huston had just died. It was fitting to me that I was dealing with a childish outburst on the set while learning of John's death. A situation where I was calling upon every lesson Huston had taught me in production politics, and I found one, the shared camaraderie of the exploited, that worked.

I finished the film on time and submitted my cut on budget. I discovered the company, though touting the songs it had licensed, had actually not done so, and the title was not available to us. They suggested other songs they owned, including Kate Bush's "Running up that Hill," which, though a great song, was not appropriate for any point of the story. But since the company owned the rights, it was used anyway, relevance be damned.

My position was that the film needed the right music and atmosphere to work like Lolita did, with everything played as a melodrama but underplayed until it gets dangerous. The producers, however, were too intimidated by the risk subtlety required and decided to cut the film, conceived and directed as a tongue-in-cheek dark comedy, into a serious thriller, with music to match. There were two important lessons I learned while arguing for my cut of the film: irony is confusing to American audiences, and subtle irony is lost.

I attended a screening of the producers' cut of the film, which had been retitled as well as reconfigured. The screening was scheduled for a potential buyer, who delayed it by fifteen minutes while conducting a personal phone call everyone could overhear. When the buyer hung up and the lights dimmed, the producer stood up and exclaimed, "It's a comedy." My chin hit my chest. If that required explanation, I didn't have the strength to watch what I knew would be an enigmatic exercise—not working as a thriller and hardly perceptible as a comedy.

I left, which was the last I saw of them and the film.

CHAPTER 28
THE ABCS OF (POSSIBLE) ESPIONAGE

Soon after *Riders* was completed, the contract between the Writers Guild of America and the Alliance of Motion Picture and Television Producers expired. The Writers Guild went on strike, mainly to demand an increase in residual payments for television writers.

This had very little effect on feature films, but in solidarity, I manned the picket line with other writers. Feature writers, however, were being offered work in Europe and Asia, so I received several offers to work in Europe, including one film scheduled to be shot in Berlin.

I had never been to Berlin, which always interested me. At the time, the city was reputed to be a hotbed of politics, considering it was no secret that Gorbachev planned to soon remove the Berlin Wall.

The producers of the movie wanted me to travel to Berlin and Potsdam to scout locations for a cold war thriller to be shot in the winter. Fortunately, the strike ended before production was scheduled to begin, so I accepted the job and flew to meet with the department heads in Berlin.

It was October and starting to get cold in Northern Germany, but I found it the perfect time of year to walk Berlin. The director, Jeannot Szwarc, joined me as we walked and discussed my approach to adapting the novel the story was based upon. Berlin was, to me, the most exciting city I had ever seen—full of color, passion, and numerous and conflicting ideas. People would be animatedly talking art, politics, and music in outdoor cafés all over the city.

Jeannot, a Jewish Parisian who had directed *Supergirl* and the sentimental romantic favorite *Somewhere in Time*, didn't share my enthusiasm for Berlin. He perceived subtle residual effects of the Nazi era in the form of implied anti-Semitism.

At first, I was skeptical of his concerns, but after several days at the Kempinski Hotel on the Kurfurstendamm, or Krudam, I began to see why he felt uncomfortable. Nearly all the clerks at the hotel were tall, blond, and blue-eyed, with a very officious, matter-of-fact manner. But when Jeannot, who was swarthy and slight, and I would approach the front desk together, it became clear that the clerks would address me before Jeannot, with a subtle hint of greater respect.

I grew up exposed to the most brutal forms of racism in the South, but I had not seen much anti-Semitism. Jeannot pointed it out to me several times while we were in Berlin, and I must admit that I saw it as well. Hitler had only been gone forty years, and I'm sure there were Germans who still shared his views. Jeannot, whose relatives were victims of the Holocaust, came to Germany for work, and he couldn't wait to get out.

Still, despite some misgivings because of Jeannot's unease, I found Berlin to be fascinating and couldn't get enough of my research into Cold War politics, which, through my intrigue and mindless curiosity, I almost experienced the worst of firsthand.

While in Berlin and staying at the Kempinski, I had a private driver who was authorized to take me through Checkpoint Charlie into East Berlin and Potsdam. While he was allowed to drive me anywhere in the East, he was not allowed to leave the car. The production company had secured a visa for me, with certain restrictions, and my driver would submit destinations for us whenever we traveled.

My driver, who claimed to be Scottish, was talkative and friendly and would converse freely in the car. He asked about my life, current and past, and the film I was about to write. He acted as not only a driver but a tour guide who was fascinated with the film business. He took me to the tourist spots in West Berlin, such as the Brandenburg Gate, the Holocaust Memorial, and multiple points along the Berlin Wall where tributes were erected to honor East Berliners shot dead while trying to enter the West.

The towers in the "death strip" between the two walls loomed ominously between them, each manned with two soldiers carrying rifles with high-powered scopes, under orders to shoot anyone trying to escape the East. It was beyond sobering not only to witness but to realize people walking alongside the wall—on their way to work or to shop—were reminded of it every day. Their neighbors, their friends, and in some cases their families who lived just hundreds of yards away could not visit them.

Those lucky enough to live in the West not only witnessed the oppression of freedom by the threat of death but also the sporadic demonstration of it. There were numerous memorials laid out against the wall or painted on it to demonstrate the grief and respect for those who died seeking freedom. It is a condition most of us who grew up in America only read about, and we rarely give it much thought because we've never seen it. When you walk past the flowers and tributes spread across the wall, that changes.

One day, my driver, who asked me to call him "Scotty," took me to the Pergamon Museum, which held antiquities looted by Hitler during the Third Reich, including artifacts from Africa, Persia, and the Middle East. He also took me to the Memorial of the Russian war dead, with five grassy mounds, each holding the remains of 5,000 soldiers. The 25,000 buried there all died during the taking of Berlin, which was shocking. A cold reminder that 27 million Russians died in World War II.

The last stop in East Berlin was at the Grand Hotel, the most expensive hotel ever built in Eastern Europe under Communist rule, one Gorbachev proudly designed to host foreign investors, beginning with the Japanese, whose robust economy was controlling much of the world's currency. Scotty wanted me to see the hotel since it was the pride of East Berlin, and he wanted to drop something off for a friend of his who worked there.

Apparently, Scotty's friend was a bartender at the hotel, and Scotty had purchased a gift for him. It was a recipe book for bartenders titled, as I remember, *The ABCs of Cocktails*. Since Scotty wasn't allowed out of the car in East Berlin and his friend was not allowed to enter the West, he asked if I would deliver it to him.

What he was asking me to do didn't fully register until Scotty delivered specific instructions as he handed me the book. I was to carry the book, along with my personal notebook that I took everywhere, through the lobby and into the bar, order a gin and tonic, and sit in a specially designated seat. When my drink arrived, I was to set the book down on an adjacent table, enjoy my drink while making notes in the notebook, then walk out, leaving the book on the tabletop.

I listened to his instructions, and though I was unsure of what I was being engaged to do, I considered it anyway. I leafed through the book, which seemed like an ordinary recipe book with solid binders and seams, so I agreed to deliver it.

The hotel was exquisite, with gold trim and onyx countertops throughout. I walked through the lobby to the assigned open seat—a green lounge chair by the window. I sat down in the chair and put the book on the adjacent table while the bartender came to take my order. I obliged him, he nodded and smiled professionally, and then he returned several minutes later with my gin and tonic.

While I made meaningless notations in my notebook about what I had seen that day, I began to wonder who Scotty actually was. How could he possibly communicate with his friend in East Berlin? Who exactly was the friend, and why was he living in the East? Before I could work up a nervous sweat, I quickly finished my drink and walked out, leaving the book on the designated table.

When I returned to the car, Scotty asked me if I left the book. When I told him I had, he smiled broadly and turned to the road. "Good man!" he said, unable to hide that he was more delighted than he should have been over the delivery of cocktail recipes.

I tried not to think about what I had just done, but it became more difficult when we tried to reenter the West through Checkpoint Charlie. I had visited the East at least three times previously with Scotty en route to Potsdam or other locations and never had a problem coming or going, but this time, we were detained.

Without any explanation, the East German officers asked us to step out of the car and be seated in two separate interrogation rooms in a building adjacent to the checkpoint. Scotty smiled at me as we were separated and nodded in a friendly fashion, saying in a calm voice, "Just tell them why you're here."

The uniformed police led me into a room where a man in civilian clothes entered, joined by another officer in a different uniform, who I assumed to be Stasi. They took my passport and delivered it to a third man, also in uniform, and started asking me questions.

The first set was about why I was in East Berlin, what I was doing in the West, my movie, how I knew Scotty, who I worked for—what seemed like standard questions.

This continued for about a half hour; then, they began to ask about my life at home. Who was I? What was my work history? Where did I grow up? Many questions about my childhood that I couldn't understand the relevancy of. I figured they possibly could have discovered that my father was an intelligence officer, and that's why they were asking, but they never asked one question about the book of recipes. That was what confounded me. It seemed as if they didn't know.

Two hours later, I was released. Scotty was waiting for me in the car. He smiled as I climbed in the back seat.

"Ready to go home?" he asked.

When I related my story to department heads I had befriended at the hotel, they were unanimously dumbstruck by my questionable judgment. "Do you realize," they would ask, "you could have easily ended up in an East German prison for the rest of your life? Ignorance is no alibi for espionage. Good God!"

I agreed and shuddered to think of what I had risked. I never saw Scotty again. When I next needed a car, I had a new driver, who didn't know what had become of Scotty.

I finished my research in Berlin and came home to write the script, which pleased the producers. Gorbachev ended the Cold War the following year, and in a massive celebration, the Berlin Wall was dismantled and removed. A friend who attended brought me a piece of the wall, and today it sits on a shelf in my living room as a constant reminder of the experiment that became a critically consequential period of world history.

CHAPTER 29
THE POWER OF MYTH

Almost every script written in Hollywood has an undetermined shelf life, mostly because every studio and producer is looking for "the latest thing," not a story that has been circulated. The fact that another company has already had the opportunity to reject a project is nearly enough for a studio to pass.

When the budget increased for *A Good Day to Die* and we were unable to quickly raise funding, the buzz on the film cooled, and interest waned. After a year, the option Herb had taken on the book expired, and a French producer took a new one and planned to write his own screenplay, so my script became useless.

When I finished the Berlin script and had exited *Riders on the Storm*, which was retitled *Shadows in the Storm* because the company had no rights to the song, I planned to write another script on speculation but had to decide on a genre and a story.

Richard Chapman made that decision for me, with a new proposal. He was a major fan of all the novellas in Harrison's *Legends of the Fall* collection and would be interested in optioning one of them and partnering with me as producers if I would write the screenplay as my part of the investment.

I knew that John Huston was once slated to direct *Revenge*, one of the novellas from the *Legends* collection, which was ultimately helmed by Tony Scott and starred Kevin Costner, Madeline Stowe, and Anthony Quinn. John and I had discussed Harrison's work. He was also a fan of the writer.

Another novella, *Legends of the Fall*, was under option to Edward Zwick, who would soon produce and direct it, starring Brad Pitt, Anthony Hopkins, and Julia Ormond.

The one novella available for option was *The Man Who Gave Up His Name*, a story about Nordstrom, a successful oil executive and hatchet man, who, in a strong metaphor, likes to dance alone.

Nordstrom begins questioning his history of life choices when his daughter calls him a "cold fish." This accusation leads Nordstrom to reevaluate his life, causing him to give away his money and divorce his wife. He then becomes involved with a young scam artist, but when he realizes her scheme, he turns the game around, leading to a deadly confrontation on the top floor of the Carlyle Hotel.

The corporate and personal chicanery and mayhem of this world ultimately lead Nordstrom to a permanent life change as a cook in a Louisiana Gulf restaurant, where, as an epiphany, he dances in public.

When faced with a defining life choice, Nordstrom chooses the one he had always miscalculated and avoided. It seemed all of Harrison's works involved an older man falling in love with a younger woman, but it was a conversation we never had.

Richard optioned the book. I wrote the script, and everyone, meaning Richard, Jim, and his agent Bob Dattila, was happy with it. Richard's agents at William Morris were also happy, and he brought me to meet with all the department heads. They offered to sign me right away.

Now with William Morris's backing, I handed the script to producer Trevor Albert, whom I was meeting with about another project. When I mentioned *Man Who*, he asked if he could give it to Bonni Lee, who was running Robert Redford's company at the time. With Richard's approval, we gave Trevor a green light.

Lee read the script and passed it along to Redford, who apparently also "liked it" and was considering whether he would prefer to direct or just produce and star in it.

While Redford was considering, Bob Dattila met with Sydney Pollack, who had hired Bob's client Harrison to rewrite another screenplay. Sydney mentioned to Bob that he loved Harrison's books but could never find a screen adaptation that seemed to capture the spirit of Jim's prose. Bob gave Sydney my adaptation of *Man Who* to take home with him, telling him Redford had read it and liked it.

Sydney was coming off his Academy Award triumph with *Out of Africa* and looking for his next project. When he read the script, Sydney called me at home the next morning, which was Saturday.

"Terrell, this is Sydney Pollack. I hope I'm not bothering you."

"No, sir. Not at all."

"Listen, I read your script of *The Man Who Gave Up His Name*. I think it's great, and I want it to be my next movie."

This was the kind of call no young, not famous filmmaker in Hollywood is ever prepared for, no matter how much you like to think you are. Prepared for rejection, you're a veteran. Prepared for *we like it but will see what the big boss says*, you also know well. Prepared for an Academy Award-winning director whose work you've always greatly admired to say, "This is my next movie?" Never happens, and it is impossible to manufacture the right response other than "Well, that's very good news. Thank you."

"Do you own the rights to the script and the book?"

"With a partner, yes, sir."

"Good. Who represents you?"

"Ron Mardigian at William Morris."

"We'll call him Monday. Don't sell it to Bob Redford."

"I'm sorry?"

"He'll never make it. He'll sit on it so he can own it forever. I'm going to make it."

"Well, he hasn't made an offer—"

"Once he finds out I want it, he will, and he'll find out before the weekend is over."

"Well, okay, I—"

"You don't want to sell it to an actor, believe me. They develop things to death. You want a director."

"Okay."

"I'll handle Bob. If he wants to act in it, we'll make that happen. Have you talked with him?"

"No, not to him."

"There's no problem then. I'll call William Morris on Monday. In the meantime, don't sell it. Let's win an Oscar. Let's win a lot of them!"

He laughed and hung up. That was the call.

Sure enough, I didn't know how the grapevine worked in Hollywood, but word was out over the weekend. Sunday night, I heard from an angry Trevor Albert, who wanted to know if I was going to sell the script to Sydney. When I told him most likely, he proceeded to guilt me the best he could, but not successfully.

I did feel bad since Trevor was there first, but Sydney claimed he was going to make the film, he had a great track record, and his last movie did win Best Picture. I hadn't even talked to Bonni Lee, much less Redford. Like Walter Kohner, Sydney had called me before 9 a.m. on a Saturday morning while I was reading the newspaper. I liked the signaling.

I made the deal with Sydney's company Mirage Enterprises, financed by Universal Pictures, and began to prepare for our success.

The following week, *Variety* published a front-page story about how Sydney Pollack had spent four years searching for a script to make as his follow-up picture to Academy Award winner *Out of Africa* and had finally decided upon Terrell Tannen's adaptation of the Jim Harrison novella *The Man Who Gave Up His Name*.

Following that article, I became a hot ticket, pursued by producers and studios, either to adapt literary novels or rewrite existing scripts that needed something indescribable, often sought in Hollywood.

Sydney suggested I leave William Morris and go with his agents at CAA, which I did.

Sydney and I met to discuss the rewrite of the script with his notes, and he had a request for me before I began.

Sydney and his wife had just spent two weeks at the Esalen Institute in Big Sur, where they attended daily lectures by Joseph Campbell, the Sarah Lawrence literature professor who had just published his highly influential book, *The Power of Myth*.

Like Campbell's earlier book, *The Hero with a Thousand Faces*, *The Power of Myth* discusses the three stages of "The Hero's Journey": the Departure, the Initiation, and the Return. As Campbell described it, "A hero ventures forth from the world of the common day into a region of supernatural wonder: fabulous forces are there encountered, and a decisive victory is won: the hero comes back from this mysterious adventure with the power to bestow boons on his fellow man." These "boons" begin with wisdom gained from the experience.

In *Finnegan's Wake*, James Joyce called the hero's journey the "monomyth," a term Campbell enlisted as well. Many psychologists, anthropologists, and storytellers since the nineteenth century have since referred to this story structure as "the archetypal narrative." Phil Cousineau, in his introduction to the companion book of Bill Moyers's interviews with Campbell, titled *The Hero's Journey*, referred to the monomyth as "the story behind the story," which, if accepted as truth, makes it not only universal but eternal.

Growing up, Sydney was an avid reader of mythology, as was I, and he wanted Campbell's ideology to guide us through the making of our film. Sydney was taken with Dr. Campbell's lectures and didn't just want me to read his book, which I already had, but he actually gave me an assignment.

At Esalen, Sydney had recorded all of Campbell's lectures and wanted me to listen to his tapes, which were probably twenty hours in total. But Sydney felt that the environment in which I listened was very important.

Most of the story, including pivotal points, takes place in Manhattan. In the novella, Nordstrom spends much of his free time walking about the city while pondering his place in the world. This becomes a personal narration for the story, which I included in portions throughout the script. For inspiration, Sydney wanted me to walk all of New York City, including Central Park and the zoo, while listening to Campbell's lectures, just to see what developed. Sydney knew how to motivate a writer.

My instructions were to check in to a high-end East Side hotel and spend however much time I needed on my walks, listening to Joseph Campbell's lectures on the hero's journey through a Sony Walkman cassette player. I was to live like Nordstrom, who enjoyed a very entitled life, and eat like Nordstrom at his favorite restaurants, meaning Jim Harrison's, with all expenses charged to Universal.

Painful as it sounds, I did as I was instructed to do, spending two September weeks at the Lowell Hotel, living, sleeping, and eating like Nordstrom. I walked his museum routines, warmed his park benches, ate at Elaine's, and downed nightcaps at Bemelman's Bar at the Carlyle. I stared at the people passing by, considering them the way Nordstrom would, sensing their lives and purpose. I put myself in Nordstrom's place, imagining his despair, disillusionment, inner questions, and quest for resolution.

It all took, as far as I was concerned. I absorbed the lectures, contemplated the hero's journey, and returned home to rewrite the script. It was hard for me to relate to a man who was reevaluating his life and considering a major change when my life seemed so good. But I put my feet in Nordstrom's shoes and my head on his shoulders and set to work.

Nordstrom was a man who had achieved his success through his ability to coolly determine who would be the first to go in any corporate restructuring. He destroyed lives by doing this, but he managed to avoid emotional responsibility because it served the company so well. He was very successful, praised for his work, highly compensated, and given pretty much anything he asked for.

He had the perfect setup except for two things: a sense of belonging and a true sense of place. Nordstrom was tied to a chair in his very comfortable and extravagant world, but this world was empty. His daughter's comment brought all that home for him.

I felt I understood at least Nordstrom's ennui, remembering my previous life in Washington, and tried to address it in the writing. He was trapped in a sterile environment, gets called out for it, and decides to escape. I knew the feeling, and I felt as if I knew how to communicate it visually as well as with dialogue.

It was hard to contain the urge to celebrate this project, and I rarely succeeded in doing such a thing, but I was experienced enough to know that films don't always work out the way we hope, so I tried to temper it as best I could.

When finished, I was very excited with the result and felt everything was coming into focus. Sydney joined in my excitement, we shared a celebratory lunch, and we began our quest to win his next Oscar.

The following Monday, Sydney sent the completed draft to Robert Redford with an offer to play the lead. He declined. When I asked Sydney how this could be, he explained, "Ah, we're best friends."

"But he wanted it himself. I don't understand."

"It's complicated."

Sydney then offered it to Jack Nicholson, a friend of Jim Harrison's, whose seat Jim was occupying the night I met him, and an actor I had visualized as Nordstrom while writing the script. Jack also passed.

I assumed more "friend" complications but realized there were political dynamics in Hollywood that I couldn't comprehend. One of the first things I remember an actor telling me was "It's not enough to succeed. Your friends have to fail as well."

I neither believed nor understood it at the time but soon learned that that particular cynicism was the foundation of a very elaborate relationship between success and neurosis. Everyone made a joke of the notion, but among even the most evolved, it can be a sad reality.

Like my previous Harrison script, *Man Who* died of exposure after a few months, with Sydney Pollack deciding to abandon it to make *Havana* with, ironically, Robert Redford playing the lead.

Our relationship continued, though, and he asked me to read scripts he was considering and view cuts of *Havana* when they became available. He hired me to adapt another Harrison book, *Farmer*, which sent me to Australia to consult with Phillip Noyce, an Australian director Sydney was interested in. I spent an extended time in Australia with Phillip and his family, returning to write the script, which never got made through Sydney's company, Mirage, and the option expired, to be immediately picked up by Bruno Barreto, who wrote his own script and directed the film starring Dennis Hopper and Amy Irving, released under the title *Carried Away*.

I suppressed the disappointment of having come so close to what I had been striving for, just to have it dissolve for reasons I couldn't understand. Heeding the words of John Huston, I moved forward.

The result was an onslaught of writing assignments, many for prestige projects, all of which paid well, but for one reason or another, often the shuffling of studio executives or actors or directors who would be offered a greenlit project (meaning cleared by the studio to begin production), none of these films would get made.

These assignments, most of them working with successful directors and producers, put me back in the dangerous territory of having a large income with the confidence it would continue. So, like many of the television writers I swore not to emulate, as my income increased, so did my monthly nut. I avoided the family, but my English bulldog was nearly as pricey.

Apparently, when I returned from New York, I brought Nordstrom's previous life home with me.

CHAPTER 30
THE MUSIC IN THE GREASY GRASS

Jim Harrison's agent, Bob Dattila, called me one afternoon with an invitation to meet Mickey Rourke for lunch. Bob had given a script of mine to Mickey, who was looking for a writer for a personal project with private financing. Mickey liked the script and wanted to meet me.

Mickey's younger brother Joey had been diagnosed with lung cancer. Mickey and Joey were close, and both were motorcycle enthusiasts. Mickey had an idea to make a film with Viggo Mortensen, who wasn't yet a star, about two brothers, one of whom is dying of cancer, taking one final trip on their Harleys from the northwestern corner of Montana near Flat Head Lake, across the state to Sturgis, South Dakota, to celebrate the annual motorcycle rally. The event draws hundreds of thousands of enthusiasts each year.

Bob brought me to meet Mickey over lunch by the pool at the Sunset Marquis. Among a cavalcade of French models who were staying at the hotel for a photo shoot and thrilled to be around the star, Mickey explained why he wanted me to write the script for this film, why it was so important to him, and why his Japanese investors would be honored to pay whatever it cost.

I had not been in the position where someone essentially told me to "name my price," but it was a comfortable one. It's not easy determining a figure when there is no precedent or established quote, but I also had not been in a position where an actor, who I didn't know but had a reputation of being temperamental, was calling all the shots. I had to price my services accordingly.

I quoted a figure that was high enough that, if he said yes, I assured myself that there was nothing that could misfire so badly that I would complain about it. The money would just be too good, and I felt confident I could do a good job with the script, ideally a story I could get behind.

Mickey immediately said yes to my quote, and we had two quick meetings at the office of the director, Leslie Dektor, to talk about the story. Mickey suggested that he and I take the same trip as the brothers across Montana and find people and places to base our episodic story on. This worked for me, so we scheduled the trip.

Over the next week, I took several meetings with Leslie, but Mickey would send his manager and call in to join on speakerphone, saying he wasn't feeling well. We would wish him better health and continue with the meeting while Mickey offered his thoughts over the phone.

I also met several times with Viggo, who knew the area fairly well because he had lived in nearby Orofino, Idaho, and had briefly been a biker himself. He brought me to a poetry slam where his wife at the time, Exene Cervenka, the former lead singer for the band X, performed a poem she had already written about the character Viggo was intended to play, even though I hadn't yet written the part. That immersion impressed me.

Within a week, I was on my way to Kalispell, Montana, where I was to meet Mickey and ride across the state to Sturgis, where we would scope out the town as a location for the finale of the film.

The idea was for Mickey and me to simulate the ride and stay in the same towns as the characters in the story, starting with Whitefish, MT, and ending in Sturgis.

I flew into Bozeman, MT, and visited with Bob Dattila and

friends in Livingston before driving to Kalispell to meet Mickey. I passed time in the airport until Mickey's flight landed and passengers disembarked, with no sign of Mickey. I called his manager, who returned the call five minutes later with the news that Mickey wasn't feeling well and wouldn't be making the trip.

I called Bob, who lived in Livingston, and asked if he wanted to fly to Kalispell and join me, which he was game to do. I spent the night in Kalispell and picked Bob up the following day. We set out across the state, looking for promising locations, characters, and a story.

Our first stop was Whitefish, a wintry town with a nineteenth-century feel and strong Western flavor. We stopped for lunch at the Bulldog Saloon, housed in a stretch of adjoined two-story wooden buildings, with a large EAT sign by the door, directly underneath a second-story bar sign at least ten feet high, displaying a hand-painted bulldog standing on hind legs in a human's fighting posture, wearing boxing trunks and shoes. As a bulldog owner, I was moved to stop in.

The bar was filled with photos and drawings of the dogs, reflecting a fascination any bulldog owner can easily understand, being a breed that looks threatening yet acts childlike and innocent. Even the men's room was covered with bulldog paraphernalia, with photos and graffiti scribbled on the wall addressed to one's favorite bulldog, a creature with a face and personality somehow designed to elicit a smile. Even the names on the pinups, such as Tulip, Julius, and Lulu, summoned that effect.

I asked the bartender what relationship the breed held to the bar's history, and he replied, "Attitude." Confused, I asked him to elaborate. "We're a nice bar," he said. Got it. I further understood when I later went to the bar's website and discovered the web address was "fart-slobber.com." Definitely got it.

The character search continued through Flathead Lake and across the state, stopping in fishing grounds, reservations, and saloons, including one in Missoula, where we were denied an open seat at the bar because it was reserved for Jim Crumley whenever he decided to pop in. Crumley, the author of *Dancing Bear*, among other books, was an iconic figure in Missoula, a notable writer revered in not only that bar but others in town. The stool was rarely empty, for Crumley kept a sizeable tab working.

We stopped at famous trout fishing rivers and streams, mountain viewpoints, and interesting merchants and hotels along the way. One general store on a side road had dozens of elk antlers stacked twenty feet high off to the side of the building. I went in to buy whatever they were selling and struck up a conversation with the owner, who wore a scowl like he was born into it. He was perched in a chair by the door and never moved the whole time I was inside, eyeing me like a bird of prey, with a likened sense of humor.

"Did you shoot all those elk yourself?" I asked him.

"Don't need to when they layin' on the ground."

"You just comb the forest and pick them up?"

He nodded.

"How often do they shed?"

His eyes narrowed. "Why you askin'?"

"I'm just curious. What do you do with all those antlers?"

"Sell 'em to the Japanese."

"What do they do with elk antlers?"

"Grine 'em inna afedeezyacs."

"Really? What do they pay for those?"

"That stack? Three hunnet thousand."

"Dollars?"

He nodded.

"That's an expensive pile of bone. How do you keep it from getting stolen, just sitting out there?"

At that, he smiled for the first time.

"Well, to get them antlers, you gotta go through my dog, me and my M16." He gestured behind the counter.

That was my lesson for the day, and those stacks were an impressive sight by the side of his store.

Bob and I continued through Butte, Bozeman, and Billings, where the railroad roundhouse reminded me of all the films I saw growing up where trains were such an integral part of industrializing the West in the nineteenth century. As we drove across the plains, herds of antelope, like a colorful high-speed marathon, would race alongside the road, threatening at any point to cross in front of us.

We stopped in numerous bars to soak up the local personality and were rarely disappointed by what we found. The only trouble we encountered was at a rough bar not far from Livingston, where two sizeable women exited the restroom and accused us of taking their seats at the bar, which was odd considering the barstools were nearly empty. But we would have been happy to give them up.

The larger of the two, however, wanted to administer a little punishment to at least one of us, even if we didn't care about the barstools. This was a new situation for both of us, and neither knew how to handle it. We left, making the choice easy. Neither one of us wanted to be tossed from a bar or pummeled by a woman bigger than us, but it made for an interesting discussion regarding how it could have been described later.

Before entering South Dakota, we stopped at the Little Bighorn battlefield, close to the Little Bighorn River, where General George C. Custer suffered his famous defeat.

The battlefield is now part of the Crow reservation, but it is a historical monument that has the penetrating solemnity of a church. There are no signs, no gift shops, no lights. Just gravestones and a sculptured memorial to the soldiers and Indian warriors who died there. There is an eerie quiet—one that artfully describes what happened. Custer's 268 men were wiped out by 3,000 Sioux and Commanche fighters, under the leadership of Sitting Bull and Crazy Horse in what the tribes called "The Battle of Greasy Grass."

One doesn't even want to talk when visiting this hallowed piece of land. You can sense the ghosts on the battlefield and feel the gloomy presence of violent death as you walk among the gravestones, quiet but for the wind gently blowing through the "greasy grass," its soft whistle creating its own music, giving the name life.

The sky was full of clouds without definition or rain, creating an ominous silence but for the wind. One assumed the sky over Little Bighorn was always filled with these very same clouds since the massacre. When standing on those hilltops, it's easy to see the battlefield of 150 years ago, requiring no imagination, a landscape unchanged but for generations of the same greasy grass, an eerie magic floating in the fields.

Bob and I finished our journey in Sturgis, which, without the bikers, was not unlike most nondescript Western towns. It was unremarkable in most respects, and I realized I'd have to come back for the rally, probably with Mickey.

That never came to pass. I turned in the script, and Mickey's Japanese investors paid off the entire fee and never asked for a second draft. The project was scuttled for some undisclosed reason, and I was happy to keep it undisclosed. I had been well paid, enjoyed a gorgeous and enlightening drive across Montana, and fell under the spell of the greasy grass. If only the elk knew what they carried on their heads.

CHAPTER 31
A BIGGER HOUSE WILL SAVE YOU MONEY (AND OTHER HOLLYWOOD ILLUSIONS)

I was extremely busy for the next few years, and my income grew to a point where I started looking for some form of tax shelter. I was paying 10 percent of everything I earned to my agents, 5 percent to a lawyer, and 5 percent to a business manager, which I was still uninitiated enough to believe was necessary to manage my money. This was before the enormous tax bite of more than 50 percent of my adjusted gross income, which was a painfully large check to write every quarter, understandably because I had been so fortunate.

When I approached my business manager with a request to find me somewhere to invest my money rather than just pay it immediately to the government, he told me that I already had a 401K that I maxed out each year, I was incorporated, and I contributed to several charities. His advice was this: the best way to invest my money was to buy the biggest house I could find, in the neighborhood I most wanted to live, and take out the biggest mortgage available. The bigger the house, the more it will appreciate, and in the end, make me money instead of paying it in taxes.

Okay.

I loved the house I lived in at the time, which was a Spanish home built in 1935, about 1,700 square feet, with a beautiful view of the

Silver Lake reservoir and a large fenced-in yard for my bulldog Gus. It had two productive avocado trees and a lovely garden.

I had paid $229,000 for the house in 1986 and could easily pay off the remainder of the mortgage principal whenever I chose and, with a car I fully owned, be debt free. But I was paying a business manager for advice, so why not use what I was paying for? Or at least, as I remember, that was my logic. I set out to find an expensive house.

I decided on a neighborhood close to the Griffith Observatory and found a Mediterranean house that fit the bill. It had ostensibly been built by Hal Roach, creator of *the Little Rascals* and *Laurel and Hardy* series in 1927. The house was 5,500 square feet and had five bedrooms, two kitchens, and three terraces with original cast-iron hanging fixtures. It featured vaulted ceilings, a circular staircase leading up to a double-sized bedroom with amenities I had never imagined, mahogany and Spanish tile throughout, and a driveway that led through an electric iron gate and around the side to the rear of the house, crossing over the nearly Olympic-sized swimming pool with waterfalls in the cove hollowed underneath. Across the pool, the drive ended at a three-car garage with an attic space that I converted into a writing studio with French doors and a Ben Franklin stove on a brick pedestal. The house could have comfortably housed at least six people. I lived alone with Gus, who, at times, chose his own bedroom.

My immediate neighbors were all successful television people or prominent physicians from USC. Danny Devito and Rhea Perlman lived two doors up the hill, Anthony Edwards across the street, and Stevie Wonder around the corner. My friends called the place "the mansion," and Gus and I were like kids in a giant bounce house, gravitating to one corner. It wasn't long before I realized I basically lived in five rooms out of eighteen. I cooked and ate in the kitchen and occasionally on the adjacent terrace, watched television in the den, slept in my bedroom, used the bathroom, and wrote in the garage perch I had paid $150,000 to turn into an office.

Gus seemed to be getting more out of the place than I did, snarfling about those unused rooms, seeking creatures and toys. I used them for storage when I had something I didn't know what to do with, and we all know what happens to whatever is in storage. Never to be touched again—until the Salvation Army truck arrives.

As a cut-from-the-cloth child of civil servants and Georgia farmers who had lived the middle-class existence pretty much all my life, I didn't know what to expect from stepping up in the world. I would learn soon enough: my luxurious space didn't go unnoticed. I had more dinner guests and houseguests than I ever imagined. I had more expensive dates, had more expensive friends (and more of them), and felt compelled to eat at more expensive restaurants.

As a single man in such a house, I'd never been so obviously and strongly flirted with. I drove a new Porsche Carrera, stored fine Bordeaux wines by the case, and bought my jackets at Armani, my shirts at Maxfield, trousers at Fred Segal, and my shoes at Varda. I treated my friends to dinner, clothes, and vacations when I could. My income exceeded my expenses, so I just lived as well as I felt like living and assumed that it would, of course, continue, for why wouldn't it?

I had more calls to return every day and things to learn about home ownership that I had never considered before. I soon discovered that the more expensive the neighborhood, the more extreme (and petty) the neighborhood squabbles, which meant the more disturbed the behavior. At Halloween, I entertained more trick-or-treaters and discovered many of the families had come to the neighborhood because it was much safer than where they lived, the quality and healthiness of the treats was higher, and the odds of getting tainted or old candy was much less. I was happy to oblige and always prepared for the numbers. I had far more solicitors for nearly every service performed, and they were far more engaging and respectful than those from my more inclusive neighborhood. I had never been called "sir" so often.

In short, all the clichés about money, and the perception of it, regardless of what the songs and feel-good Hollywood dramas would have you believe, turned out to be true.

I could, however, deduct the interest to the mortgage, and that was the logic that drove me, or at least it was intended to.

In terms of my daily routine, all that changed was the route of my morning walk. I was now close enough to the Observatory that I could walk a loop with some of the prettiest panoramic views in all of Los Angeles. What my business manager and I had overlooked was the expense of maintaining such a house, including taxes, utilities, pool maintenance, gardeners, gifts to community associations, and housekeeping for an estate nearly four times the size of my last. But as long as I kept earning money, it wasn't a problem.

I had fallen into the trap that I had so studiously avoided five years earlier while working for Universal. The difference was that I was working on what I wanted, so it wasn't a compromise. The journey can become more justifiable, but the potential result? No rosier.

CHAPTER 32
YOU SLOW DOWN, YOU GO DOWN

My first assignment after moving into the big house was for MGM and Hugh Hudson, director of the Best Picture Oscar winner *Chariots of Fire*. The studio sent me to Key West to research *Bones of Coral*, an adaptation of the novel by James W. Hall. Hall's book was a fascinating story on the relationship between US Defense Department testing of chemical-warfare weapons in the 1950s and the elevated incident rate of multiple sclerosis in Key West forty years later.

Writing the script and learning the background to the story Jim Hall had written was a great experience. I loved Key West and returned several times to stay at a secret rental that Jim Harrison arranged for me. It was a beautiful house, converted into four apartments, with its own private beach belonging to Jim's publisher Seymour Lawrence. He rented only to writers, and the rent was less than minimal for what I would argue was the best spot on the island.

Each morning, I would say hello to the Pulitzer Prize-winner John Hersey, author of *Hiroshima*, who lived next door and would be having breakfast with his friends on the terrace, as I left for my daily bike ride to collect the day's grouper, crab, and produce to cook that night on the beachfront grill.

Part of my research, which was a significant part of the story, involved getting to know actual smugglers who took me on the vessels they used to transport product, mostly cocaine and stolen salvage, from the Bahamas and reef islands to Florida coves. They could elude Coast Guard ships because of their speed, maneuverability, and adaptability.

I found it almost ridiculously easy to find these outlaws, for most all the locals knew who they were, and even easier to befriend them as a representative of the movie business. As seems to be the case most everywhere I have scouted for a film, everyone was happy to show off what they could do to someone who made movies and, in this case, eager to demonstrate their high-performance, customized boats. The Coast Guard was around, but only on ships, and there never seemed to be any other form of law enforcement about. I did hear stories about the one patrol cop giving drunken drivers a lift home. This was before strict DUI enforcement.

The smugglers' boats were double-engine, high-speed vessels, similar to Cigarette racing boats but with altered engines and holds, adapted to carry large loads while skimming the surface at very high speeds—much like a Florida Keys version of *Thunder Road*.

I got a harrowing lesson in the importance of skimming the surface while piloting a boat myself. While cruising offshore, a smuggler had given me the controls to see how I could handle it. I was a novice, and if I was going to make a movie about fast smuggler boats, I ought to know what it felt like to steer one. So, he had me pilot the boat at full throttle through the shallow mangrove flats of Key West, the routes commonly used by smugglers to evade the bigger Coast Guard boats, which needed deeper water to keep from running aground.

I'd been given a beer and no prep. I piloted the boat through the lagoon, which wasn't difficult, then into a shallow inlet leading back to the ocean. The smuggler told me to keep the speed up, but he never mentioned the importance of it, and I thought he was just a boasting joyrider who wanted to stay clear of the Coast Guard. As we turned into the inlet, I saw we were approaching a bridge about two hundred yards ahead, traveling at full throttle.

The smuggler instructed me to weave my way between two piles spread about twenty feet apart. From the spacing between the piles, it was clear there was no anticipated boat traffic in this inlet other than small flatboats or rafts. I was approaching this bridge around 60 mph, which was an unsafe passage even for an experienced pilot, so as I got close, I reached for the throttle to slow down before threading the needle.

As my hand closed around the red lever to pull back, the smuggler yelled, leaping from the back of the boat and pushing the throttle back to full speed in one motion. "Christ, man. You want to kill us?" He held onto the throttle as I successfully steered the boat between the piles, which flew by in a blur, just a few feet separating us from solid concrete.

"What are you talking about?" I asked.

He pointed at the water. The bottom, visible just below the surface, was a layer of rocks. He hadn't mentioned the danger when he gave me the throttle. I thought he just loved speed. "That's why the Coast Guard can't come in here. But this boat can."

I kept looking at the rocks below us, hurtling by at high speed as we flew across the surface. "We slow down, we go down," he said, almost with pride, and added a laugh.

I was certain that had been the fate of more than one of his colleagues. All it would take is a piece of grit in the fuel line. I didn't feel like laughing. I only felt like getting off the boat and onto my bike.

After working through the hottest part of the day, I would take a second bike ride around the island, stopping at the Full Moon Saloon and Sunset Pier for a margarita and some conch fritters or possibly a grouper sandwich. European tourists would file off cruise ships onto the pier around 5 p.m. daily, and there was always a conversation available. I found many character sources in those crowds.

Adjacent to the rental house on the beach was Louie's Back Yard and the Afterdeck Lounge, an old waterfront restaurant popular among Key West's numerous expats. Hanging each night at the Afterdeck after dinner, I learned all I needed to know about drug running, ocean salvage, checking shoes for scorpions in the morning, and living outside the fringes—popular in Key West at that time. I even became involved with the famous treasure hunter Mel Fisher, the man who recovered the Atocha, by investing in his expedition to find a sunken Spanish galleon loaded with gold bullion.

Fisher's salvage team found the galleon, but unsurprisingly to anyone familiar with ocean salvage teams, there was a very high turnover among the divers, and much of the gold in the ship's manifest turned out to be "missing." I did get a cannonball, some gold and silver Spanish coins worth only their weight, a few emeralds, and other keepsakes, which I found not that keepable. But the hunt was fun, though expensive.

Bones of Coral didn't get made, and the option expired. Partially due to my newly acquired fascination and experience with the treasure-hunting culture, I was hired to write another tropical story, this one set in the West Indies.

CHAPTER 33
INNOCENT MILLIONAIRES

Steven Vizinczey's clever and insightful 1983 novel, *An Innocent Millionaire*, is the story of an enterprising yet earnest young man who finds a sunken Spanish galleon off the Bahamas with $350 million worth of gold bullion aboard—a fortune even now. Between the assaults of governments, lawyers, unscrupulous art dealers, and criminals, our protagonist loses the money, but he finds love in the process. In the realist tradition of Balzac's *Lost Illusions*, it is a cynical book about a genuine hero, written without cynicism.

I was hired by MGM to write a screen adaptation for director Jon Avnet, with Tom Cruise intended to play the lead role. Avnet and Steve Tisch had produced *Risky Business*, which first propelled Cruise to stardom.

To create a setting for the story, I flew to Harbour Island, a small, quiet, family-friendly resort destination in the outer Bahamas, which had been recommended to me by a friend who was a native. Tourist access from the US required flying to Nassau or Eleuthera and ferrying to the island, so it was much less traveled than most of the Bahamas.

I checked in to a modest but comfortable hotel, the Coral Sands, removed from most others and nestled among private homes on the pink sandy beach. I would venture out daily and walk the island as far as I could in all directions, discovering the personalities and lifestyles of permanent residents. Famous for its smooth, pink sand beaches, Harbour Island was known as a vacation destination for families and much quieter than most of the commercial vacation spots in the Bahamas. There was no night life, very few restaurants, and simple markets where locals shopped.

One discovery I made on my walks was an off-road country Baptist church. I grew up in the South, attending Baptist churches, with a personal background in music. What emanated from that building was the most inspired Africa-themed gospel music I had heard since moving to California, and the talent inside was extraordinary. Not just the players but the whole congregation. This was something I had not anticipated, and I returned several times just to stand outside the small, weather-beaten chapel and listen to the magic being created inside.

Outside the church, I couldn't help but move to the music. Here I was, on a desiccated coral key in the Caribbean, outside this rustic wooden building with peeling paint and rotting steps, nestled in the sand and scrub off a side road hosting only foot traffic, gyrating and tapping to electric guitar, organ, bass, drums, and powerful voices giving it all they had. The energy was infectious, and when a service was scheduled, I wanted to be there. I never entered the church, for I would be a clear intruder on the sanctity of their worship, but I was experiencing my own outside the window.

Each day, I would spend a few hours in my room working on the story outline, and if there was no service at the church, I would take a walk along the beach up and down the key, admiring the unique colors of clear water on pink sand. I would then take a swim and sit on the beach to dry off and stare out to sea before returning to work.

One afternoon, I noticed an unusual yacht anchored possibly a half-mile offshore from the hotel. It was the biggest private yacht I had ever seen, and soon, a tender ferried two men and a teenage boy from the yacht to the shore in front of the hotel. The tender dropped them at the beach, then returned to the yacht.

The boy and one man walked across the beach to the hotel while the other spread a towel in front and sat. The boy was disabled, with obvious difficulty manipulating his left side. He walked with a distinct limp, and his left arm and leg were considerably smaller than his right. He was a handsome boy, somewhat slight, and always in the company of at least one of the two men.

This ritual continued for the next three days. The tender would drop them off, then the boy and one of the men would enter the hotel, and the other man remained on the beach. The two would occasionally come out of the hotel, visit briefly with the second man, then return inside.

Later in the day, the tender would return, and the three would climb aboard and return to the yacht. I watched this routine for two days, curious as to who they were and what they were doing. At night, I looked out at the yacht anchored offshore. It was brightly lit, like a party boat, and I wondered who was aboard. Was this some kind of commercial venture? But who were the men? And who was the boy?

On the third day, when the three arrived and two of them entered the hotel, the third man stared at me a little longer than sheer curiosity allowed. I was sitting in the same chair I always did, for the beach was never crowded at the hotel, particularly offseason. When it was clear that he wasn't being surreptitious, I nodded a greeting to him. He got up and approached me, as if he'd been awaiting a signal.

The man smiled as he asked if he could join me, then casually began a series of friendly questions. He wanted to know if I was on holiday, was I enjoying myself, why was I visiting the Bahamas alone, and several seemingly irrelevant questions. I answered directly, figuring I would, in turn, get what I gave, and when I told him I was a screenwriter researching a story, his manner brightened, and he seemed as happy to share his story as he was to hear mine.

The yacht belonged to the Aga Khan, spiritual leader of the Shia Ismailli Muslims and one of the richest royals in the world, considered to be a direct descendant of the prophet Muhammad. The boy was his Highness's youngest son Hussain, a sixteen-year-old student at Deerfield Academy who had a fascination with marine life and came to this hotel every year to visit the owners' private aquarium.

Hussain's entourage kept rooms in the hotel for privacy and a rest stop on the beach while the yacht was anchored offshore. His Highness the Aga Khan was a yachting enthusiast, and this particular craft was at the time the most expensive in the world, powered by two flanking jet engines. In 1992, it was still considered an experimental vessel capable of speeds over 50 knots.

The man told me he was Hussain's tutor, which I read to mean bodyguard, which seemed to explain why he was curious about me. Since childhood, Hussain had harbored a love for the sea and its wildlife. When Hussain was thirteen, the tutor told me, he was jet skiing with a friend and fell off his ski into the water. The friend, directly behind Hussain, couldn't veer away in time and went over the boy's neck, the prop cutting into Hussain's spinal cord. Even with the best medical care in the world, the injury left him permanently disabled.

The tender arrived, and Hussain and his second attendant came out of the hotel. I was introduced, and they said goodbye, for the yacht was leaving the next day.

As I watched the boy amble across the sand, then being helped aboard the tender, I thought about the fragility of our fortunes. The obvious truth of the maxim we hear from childhood—one we all understand but never more clearly than when it's exemplified in front of our eyes—"All the money in the world can't buy health and happiness."

That evening, a group of young men arrived from Paris and checked into the hotel. It was the German electronic rock group Enigma, who, in the previous year, had created a sensation by adding synthesized sounds to Gregorian chants. The group was looking for a getaway to relax and enjoy the sun, sand, and water and had never been to the Bahamas. We met at the bar, and they invited me to join them for dinner, where they asked me a series of questions about Hollywood. None of them had been to LA, much less the South, and they were all interested in my musical background, for they knew very little about Southern music.

I asked if they were aware of the Baptist church on the island, and of course, they were not and were fascinated by the concept of amplified instruments rocking a church. None of them had heard real gospel music performed in the proper environment. I told them they were in for a very special treat, and since it was Saturday, I arranged to meet them in the lobby just before the following day's service.

The next morning, we walked over to the church and could hear the spirit long before we reached it. When we did, I asked my new acquaintances to stay outside, stand in my spot beside the steps, and covertly watch through the window so as not to distract the congregation.

The entire band was astonished. None of them had heard anything this spontaneous, original, inspired, heartfelt, and just plain moving. They were like smitten teenagers, excited to get back to the hotel and start making phone calls to share their discovery.

Before I left two days later, Enigma informed me that they had arranged for their recording equipment to be shipped to Harbour Island and were planning an album based on the music they heard at the church, which they were now attending for every service.

I was pleased to hear of their plans and was again reminded of the fragility of our fortune, this time for the good. Enigma's next album, *The Cross of Changes*, was a major success worldwide.

I returned home and wrote the script, reliving my encounters to enrich the story I was telling. In my interpretation of Vizinczey's novel, I wrote our hero as being robbed of his discovery because, like most of the world, he is emotionally unarmed for legal combat and too innocent to recognize sophisticated grift. This perceived vulnerability was exploited by all capable and cost him his sunken treasure. But our hero's stamina and unflagging spirit in the face of so much corruption, even as the impending sacrifice became inevitable, provided him strength and won him the love he had sought.

Everyone involved loved the story, including at MGM, but scheduling never aligned, the option expired, and *An Innocent Millionaire* never got made. Despite the misfortunes within his adventure, our hero evolved and returned with something of value, as did I.

CHAPTER 34
A WORLD AGAINST CHANGE

In the eastern Gulf of St. Lawrence, it is a centuries-old rite of passage for Canadian men and their young sons to walk onto the ice floes where harp seals gather to give birth every spring.

The men carry large, spiked wooden clubs called "hakapiks," Medieval-styled weapons with protruding nails, and seek out the hollowed folds in the ice where mother seals settle to nurse their babies. These young seals are called "whitecoats" for their soft, fluffy fur that develops the first two weeks of their lives.

When the hunters find a mother and her pups, they quietly approach, and when close enough, they bludgeon the babies to death with the hakapiks, often the mother as well if she is aggressive, pile the bloody corpses onto a sled, and pull them off the ice. Thousands of seals are slaughtered this way each year. It is sickening to witness—and haunting.

Brian Davies, a Scotsman who founded the British based nonprofit International Fund for Animal Welfare (IFAW), was determined to end the Canadian seal hunt. He and Director Hugh Hudson hired me to tell his story in a screenplay.

The research took me across Newfoundland, where many of the seal hunters resided, west to the Magdalen Islands, centered in the

Gulf of St. Lawrence between Newfoundland, Nova Scotia, and New Brunswick, close to the ice floes where the seal hunt occurs every spring. I titled the script *Red Ice*. It was a brutal story to tell, and at times dangerous.

Many of the hunters would gather on the Magdalens in March, when the seals would be nesting on the floes. I was also there, and if the hunters had known why, it would not have been safe for me. They knew about Brian Davies's campaign to end the hunt, threatening violence against him and those who worked for him.

Most of the hunters thought I was a filmmaker who wanted to document their stories because I asked so many questions about the history of the hunt, how many generations of their families had participated, and how they felt about it. Considering this to be a major part of the story, this is what I accentuated when I talked to them on the ice, and at the bar afterward, where they would stay long after I returned to the only motel on the island.

Though I never saw them, I was told Paul Watson of the Sea Shepherd Conservation Society was also on the island with actor Martin Sheen, an animal rights activist, with the intent to protest the hunt. Talk around the island was that Watson had arranged for international television news crews to document the protest.

Hunters told me Watson and Sheen had arrived in a helicopter, as had I, piloted by Brian Davies. But after dropping me off on the ice, Brian returned to Prince Edward Island. He was a known face targeted as an enemy by the hunters, so he never spent a night in the Magdalens. The hunters, however, told me they had seen Watson and Sheen's chopper parked behind the motel where I was staying, and the two were not welcome on the island.

The night before the hunt, after interviewing the hunters in the bar, I returned to my room around 10 p.m., made some notes, and went to sleep.

Around 2 a.m., I was awakened by drunken shouting and banging of clubs on walls. I knew what type of clubs these men carried, and they were designed to kill large, wild animals. When I could make out voices, I heard, "Where the fuck is Watson?" "Watson, we want you!" "What room is Watson in?" Each yell would be accentuated by the banging of a club against a wall. There were a number of voices in the hallway, and the clamor was loud, intense, and threatening. As a precaution, I dressed and checked the window, in case the hunters had discovered my connection to Brian and decided to come after me as well.

When I opened the sash, I heard rustling and scraping behind the motel, and less than a minute later, a helicopter sprang to life and quickly lifted off. The noise in the hall faded as the men moved outside, still crying violence. I don't know who was in the chopper, but if it was Watson and Sheen, they most likely fled to PEI. Still fully prepared for a quick escape, I eased back into bed and waited for the mercy of daylight.

Though I was a bit nervous to be on such dangerous grounds, none of the hunters treated me with suspicion the next day on the ice, nor later at the motel. The following day, I left the islands to begin the first draft of the script, reliving the experience in my thoughts as I traveled. My time in the Magdalens and on ice floes had been alternatingly sad, exhilarating, awe-inspiring, eye-opening, and unquestionably heartbreaking.

Between drafts of the script, I had to discuss the approach with Brian and interview him about his experiences, but his schedule was so tight that he had no time to meet with me in one place. The only solution was for me to follow him for weeks, taking advantage of his free time between speaking engagements and meetings with donors, which he would be doing in Italy for the next month.

This required me to fly to Florence, rent a car, and follow Brian wherever he went. Since his daily schedule was so tight, this left my days free to explore Tuscany and Umbria, the Medieval cities of Todi, Assisi, and Perugia, vineyards, olive groves, sunflower fields, and a Tuscan cashmere factory, all while staying as the lone occupant in an ancient castle-turned-hotel in Montecastello di Vibio, a walled city close to an estate of olive groves and vineyards where Brian was staying.

When I checked into the hotel, the clerk informed me that the hotel employees left for the evening at 8 p.m. If I was out of the hotel, I would not be able to get in, and vice versa, so please be inside by that time and plan to be there for the night.

What the clerk didn't tell me was that I was the only guest, and when the hotel was locked at 8 p.m., everyone went home, and I would be the only person inside the old castle until 6 a.m. the next morning.

This was a dreary, dark cut stone building over 500 years old with multiple empty guest rooms off grand marble hallways. Bronze and stone statues lined the corridors, flanked by tall iron candle sconces that flickered ghostly yellow light onto the cold granite walls. Blood-red carpeting led to darkened stairways on every floor. Not a welcome venture for anyone familiar with ghost stories.

I stayed in the hotel for four days, and wasn't the only guest for the last night, but waking up at 3 a.m. in that castle, knowing I was completely alone, or maybe I wasn't, was a thrill.

I would spend the days in Umbria exploring and eating before meeting with Brian for an early dinner and script talk, returning to the castle before 8 p.m. with a fine bottle of the local Sangiovese Riserva, preparing myself to walk the empty halls and talk, sing, or maybe shout as loud as I could, simply to hear the melodic ricochet of my voice off the ancient stone walls surrounding me.

When I returned to LA, Brian called to tell me Samsung, Korea's largest corporation, was an intermittent donor to IFAW and was interested in cultivating an environmentally responsible reputation. His contacts had told him that the company could conceivably contribute a portion, if not all, of the financing for the film. The CEO's daughter was interested in Hollywood, and *Red Ice* could be her perfect entry. Brian suggested Hugh Hudson and I travel to Seoul with a budget and presentation to pitch the idea to the company's PR people.

Hugh and I flew to South Korea with Jak, an IFAW PR rep who had worked with Samsung and knew some of the representatives. Jak had spent time in the country and would ideally help us navigate potential cultural obstacles in negotiations. We landed at Gimpo Airport, originally built during the Japanese Imperial occupation by slave labor and later reconstructed in 1950 by American forces using a giant Quonset hut as the main terminal. The airport still carried a military presence, evocative of the periods of my youth spent on American bases overseas.

After we cleared customs, a group of Samsung representatives took us to dinner at a local French restaurant. While exchanging pleasantries, a friendly rep sitting across the table asked what I planned to see while in town. I asked what he recommended, and he suggested the caves of Panmunjom, a tunnel North Korea built to infiltrate the South, discovered in 1978. I thanked him for the suggestion, and he smiled, nodded, and continued eating.

The next day, Hugh and I prepared our pitch in the morning, then walked about the city visiting several ancient temples. At dinner that night with the same Samsung executives, the man who had asked what I wanted to see in Seoul remarked to me, "So I understand you didn't go see the caves of Panmunjom."

When I asked him how he knew, he replied, "Because we had a car waiting for you in front of the hotel all day."

I looked at him quizzically. "I'm very sorry. I had no idea there was a car waiting for me. My apologies. No one informed me."

He smiled and nodded again, and the dinner continued. Afterward, I approached the liaison/translator who had attended college in America (Purdue, where Samsung sent many of their

American cultural liaisons at the time) and asked her why no one told me there was a car waiting. "Because they would lose face. Once you expressed an interest, it is their obligation to provide a car for you, whether you use it or not."

This cultural gulf became a recurring problem, requiring the liaison's presence as often as possible. Whenever we were asked what we would like, for entertainment or food, we had to be very careful how we replied so as not to create unnecessary attention. We had to assume that all activity had been planned, but it had to be by our suggestion. Therefore, we had to figure out how to suggest what had already been arranged.

All dinners were reserved by the company at American or European restaurants, which were uniformly mediocre. Our hosts assumed that is what we preferred over local Korean or Asian food, and if we suggested such, they would assume we were only doing so to not insult our hosts, therefore causing them to lose face. This is how it had to be.

At one particularly bad Italian dinner, the rep asked us where we would like to go after, and we made a series of suggestions, including a geisha house where the very same rep had taken Jak during an earlier visit. The Samsung rep replied, "Oh, I'm sorry. I don't know of any geisha houses." I looked at Jak curiously. His expression didn't change.

"How about a karaoke club?" Hugh suggested, to which the rep shook his head. "I'm sorry. I don't know of any karaoke clubs."

Jak interjected, "What about a disco? Can you recommend a disco?" The rep brightened and nodded his head. "Oh, yes. I know of a disco I can take you to."

So, we traveled by taxi to a stylish night club where the doorman greeted the Samsung rep effusively and held the door for us while another club employee led us through the dance floor and into a back room where a long table had been set up, fully seated except for four empty chairs. Everyone at the table, all Samsung employees, was in party mode and welcomed us as if they had been waiting all night.

There were small bottles of whiskey in front of our seats, and the waiters already had our dessert and sides prepared. There was never a question about where we were headed, but we had to suggest it. Jak apparently knew this from prior experience.

When time for our pitch meeting with the Samsung executives arrived, we felt prepared. We had assembled what is now known as a "deck," which included extensive material regarding us, our subject, proposed actors, and the story we wanted to tell. We included box office projections based on similar movies and a passionate approach to the storytelling. Sadly, the executives were not so interested in our story but rather in a realistic income projection for the investment, and we couldn't provide that in good conscience, only best-case scenarios. As we knew, there are very few investments with greater risk than films, one possibly being a hunt for sunken treasure.

We gave the executives examples of similar films with a successful box office, but they didn't seem convinced that we could guarantee a major return. Hugh's Academy Award win and the strength of the story didn't carry any weight. It was clearly a business they neither knew nor understood. So, they told us thank you for coming, please return to your hotel, and we will let you know if another meeting is necessary in the next few days.

Hugh, Jak, and I returned to the hotel, where we waited for a week. The Samsung people took us to lunch and dinner every night, and though we deeply appreciated our hosts' kindness and consideration, we dined daily at some of the worst Italian, American, and French restaurants. The only Korean meal we were lucky enough to savor, other than breakfast in the hotel, was when Hugh and I told our hosts we weren't eating lunch and surreptitiously left the hotel for a private walk through downtown, where we discovered a Buddhist vegetarian restaurant, and that lunch was superb.

After a week of waiting in the hotel for a response to our pitch, Hugh and I both felt it was time to return home, which we did. Gauging from our experience with the culture, I suspected "no" was a word we would never hear, and it was becoming apparent we weren't going to hear "yes" either. Jak agreed that it was possible we would never get an answer from Samsung, and true to our suspicions, we never did.

It was a worthy effort, with strong cinematic possibilities. A lot of development money had been spent on Hugh, me, my research, and our pitch trip to Korea. We were prepared, anxious, and ready, and as is most likely with movies, that is where it ended.

CHAPTER 35
THE BELLWETHER VEAL CHOP

Over a period of probably twenty years, I worked on numerous projects that were fun, educational, inspiring, and enriching on many levels. I was receiving great feedback and was proud of most of my work. My problem was that my screenplays weren't getting produced, and this could only go on so long before the well ran dry.

My agents understood that I only wanted to meet about projects with the likelihood that I would be attracted to them creatively. I asked them to please not send me to meet on a potential film I would have no interest in watching.

As a result, I said no to meetings about sequels, comic books, and action movies. Most of my meetings, as well as my assignments, were adaptations of serious books that had been optioned or rewrites of famous screenplays like David Lean, Christopher Hampton, and Robert Bolt's rendition of *Nostromo*, which, since I was a fan of Joseph Conrad, I did with great enthusiasm. But like the others, the financing collapsed, and the film was never made.

I met on projects for original stories or what I considered the best books of the present and the past, and I was hired to adapt several, but none got made, and my agents made it clear that I had to get something made soon because that is how the agency made their money. The idea was to package their actors and director with me, along with the inflated "back end" of a writer's deal, meaning the production bonus the writer receives on the first day of principal photography.

I asked my agents what I should do differently in my approach or style of writing. The answer I consistently got from them was "don't do anything different. They love what they're getting. It's just bad luck. It will change."

I think there was a particular point where my fortunes took a distinct turn, and I attribute that to a project that should have served as a prognosticator of things to come.

I was called in to meet with producer Raymond Wagner regarding a project he was very excited about. Ray had shepherded *The Passenger*, *Network*, *The Champ*, and *Logan's Run* at MGM and produced *Petulia* as well as many other highly regarded films of the 1960s and '70s. He had given Sherry Lansing her start in the business as a $5 per hour script reader, and when I was called in to meet with Ray, Sherry was the head of Paramount Pictures. This was a Paramount project we were to discuss, so I felt that whatever Ray had in mind to develop stood a better than remote chance of getting made.

The proposed film was an adaptation of the book *Gaudenzia, Pride of the Palio*, the story of a boy, a horse, and a very big race. Fifteen-year-old Giorgio helped raise filly Gaudenzia on a small farm in Tuscany, training the horse to race in the Palio, the fabled annual fest in the Piazza del Campo in Siena, touted as the oldest horse race in the world.

Gaudenzia, a mare born in 1942, much smaller and less muscular than most horses chosen for the race, won the Palio three times with Giorgio on her back, the only mare in a race against much bigger and stronger stallions. The Palio was notorious for cheating, sabotage, and any form of skullduggery sponsoring guilds could use to get an edge. Given this advantage, after three wins for Gaudenzia, the competing guilds had Gaudenzia banned from running again out of fear no horse could beat her.

Our film was to be a love story between the boy, his horse, and their small, rural community in the hills of Tuscany. Giorgio confronts the powers of the race itself, as well as the guilds representing it, to emerge victorious.

To me, this was a story with genuine heart that only required subtlety to make it work, and if done right, it was a sure winner at the box office. Finally, I had found a project that was a family film, blatantly commercial but not overblown or sappy, and one I would like to see. More than that, the studio would pay all expenses for my research in Italy. It was excitement I hadn't felt in some time. As John Huston told me with such optimistic foresight, "Frankly, I don't see how you can lose."

One of my agents at CAA called the next day with news that Paramount had agreed to the deal and paperwork would immediately follow. I would receive a generous fee for each draft with a hefty production bonus on first day of principal photography. The sweetest part of the deal, though, was that they had agreed to subsidize up to six months in Tuscany for me to research and work on the script, living in the countryside so I could imagine the life of Giorgio in the 1940s and '50s. They would use studio resources to secure a rental property for me and asked when I would like to go.

This was true cause to celebrate. Of all the screenplays I had written, aside from Sydney's embrace of *The Man Who Gave Up His Name*, I felt this one had been given the best chance of both commercial and critical success. If I could keep it simple and honest, hold the sentiment to a bare minimum as the author of the book, Marguerite Henry, had done, and keep it subtle enough to appeal to an accomplished director, I didn't see how I could lose. The story itself was so basic and appealing—my job would be to keep it that way.

When the contract was executed, I called a friend to invite him to join me in my celebration. "I just got a dream job. Veal chops and Margaux at Celestino, on me! Are you in?"

Who wouldn't be? I can nearly recall the entire meal we enjoyed that night at my favorite Italian restaurant. Champagne to start, followed by the promised Chateau Margaux, with an extra glass to savor over dessert. Chicken livers, bruschetta, antipasto, and tricolore, the perfect warmup, veal chops and broccolini even better than envisioned, the additional sides plentiful, and the desserts superfluous, all of them.

The indulgence stretched until closing time, as most great dinners do. The vintage Margaux alone cost several times what the dinner should have totaled, but it was one of those nights when, considering my joy, no indulgence would be extreme.

This was the job that felt like deliverance, at the perfect time, in the perfect place. I loved Italy, had lived in Naples as a boy, and had spent a lot of time driving around Tuscany and Umbria when I was working with Brian Davies. Aside from the tailgating drivers, I was comfortable in that province, could almost predict my nightly menu in my rental house or local inns, and was preparing a mental list of who to invite for a visit.

A week later, while arranging house-sitting, dog care, and intensive Italian lessons, I received another call from the agent at CAA. "I'm afraid I have some unfortunate news," he began, then proceeded to tell me that the book we were to base the screenplay on had entered public domain, and Paramount had a clause in every contract that stated if the studio were unable to acquire rights in perpetuity to any source material, the contract was null and void.

Apparently, Marguerite Henry, the author who was in her nineties and in poor health, had failed to renew the book's copyright when it expired after twenty-five years. Exclusive rights to the book were no longer available. What this meant was that anyone could make a film of the book, and anyone could also make any number of sequels.

I called Ray Wagner. He apologized for his error, didn't understand how it could have happened, and was just as disappointed as I was. There was nothing more to say.

I asked Ray if he wanted to try other studios or independents. He did not. I realized his wagon was harnessed to Sherry, and Sherry was the horse he could depend upon. He'd rather find another project, meaning one he could own, and I couldn't blame him.

So that was it. The project was dead before taking a breath. What I would always refer to as my "veal chop job" was gone before I had a chance to pack. Only years later would I assign its loss greater significance, but it was clearly the turning point for my career—and a very expensive celebration.

The vanished windfall in Tuscany became my fortuitous whale in the ocean.

CHAPTER 36
WHAT GOES AWAY

Several ominous events occurred soon after the veal chop experience, including the Northridge earthquake in 1994. My house survived the quake well, with only cosmetic damage, but it was the beginning of a real estate collapse in Los Angeles.

Japanese investors had purchased properties across the city in the 1980s, creating a real estate boom like nothing the city had seen. By 1988, many of these investors had pulled out of the market, sending prices tumbling, which I had taken advantage of in 1990 by buying my house out of foreclosure at what I considered an excellent price.

Prices fell even further after the Rodney King verdict and ensuing riots of 1992, bottoming out after the Northridge earthquake in January of 1994. By March, my house was worth far less than my mortgage. My expenses remained the same, and after the veal chop mirage, the jobs diminished while my expensive house was hemorrhaging money. I realized that I couldn't continue to maintain the lifestyle unless I looked for a job that would pay for it, which would mean a job I didn't really want.

I had three options: 1) continue funneling out money while looking for a writing job I didn't want, meaning television, action, or fantasy, 2) rent out the spare rooms in my house to pay the mortgage while seeking independent films to write for far less money, or 3) walk away from the mortgage and look for a smaller house that could double as an income property while continuing to look for the work I wanted.

I decided on the third option. I would get rid of the house while I still had money for the down payment on another one. But how would I get out of my mortgage when I would still owe several hundred thousand dollars after the sale? If my credit was tainted, how would I qualify for another mortgage? Houses were being foreclosed on in multiples in Los Angeles, and banks were overburdened with properties they were forced to resell. The foreclosure signs were becoming more prevalent across the most expensive areas in Los Angeles, including where I lived in Los Feliz.

These properties quickly became unsightly due to the neglect caused by the sheer numbers. The banks just couldn't maintain so many empty properties, which is another reason their value kept plummeting. When I inquired to people working in the real estate industry, I was told banks were overwhelmed with foreclosures, and since the prices kept dropping, people were waiting to buy until the market hit bottom. No one had any idea when or where that would be. In the meantime, it was costing banks more each month to maintain empty houses. When would they decide not to invest in a declining property?

I had an idea about how to try to get out of my mortgage, sell my house at a loss, and still maintain my credit. It was at least worth a try.

My loan was with Chase, so I located the mortgage head in Southern California and was able to get him on the phone with a proposal. I told him I would stop paying my mortgage and give the property to Chase to sell. While the house is on the market, I will continue to live in the house and maintain the property in perfect condition, arrange for the house to show at the realtor's discretion, keep the house and gardens perfectly manicured and maintained, including paying all maintenance, gardening, and utility bills (which were sizeable)—but no more mortgage payments.

If Chase allowed me to do this, I would also keep the house presentable according to the realtor's discretion (staging was not yet the standard) and vacate as soon as the house was sold. What I asked from Chase in return was a guarantee in writing that my credit would not be affected by my default so I could qualify for another loan without waiting the usual period to reclaim a solid rating.

The mortgage head agreed to my proposal. He told me no one had asked for this previously, but these were desperate times, and he would accommodate me, with one exception. On my credit report, the loan would not be listed as a default but as "closed without being satisfied," which was apparently a new designation to create a gray area between paid and defaulted since so many loans were being abandoned.

I asked him to sign an agreement and fax it to me, which he did. I stopped paying the mortgage but remained in the house, paying utilities and caring for the property. I found a realtor for Chase, the same person who sold me the house, and within three months, the house was sold for two-thirds of the price I had paid four years earlier.

I loved living at the house, but not the house itself. Since the beginning, nothing about it felt right for me. It was too expensive, grandiose, and demanding.

I am friends with my neighbors who lived behind my old "mansion." They tell me the current owners, a successful stand-up comedian and his television producer wife, bought the house in 2018, paying fifteen times what I sold it for in 1994. If I had chosen option two and rented out the rooms to pay the mortgage, I would have a substantial annuity available to me now, but that wouldn't come close to making the house right for me, which would have driven me from it eventually, regardless of my finances.

My life changed dramatically when I left that house, and I learned from the experience. Along with the house and the equity, I lost a certain cloak of privilege, never to be regained. This could be viewed as a gift as easily as a loss.

I still like veal chops, but I don't order them in restaurants.

CHAPTER 37
THE MYSTERY

Most of us have seen a sundog, perhaps with no comprehension of what we are looking at. We may dismiss it as an optical anomaly and go about our day. A sundog is essentially a halo around the sun, or the illusion of three suns together caused by the sun's reflection on ice crystals in the atmosphere. Apparently, the accepted spiritual interpretation of this is that the appearance of a sundog represents nature speaking in magical and mysterious ways, if we are willing to listen. It is a sign of change.

The last Jim Harrison novel I adapted for the screen is titled *Sundog*. It is the story of a jaded journalist, our narrator, who is tiring of his self-indulgent existence and struggling through a divorce. He sets out to interview Robert Corvus Strang, a man who, though impaired by epileptic seizures since childhood, is self-educated in numerous fields. He is an accomplished engineer, a builder of dams, wealthy, motivated, capable, and, unlike our narrator, technologically adroit. A man our narrator describes as "someone who does things."

As the narrator comes to know Strang, he discovers what he refers to as the "mystery of personality," which he considers the core of what separates those who do from those who cannot and, as related to our narrator, the accomplished from the failed.

One fall afternoon, Bob Dattila introduced me and producer Richard Chapman to the director Hal Ashby in a Brentwood restaurant, with the topic being Jim's novel and how we could approach a screen adaptation. Jeff Bridges, who Hal knew well, was interested in playing the role of Strang, and we aimed to have a completed draft ready to present to him by the new year.

Hal, who had directed a number of famously humanistic and successful films such as *Harold and Maude*, *Coming Home*, *Shampoo*, *Bound for Glory*, *The Last Detail*, and *Being There*, split his time between Malibu and New York, and considering we lived so far apart, we would hold most of our script discussions over the phone, figuring we would meet when the first draft was done.

I got to know Hal during this time, at least superficially to start, and discovered he was extremely human, with deep streaks of kindness, humor, and consideration. He made no effort to impress, though he was an accomplished filmmaker, beloved by actors and crews. Like me, he was also an admirer of Jim Harrison and the referenced "mystery of personality" that made Jim larger than life.

When I finished the first draft of the script, I flew to Washington to spend Christmas and New Year's with old friends, planning to train from DC to New York, where I would meet with Hal and go over preparations for the next pass before we submitted it to Jeff.

The day of my trip to New York, I waited at Union Station for the incoming Colonial train, destined for Boston, on the outdoor platform with two teenage sisters who had invited me to join their game of hearts on a flattened suitcase. When the train arrived, we boarded together, and the girls, aged thirteen and sixteen, sat behind me, in the middle of the third car.

On the train, the girls talked about a letter the older sister was writing to her best friend. She had said something insensitive to the friend and was considering whether to apologize. Her younger sister advised against it, claiming it would give the friend an emotional advantage, or "upper hand" in their relationship. I voted for the apology, claiming there was no such thing as leverage in a true friendship, which is invaluable.

Before a decision was made, the girls stood up to visit the café car, and as I advised they were headed in the wrong direction, the front of the car exploded as if hit by a missile, sending a wave of victims and debris throughout the car, followed by the blast of smoke and the suffocating stench of diesel fuel.

At that moment, a number of lives ended, including both sisters, and others forever changed, including mine.

Traveling 135 miles per hour, our Amtrak passenger train had collided head-on with a freight engine. Our locomotive left no single piece larger than a wheel at the crash site, the first passenger car was flattened into the rail ties, the second thoroughly demolished and burned with no survivors, and the third car, our car, split apart at impact and overturned, skidding across the scattered ties. Only two of us, as I recall, were able to escape the carnage unassisted and return to help injured passengers.

For me, it was a day that would remain momentous, yet undefinable beyond the context, at least for a time. As anyone who has experienced that level of destructive power, through whatever fashion, can attest, there is no fair description of, nor calm escape from, the trauma. The power of shock is so strong that I wasn't even aware of my own injuries, which were not severe. The experience was transcendent enough to make this secular person fully aware, if not accepting, of the power of God.

While helping injured passengers escape, I witnessed the haunting remains of not only my two traveling companions but dozens more that winter afternoon, including children, their heartbreaking belongings lying open in the tainted snow, images that meticulously prepared me for the following day in New York.

I arrived in the early morning hours after survivors were bused to Penn Station from the accident site in Maryland. I hailed a taxi to a friend's apartment on the Upper West Side of Manhattan, where I would stay while he was out of town.

Living in a surreal fog, I fell into an exhausted sleep, but the alarm awakened me early enough to call Hal Ashby and cancel my scheduled script meeting. I explained to Hal what had happened, and his impulsive voice nearly came through the phone and lifted me from under my shoulders.

"What? My God, you were on that train? Where are you? Are you alone?"

I told him I was, and he didn't hesitate.

"Give me your address. I'm coming to get you."

"That's very kind of you, Hal, but I'm okay. I just can't meet about the script today, if you don't mind."

"Forget that. I'm coming right now. Don't go anywhere."

And he did, arriving in his Corvette from his downtown loft in a matter of minutes and depositing me into the car.

"All right, where do you want to go?"

"Nowhere, Hal. I can't think of anywhere I want to go today. Don't want to think at all."

"Nowhere it is."

He put the Corvette into gear, and we began our journey to nowhere. I looked around the interior of the car, which was only months old.

"I used to own one of these. When I was eighteen."

"Good age to drive," he told me. "You're ready to travel."

I thought about that, deciding he was dead on, and we drove.

Over the course of the day, we traveled New York, New Jersey, and Connecticut, stopping at diners and bars, ultimately arriving at Hal's loft where we ate again. The day was a blur, but his presence was not. A relative stranger had presented himself as an angel whose mission was to care for me, completely selfless, without regard to the business we had together.

We had scheduled a breakfast meeting to discuss the script. I asked to cancel because of personal injury. He could have easily and remorselessly spent the time doing whatever slotted into his daily life. Instead, without hesitation, he devoted the entire day to my comfort and well-being, someone he hardly knew, as if our business relationship had become irrelevant, except for one salient detail.

We talked about Strang, and why did either of us think Jim created him? This initiated a series of questions, which seemed fitting for this day. I was vulnerable and wounded, and he had come to me like a medic on the battlefield. It was an immeasurably raw moment in my life, which had suddenly bled into his.

We agreed that to Jim, Strang represents someone we want to be—but cannot—and the question is why should that be a goal? Why do we want to be what we are not, and why choose someone like this to admire? Simply because we cannot be this person? Is this person truly admirable, or only because he/she is not us? If we can't be that person, why is it so important to us just to be close to his/her accomplishment? And finally, don't we know the answer to this question, but we keep asking it anyway, proving there is no answer?

Hal told me that in retrospect, he understood this question was something he had dealt with all his life; his father killed himself when Hal was twelve years old, and Hal hitchhiked to Los Angeles seeking something, anything, but his life in Ogden, Utah. My father died when I was eleven years old, from a heart attack, and I understood that the need for Hal to hitchhike was the same power that propelled me to pack up my Corvette and drive it from Georgia to Virginia when I was eighteen and drive to Hollywood twelve years later. Why do we feel the need for change, to escape whatever drags us into our doldrums, rather than creating our own intellectual avenues out? Why is the drive to step off the front porch greater than the need to determine a destination?

Hal felt compelled to find the path to acceptance. His own acceptance of what he had become, what he had both succeeded at and failed at. I argued that he had only succeeded, but he told me about nearly ten years of perceived failures in every aspect of his life and how he had learned to accept all of them—personal, professional, intellectual, and spiritual. In his own words, he implied that external factors such as drugs, alcohol, and fate will always play a role, but they are only distractions from the truth of who you are. Is ambition just another form of escape?

What we desire to be can sometimes be a mirage, so can recognizing that mirage possibly be a major goal in life? Is it one of the steps of Buddhism? The realization that the foundation of suffering is desire? Was this what Jim was seeking, or Hal, or me?

Hal took me back to the apartment late that night. I returned to LA and rewrote the script. The financing fell through, Jeff Bridges went on to another project, and Hal stopped returning phone calls.

The reason he didn't return not only mine but anyone's calls, I soon learned, was that before I saw him in New York, he had been diagnosed with terminal cancer and was getting progressively worse for months. Soon after, he died at his home in Malibu.

The thoughts he relayed to me that day regarding ambition, acceptance, and Strang's role in all of it were those of a condemned man, and Hal never mentioned it.

I went to a Memorial at the Directors Guild, where several stars went on stage to tell stories about Hal as their guardian angel on set, closing with his favorite song from *Bound for Glory*, "Hobo's Lullaby," which the performers, Ronny Cox and Melinda Dillon, were too emotionally overcome to finish, so the audience did it for them. After that, I met more actors with similar stories about Hal. He was a guide, a presence, seemingly there for a reason greater than making a movie.

Hal Ashby's career hit a wall after the highest level of critical and financial success. Buzz around executives in Hollywood could (then and now) make or break careers. Hal's opinion was that due in large part to power brokers whom he could not relate to, and who could not relate to him, his star fell and never got the chance to recover. He was hoping that *Sundog* would have given him that chance; it was familiar territory for him, a chance to say something heartfelt and true.

Jim Harrison told me that not long after I returned from New York, Hal drove his Corvette cross-country back to Malibu, which would be his last journey. On the way, he detoured over 500 miles north, then again south, to come see Jim at his cabin in Grand Marais.

A Corvette is not built for travel across the Upper Peninsula, and it bottomed out in the drive leading to Jim's cabin, breaking an exhaust pipe and creating havoc for Hal's trip, causing him to shorten the visit in order to see a mechanic in Grand Marais who could patch it enough for Hal to drive to Marquette before dark.

Jim, who died in 2016, told me Hal had two goals for his brief visit he had so painstakingly detoured for. One, to see the cabin where Jim worked and ask what made it special to him, and two, to talk about *Sundog* and the significance of Strang.

Essentially, Hal did precisely what I had done the previous year. It was why I spent days at the cabin with Jim and nights at the Dunes Saloon eating whitefish, drinking bourbon, and talking to regulars. I wanted to catch Jim, or Strang, in his element and reap something, but more important, I wanted to understand why Jim created a narrator who wanted to be Strang, and not himself, and was at peace with that. To understand, as Jim put it in the book, the "mystery of personality."

It could be what haunts me over my inability to meet John Huston's expectations. The day I told him I had been fired and he looked me in the eye and told me not to despair but move on because I was "going to go places."

I did. I set out on the roads he envisioned, but I never reached my destination—or at least what most people in Hollywood would define as success, measured by the acknowledgment of your peers. Those outside of the business would assume success means creating top grossing movies or winning an Oscar, which every person in the film industry wants to do and understands is life-changing. But what really counts is the buzz, the general acknowledgment by your peers that you are among the best at what you do. This is the goal of every actor, director, writer, producer, and technician. What they all seek. It is validation, which requires no awards.

I had it when Sydney Pollack announced in *Variety* that my script would be his follow-up to the Oscar-winning *Out of Africa*. I could get most anyone in Hollywood to take my call or meet me for lunch. But I lost it when not only did *Man Who* not get made, but neither did any of my scripts over the next ten years. So much of it is simple kismet.

To truly make it, you must get films produced, and they must be critically or commercially successful, no matter what your role. The early ones were part of my learning experience, controlled by producers with a conflicting approach to filmmaking. I don't believe the films were reflective of my work, and every writer or director has movies like that in their résumé. Sadly, yet understandably, pretty much nobody outside of Hollywood will ever read a screenplay, which is simply a blueprint, but pretty much everyone will watch a movie.

After my documentaries, I never made a film that I could be proud of. It became my grail, and I never doubted it would happen, but it did not.

I live easily with the turns in the road, but I don't know if I will ever understand the *story* behind the story. Ambition—and the cruel yet enticing irony it holds.

EPILOGUE
WHAT COMES BACK

After leaving the mansion, I moved to a house in a historic neighborhood in the Hollywood hills with a view of the Cahuenga pass, Hollywood sign, and Hollywood Bowl. It is not a big house, but it is a unique three-level hillside duplex, with a lovely apartment on the ground floor and substantial outdoor living on tiled terraces and a large redwood deck. The upper two levels also have a tiled balcony extending nearly the length of the house, with an extended terrace for work and dining. The view is over and through the numerous trees on the hill, giving it the feel of a tree house.

When I applied for a loan to buy the house, I was initially declined due to a default on my credit report, listed by Chase Mortgage. Through a series of phone calls and employee directories, I was able to locate the Chase executive who signed the original agreement.

Chase had moved the executive to Denver into a new, unrelated department, and he claimed to have no memory of our arrangement. However, when I faxed him the agreement with his signature, within two weeks, the default on my credit report had been adjusted to read "Loan Closed Not Paid in Full." Apparently, this was a designation created to include those who, like me, got caught in the post-earthquake real estate collapse and lost their home but who, without a default, could qualify for a new mortgage. This enabled me to live where I do today.

I don't miss the mansion, the space, the clothes, the office, the Porsche, the gardens, or the pool with the waterfalls under the drive. I do miss Gus, who died from a heart attack at age ten. I rescued a litter of feral kittens born under my deck to help occupy the cavern of his loss. I know that I am one of thousands of writers, directors, actors, producers, and support people with the same "almost" story, though I believe I came closer to realizing my goal than many do.

When opportunities come along, I'm paid far less now, for far lower profile projects, with lesser-known producers, directors, and stars, and I spend more time on non-income producing projects like this one. I wrote a memoir about my family, and now these observations about the experiences that led me here.

I still travel for some projects, and one recent trip restored memories of the veal chop—and why lessons learned can't be forgotten.

Scott, a producer who I worked with during my early years in LA and have remained in contact with since, approached me with a proposal from the oldest television network in the Philippines, ABS-CBN, that was looking to get into the international movie business.

Scott had been hired to oversee a slate of films the network wanted to produce, their goal being to make five-million-dollar (US) movies in the Philippines, a budget that would equate to several times that in the US. Their plan was to hire an American writer, director, and star for each film and shoot for worldwide distribution. I would be the first American writer, and potentially the first director.

ABS-CBN had optioned a script about an older man whose beloved wife of many years dies, and following her funeral, he discovers a passionate love letter his wife had written years earlier to another man. The husband sets out to find this man, and his journey becomes the movie. The script had been written by a Filipino, for a Filipino star.

Scott brought me in to rewrite the film with an American approach, for an American star, in a fashion that would appeal internationally. I did so, beginning the film in the Claremont area of the Los Angeles suburbs, with a retiring American music professor who loses his Filipino wife of forty years, a former student of his who moved here to marry him. Following his deceased wife's memorial, he is sorting through her belongings for keepsakes and finds a journal he has never seen, with entries declaring her love for an obscure and mysterious man back in the Philippines.

Our hero, who has never been to the Philippines, sets out to find his adversary and encounters interesting, extraordinary, and sometimes exhilarating challenges trying to satisfy his quest, including joining an alt-rock young Filipino band, leading him to find what he is looking for.

ABS brought me and Scott, who was involved in other projects in the Philippines, to the islands to meet and scout locations. We traveled with network representatives and crew members to document the locations for my benefit while writing. This travel enabled me to see several of the most tropical and remote islands, including Culion, an island in the municipality of Palawan, that housed the American-run leper colony established in 1906.

Culion was declared to be leprosy-free 100 years later in 2006, and upon visiting in 2020, I felt a peace and harmony unlike anything I'd experienced. A calm that, like music, cannot be justly described, only felt. Everyone in our entourage had the same experience on this island, and it served as both inspiration and setting for the conclusion of our story.

I returned to LA and began to work. It is always a pleasure to feel motivated as one begins, and I was fully, with distinct memories and a catalogue of photos to aid me. When finished, I tweaked it according to Scott's suggestions and sent it off to ABS.

Scott and I were feeling celebratory, happy with the script, enthusiastic about a meaningful, resonant story in an extraordinarily beautiful setting, and excited to work for a network that produced everything they developed. This would not end as a script—but as a movie.

I loved the Filipino people I met during our research; Scott had business dealings and personal relationships in Manila, and both of us began making plans to spend additional time in Palawan, a province full of magnificent lagoons, islands, and beaches, adjacent to Culion and a popular vacation destination for much of Asia. In truth, the whole project felt like a vacation. Who could ask for more?

The network accepted and paid for the first draft, and we waited for a Zoom conference to go over their notes before beginning the next. In the meantime, I began pricing long-term rentals in Palawan.

The wait kept extending, and Scott contacted ABS several times, but we couldn't get any response. After a month, I sent them a bill for the next payment, which was contractually due whether the second draft had been written or not.

That's when I was delivered what could accurately be described as veal chop, the sequel.

In an email, the network executives told us there were some "administrative" issues holding up the production of the film, and they anticipated getting them worked out very shortly and please give them some time. I responded that, contractually, they were obligated to pay for the next step, and it wasn't my negligence holding up the project, so I'm happy to give them time, if they meet their obligation first.

I got no more responses, so I looked for the real news, and I found it in the international press.

ABS-CBN supported opponents of then President Duterte. The network had apparently been threatened by the president but had not capitulated and was essentially being shut down. Duterte claimed this was due to "license anomalies," but few outside of the president's press corps ascribed to that. The network had been strong-armed, and our project was dead.

Not a reason I would select in a multiple-choice quiz for why a project might disappear before it begins in a Democratic state. Financing pulls out at the last minute? Check. Network shut down by a dictator for lack of political support? Veal chop redux.

But this time, it nearly brought a laugh, and there was no mansion, pool, or Porsche to give up. That was another life.

ACKNOWLEDGMENTS

This book exists as a testimonial to the tireless efforts of all the creative, technical, financial, and support people who are driven to contribute to the writing, planning, financing, and production of any completed motion picture, regardless of scope, budget, and length. There are thousands of these workers, covering every pay grade throughout the industry. Those who perform the labor that creates what is seen on film and television yet are often unacknowledged and in so many instances uncompensated. But we all continue on, eagerly anticipating what might come next.

We do it for the thrill of sitting back and focusing on the product of so much combined hard work displayed on the screen in front of us, representing the elusive dream that keeps us going regardless of our failures—with the hope that this one just might make it.

Many thanks to my family and friends for all their encouragement and critical input. To Jeff Severson for expanding my cultural horizons northward, to Judson Mitcham for his keen and challenging insight, and a very special thanks to Ken Wells for lending this book his creativity, wisdom, and finely honed editorial gift.

I am also extremely grateful to Charles Kaufman and Richard Parli for their heartfelt encouragement and support in helping turn this musing into a reality.